FOOTBA
FOOTB

RIVA

C000024721

# EVERTON

VS

# LIVERPOOL

*Classic*
## MERSEYSIDE
### Derby Games

First published in 2013

A catalogue record for this book is available from the British Library

ISBN: 978-0-85733-207-3


Published by Haynes Publishing, Sparkford, Yeovil,
Somerset BA22 7JJ, UK
Tel: 01963 442030 Fax: 01963 440001
Int. tel: +44 1963 442030 Int. fax: +44 1963 440001
E-mail: sales@haynes.co.uk
Website: www.haynes.co.uk

Haynes North America Inc., 861 Lawrence Drive, Newbury Park, California 91320, USA

Images © Mirrorpix

Creative Director: Kevin Gardner
Designed for Haynes by BrainWave

Printed and bound in the US

FOOTBALL
FOOTBALL
RIVALS

# EVERTON
## VS
# LIVERPOOL

*Classic*
## MERSEYSIDE
### Derby Games

**Ian Welch**

# CONTENTS

# Introduction

While football as a pastime had been around for a long time – historians can trace the origins back to medieval Britain – it wasn't until the formation of the Football Association (FA) in London in October 1863 that the sport began to take on characteristics and rules that more closely resemble the modern game. It was Ebenezer Cobb Morley, a solicitor from Hull, who first drafted a set of rules and nine years later the first FA Cup was contested with the Football League kicking off its inaugural season in 1888. The game of football has evolved over the decades – one such change was the introduction of the penalty kick that came into effect for the 1891–92 season while others include the arrival of yellow and red cards in 1970 and the value of a win being changed from two points to three in 1981 – and is the most popular sport in the world in the 21$^{st}$ century.

The deep-seated intensity between Everton and Liverpool dates back to 1892 when a dispute in the ranks at Everton – tenants at the Anfield Road ground since 1884 – led to them moving the short distance across Stanley Park to set up home at Goodison Park and the formation of Liverpool FC at the ground they left behind. Everton had been founder members of the Football League in 1888 (10 years after the club was formed) while Liverpool turned professional in the year of their formation and joined the Second Division, gaining promotion to the top flight in 1894. The Merseyside derby had been born.

## Honours:

### Everton
**Premier League winners:** 0
**Premier League runners-up:** 0
**First Division winners:** 9
1890–91, 1914–15, 1927–28, 1931–32, 1938–39, 1962–63, 1969–70, 1984–85, 1986–87
**First Division runners-up:** 7
1889–90, 1894–95, 1901–02, 1904–05, 1908–09, 1911–12, 1985–86
**Second Division winners:** 1
1930–31
**Second Division runners-up:** 1
1953–54
**FA Cup winners:** 5
1906, 1933, 1966, 1984, 1995
**FA Cup runners-up:** 8
1893, 1897, 1907, 1968, 1985, 1986, 1989, 2009
**League Cup winners:** 0
**League Cup runners-up:** 2
1977, 1984
**FA Charity Shield/Community Shield winners:** 9
1928, 1932, 1963, 1970, 1984, 1985, 1986 (shared with Liverpool), 1987, 1995
**FA Charity Shield/Community Shield runners-up:** 2
1933, 1966
**Full Members Cup winners:** 0
**Full Members Cup runners-up:** 2
1989, 1991
**Champions League winners:** 0
**Champions League runners-up:** 0
**European Cup winners:** 0
**European Cup runners-up:** 0
**European Cup Winners' Cup winners:** 1
1985
**European Cup Winners' Cup runners-up:** 0

UEFA Cup winners: 0
UEFA Cup runners-up: 0
UEFA Super Cup winners: 0
UEFA Super Cup runners-up: 0
Screen Sport Super Cup winners: 0
Screen Sport Super Cup runners-up: 1
1985–86

# Honours:

## Liverpool
Premier League winners: 0
Premier League runners-up: 2
2001–02, 2008–09
First Division winners: 18
1900–01, 1905–06, 1921–22, 1922–23, 1946–47, 1963–64, 1965–66, 1972–73, 1975–76, 1976–77, 1978–79, 1979–80, 1981–82, 1982–83, 1983–84, 1985–86, 1987–88, 1989–90
First Division runners-up: 10
1898–99, 1909–10, 1968–69, 1973–74, 1974–75, 1977–78, 1984–85, 1986–87, 1988–89, 1990–91
Second Division winners: 4
1893–94, 1895–96, 1904–05, 1961–62
Second Division runners-up: 0
FA Cup winners: 7
1965, 1974, 1986, 1989, 1992, 2001, 2006
FA Cup runners-up: 7
1914, 1950, 1971, 1977, 1988, 1996, 2012
League Cup winners: 8
1981, 1982, 1983, 1984, 1995, 2001, 2003, 2012
League Cup runners-up: 3
1978, 1987, 2005
FA Charity Shield/Community Shield winners: 15
1964 (shared with West Ham United), 1965 (shared with Manchester United), 1966, 1974, 1976, 1977 (shared with Manchester United), 1979, 1980, 1982, 1986 (shared with Everton), 1988, 1989, 1990 (shared with

Manchester United), 2001, 2006
**FA Charity Shield/Community Shield runners-up: 6**
1922, 1971, 1983, 1984, 1992, 2002
**Full Members Cup winners: 0**
**Full Members Cup runners-up: 0**
**Champions League winners: 1**
2005
**Champions League runners-up: 1**
2007
**European Cup winners: 4**
1977, 1978, 1981, 1984
**European Cup runners-up: 1**
1985
**European Cup Winners' Cup winners: 0**
**European Cup Winners' Cup runners-up: 1**
1965–66
**UEFA Cup winners: 3**
1973, 1976, 2001
**UEFA Cup runners-up: 0**
**UEFA Super Cup winners: 3**
1977, 2001, 2005
**UEFA Super Cup runners-up: 2**
1978, 1984
**Screen Sport Super Cup winners: 1**
1985–86
**Screen Sport Super Cup runners-up: 0**

Head to Head:

### League

|         | P   | W  | D  | L  | F   | A   |
|---------|-----|----|----|----|-----|-----|
| Everton | 188 | 57 | 58 | 73 | 220 | 256 |
| Liverpool | 188 | 73 | 58 | 57 | 256 | 220 |

### FA Cup

|         | P  | W  | D | L  | F  | A  |
|---------|----|----|---|----|----|----|
| Everton | 23 | 7  | 6 | 10 | 27 | 37 |
| Liverpool | 23 | 10 | 6 | 7  | 37 | 27 |

### League Cup

|         | P | W | D | L | F | A |
|---------|---|---|---|---|---|---|
| Everton | 4 | 1 | 1 | 2 | 1 | 2 |
| Liverpool | 4 | 2 | 1 | 1 | 2 | 1 |

### FA Charity Shield/Community Shield

|         | P | W | D | L | F | A |
|---------|---|---|---|---|---|---|
| Everton | 3 | 1 | 1 | 1 | 2 | 2 |
| Liverpool | 3 | 1 | 1 | 1 | 2 | 2 |

### Screen Sport Super Cup

|         | P | W | D | L | F | A |
|---------|---|---|---|---|---|---|
| Everton | 2 | 0 | 0 | 2 | 2 | 7 |
| Liverpool | 2 | 2 | 0 | 0 | 7 | 2 |

### Total

|         | P   | W  | D  | L  | F   | A   |
|---------|-----|----|----|----|-----|-----|
| Everton | 220 | 66 | 66 | 88 | 252 | 305 |
| Liverpool | 220 | 88 | 66 | 66 | 305 | 252 |

# Chapter One

# The 19<sup>th</sup> Century

Everton were founder members of the Football League and won their first title in 1890–91 while Liverpool did not compete at the highest level until the 1894–95 season and their inaugural top-flight campaign ended in relegation followed by a one-year sojourn back in the Second Division. The Goodison Park team twice reached the FA Cup Final during the 1890s, losing 1-0 to Wolves in 1893 and 3-2 to Aston Villa in 1897.

## Record in the 19<sup>th</sup> Century

**Everton**

| Season | League | P | W | L | D | F | A | Pts | Pos |
|--------|--------|----|----|----|----|----|----|----|----|
| 1888–89 | Div 1 | 22 | 9 | 2 | 11 | 35 | 46 | 20 | 8 |
| 1889–90 | Div 1 | 22 | 14 | 3 | 5 | 65 | 40 | 31 | 2 |
| 1890–91 | Div 1 | 22 | 14 | 1 | 7 | 63 | 29 | 29 | 1 |
| 1891–92 | Div 1 | 26 | 12 | 4 | 10 | 49 | 49 | 28 | 5 |
| 1892–93 | Div 1 | 30 | 16 | 4 | 10 | 74 | 51 | 36 | 3 |
| 1893–94 | Div 1 | 30 | 15 | 3 | 12 | 90 | 57 | 33 | 6 |
| 1894–95 | Div 1 | 30 | 18 | 6 | 6 | 82 | 50 | 42 | 2 |
| 1895–96 | Div 1 | 30 | 16 | 7 | 7 | 66 | 43 | 39 | 3 |
| 1896–97 | Div 1 | 30 | 14 | 3 | 13 | 62 | 57 | 31 | 7 |
| 1897–98 | Div 1 | 30 | 13 | 9 | 8 | 48 | 39 | 35 | 4 |
| 1898–99 | Div 1 | 34 | 15 | 8 | 11 | 48 | 41 | 38 | 4 |
| 1899–1900 | Div 1 | 34 | 13 | 7 | 14 | 47 | 49 | 33 | 11 |

**FA Cup**

| | |
|--------|--------|
| 1878–79 | Did not enter |
| 1879–80 | Did not enter |
| 1880–81 | Did not enter |

| | |
|---|---|
| 1881–82 | Did not enter |
| 1882–83 | Did not enter |
| 1883–84 | Did not enter |
| 1884–85 | Did not enter |
| 1885–86 | Did not enter |
| 1886–87 | Walkover awarded to Glasgow Rangers after fielding ineligible players |
| 1887–88 | Disqualified after fielding 'professionals' against Bolton Wanderers |
| 1888–89 | Did not enter |
| 1889–90 | 2-4 v Stoke (Second Round) |
| 1890–91 | 0-1 v Sunderland (First Round) |
| 1891–92 | 2-4 v Burnley (First Round) |
| 1892–93 | 0-1 v Wolverhampton Wanderers (Final) |
| 1893–94 | 0-1 v Stoke (First Round) |
| 1894–95 | 0-3 v The Wednesday (Third Round) |
| 1895–96 | 0-4 v The Wednesday (Third Round) |
| 1896–97 | 2-3 v Aston Villa (Final) |
| 1897–98 | 1-3 v Derby County (Semi-final) |
| 1898–99 | 0-1 v Nottingham Forest (Second Round) |
| 1899–1900 | 0-3 v Southampton (First Round) |

## Liverpool

| Season | League | P | W | L | D | F | A | Pts | Pos |
|---|---|---|---|---|---|---|---|---|---|
| 1892–93 | Not a Football League member | | | | | | | | |
| 1893–94 | Div 2 | 28 | 22 | 6 | 0 | 77 | 18 | 50 | 1 |
| 1894–95 | Div 1 | 30 | 7 | 8 | 15 | 51 | 70 | 22 | 16 |
| 1895–96 | Div 2 | 30 | 22 | 2 | 6 | 106 | 32 | 46 | 1 |
| 1896–97 | Div 1 | 30 | 12 | 9 | 9 | 46 | 38 | 33 | 5 |
| 1897–98 | Div 1 | 30 | 11 | 6 | 13 | 48 | 45 | 28 | 9 |
| 1898–99 | Div 1 | 34 | 19 | 5 | 10 | 49 | 33 | 43 | 2 |
| 1899–1900 | Div 1 | 34 | 14 | 5 | 15 | 49 | 45 | 33 | 10 |

## FA Cup

| | |
|---|---|
| 1892–93 | 1-2 v Northwich Victoria (Third Round qualifier) |
| 1893–94 | 0-3 v Bolton Wanderers (Third Round) |

| | |
|---|---|
| 1894–95 | 0-2 v Nottingham Forest (Second Round) |
| 1895–96 | 0-2 v Wolverhampton Wanderers (Second Round) |
| 1896–97 | 0-3 v Aston Villa (Semi-final) |
| 1897–98 | 1-1, 1-5 v Derby County (Third Round) |
| 1898–99 | 2-2, 4-4, 0-1 v Sheffield United (Semi-final) |
| 1899–1900 | 1-1, 1-2 v West Bromwich Albion (Second Round) |

## The Matches

### 13th October 1894

First Division

**Everton 3**

McInnes, Latta, Bell

**Liverpool 0**

*Attendance: 44,000*

**Everton:** *Cain, Adams, Parry, Boyle, Holt, Stewart, Latta, McInnes, Southworth, Hartley, J. Bell*

**Liverpool:** *McCann, A. Hannah, D. McLean, McCartney, McQue, McBride, Kerr, Ross, McVean, Bradshaw, H. McQueen*

This was the first ever competitive match between the two local rivals and the beginning of the eagerly anticipated Merseyside derbies. Everton drew first blood when Tom McInnes got on the end of a Billy Stewart free-kick to notch the fixture's first goal on 10 minutes. Despite having to temporarily leave the field with an injury, McInnes had a hand in the second goal of the game when he found marauding winger Alex Latta, whose shot from a tight angle beat William McCann in the Liverpool goal after an hour. The third and final goal came via a Jack Bell deflected shot two minutes from the end to give Everton a convincing victory. It was the perfect result for the home side, who kept up their 100 per cent winning record at the top of the table while Liverpool were yet to record their first League victory with four draws and five defeats from their opening nine games.

# 17th November 1894

First Division

**Liverpool 2**

D. Hannah, Ross (pen)

**Everton 2**

Kelso (pen), Latta

*Attendance:* **30,000**

**Liverpool:** M. McQueen, A. Hannah, D. McLean, McCartney, McQue, J. McLean, McVean, Ross, Bradshaw, D. Hannah, Drummond

**Everton:** Cain, Kelso, Parry, Boyle, Holt, Stewart, Latta, McInnes, Hartley, Chadwick, J. Bell

Everton returned to Anfield, their old home, for the first time since their acrimonious departure two years earlier, and found their hosts a much tougher prospect in this return fixture. Both teams had chances before Davy Hannah – bought from Sunderland the previous week to strengthen the attack – gave away a penalty kick on the half-hour from which Bob Kelso scored for the visitors. Hannah himself made amends 10 minutes into the second half with a spectacular shot that Tom Cain was unable to stop and contemporary press reports allege that even the Everton fans applauded his goal. The visitors were beginning to dominate the game and seemingly had the match wrapped up when Alex Latta scored his team's second with just five minutes to go, but a foul by Bob Kelso gave Liverpool the chance to equalize from the penalty spot and Jimmy Ross made no mistake in the dying moments of the game.

# 3rd October 1896

First Division

**Everton 2**

Hartley, Milward

**Liverpool 1**

Ross

*Attendance:* **45,000**

**Everton:** Briggs, Storrier, Arridge, Boyle, Holt, Stewart, J. Bell, Taylor, Hartley, Chadwick, Milward

**Liverpool:** *Storer, Goldie, Wilkie, McCartney, McQue, Holmes, McVean, Ross, Allan, Becton, Bradshaw*

Liverpool's top-flight absence lasted just one season as they outclassed all their opposition to win the Second Division at the first time of asking and the Merseyside derbies resumed with a vengeance. Yet again, it was Everton who were the ascendant team on Merseyside and they raced to a 2-0 half-time advantage with goals from Alfred Milward and Abe Hartley. Liverpool shot out of the starting blocks following the interval and forced their first corner of the game. Within six minutes of the restart, a ball from Harry Bradshaw sent Jimmy Ross clean through and his shot screwed off the arm of Henry Briggs and into the Everton net. Both Liverpool players and fans alike clamoured for an equalizer but, despite Archie Goldie hitting the bar, they were unable to conjure up another goal and were still looking for their first Merseyside derby victory.

## 21st November 1896

First Division
**Liverpool 0**
**Everton 0**
*Attendance: 30,000*
**Liverpool:** *Storer, Goldie, Wilkie, McCartney, Neill, Holmes, McVean, Geary, Allan, Michael, Bradshaw*
**Everton:** *Menham, Storrier, Arridge, Boyle, Holt, Stewart, Taylor, J. Bell, Cameron, Chadwick, Milward*

A crowd of 30,000 turned up to watch the two sides play out the first goalless draw in the fixture's history that coincided with a debut for Everton goalkeeper Bob Menham. Liverpool started the strongest with George Allan missing the target with an overhead kick before Robert Neill headed wide. Everton retaliated with Alfred Milward sending a shot wide, but Liverpool again threatened the visitors' goal when John Holmes hit the post. Time and again both sides threatened to open the scoring but each team lacked the creativity and accuracy in the final third of the field to bring that promise to fruition.

## 25<sup>th</sup> September 1897

First Division
**Liverpool 3**
Walker, McQue, Becton
**Everton 1**
Taylor
*Attendance:* 30,000
**Liverpool:** *Storer, A. Goldie, Wilkie, McCartney, McQue, Cleghorn, Marshall, Walker, Cunliffe, Becton, Bradshaw*
**Everton:** *McFarlane, Meecham, Barker, Boyle, Holt, Robertson, Taylor, Cameron, Hartley, Chadwick, J. Bell*

Liverpool finally registered a win against their neighbours at the fifth time of asking. It was also their first victory of the season following draws against Stoke City and Preston North End and a 4-2 defeat against The Wednesday. Everton kicked off in bright fashion with Jack Taylor and John Cameron combining before Jack Robertson pounced on a loose ball to test Harry Storer in the Liverpool goal. His counterpart, Rab McFarlane, was soon in action preventing Willie Walker's header from breaching his goal and shortly after Storer saved from Abe Hartley the barriers at the Anfield Road End gave way under the pressure of the crowd and had to be repaired. After a short delay, Everton took the lead when Taylor sent his shot between the backs and into the net. Liverpool were level after half an hour when Walker followed up after Daniel Cunliffe's effort was charged down. Liverpool were in the ascendancy and, despite Frank Becton missing an open goal, took the lead when Joe McQue beat McFarlane from long range. Liverpool had Storer to thank for preventing Everton from equalizing after the interval and Becton made sure of the result by heading in their third goal.

## 16<sup>th</sup> October 1897

First Division
**Everton 3**
Williams 2, J. Bell
**Liverpool 0**
*Attendance:* 40,000

11

**Everton:** *McFarlane, Meecham, Storrier, Boyle, Holt, Robertson, Taylor, Williams, J. Bell, Cameron, Divers*

**Liverpool:** *Storer, A. Goldie, Wilkie, McCartney, Holmes, Cleghorn, Marshall, Walker, Cunliffe, Becton, Bradshaw*

Everton made a great start to this derby match with a goal in the first five minutes. John Divers crossed the ball and, while Jack Bell and John Cameron failed to connect, William Williams was on hand to drive the ball into the net off the crossbar. Both teams created chances, but the tackling was ferocious at times and it wasn't until the 65th minute that another goal was scored. Jack Taylor beat Archie Goldie and crossed the ball for Jack Bell to head goalwards. Although the ball hit the bar before bouncing down there was no doubt that it had been over the line and Everton could celebrate their second goal. Bell, Williams and Taylor combined to make progress up the field in a move that culminated in Williams netting his second to give Everton a 3-0 victory.

## 24th September 1898

First Division

**Everton 1**

Proudfoot

**Liverpool 2**

McCowie 2 (1 pen)

*Attendance:* **45,000**

**Everton:** *Muir, Balmer, Molyneux, Boyle, Owen, Taylor, Clarke, J. Bell, Proudfoot, Kirwan, Gee*

**Liverpool:** *Storer, A. Goldie, Dunlop, Howell, Raisbeck, W. Goldie, Marshall, McCowie, Walker, Morgan, Robertson*

The first Merseyside derby away win was recorded by Liverpool when they left Goodison Park with a 2-1 victory in this match. Chances abounded with first Tommy Robertson sending a shot wide and then Ellis Gee and Jack Taylor both having the opportunity to score. In the end it was John Proudfoot who opened the scoring when he headed past Harry Storer from a corner after 10 minutes. Andrew McCowie equalized in similar fashion 15 minutes later to send the two sides in level at half-time. The second half saw Liverpool pushing for a winner and they were handed the perfect opportunity when Billy Balmer tripped Robertson and the referee awarded the visitors a penalty that McCowie converted. Despite Everton being forced to play the remainder of the match with only nine fit players – Proudfoot and Gee having received injuries – the home side continued to press for an equalizer and only a superb save by Storer kept out a magnificent shot from Jack Kirwan.

## 21st January 1899

First Division

**Liverpool 2**

Walker, Robertson

**Everton 0**

*Attendance: 30,000*

**Liverpool:** *Storer, A. Goldie, Dunlop, Howell, Raisbeck, W. Goldie, Cox, Walker, Allan, Morgan, Robertson*

**Everton:** *Muir, Balmer, Molyneux, Boyle, Taylor, Hughes, J. Bell, Proudfoot, Crompton, Chadwick, Kirwan*

Liverpool registered the fixture's first double over their neighbours with this win, although it would prove to be the home side's last victory at Anfield until December 1919. The win also leapfrogged Liverpool above third-placed Everton although they were level on 29 points, four behind leaders Aston Villa who had played three games fewer than both Merseyside clubs. This match was evenly contested at first, despite the state of the turf, but it was Liverpool who opened the scoring when John Walker netted after 10 minutes following good build-up play by Jack Cox. Everton were disadvantaged in the second half by having to play with the sun in their eyes, and they still couldn't find a way through the Liverpool defence. Jack Kirwan produced an excellent shot which Harry Storer managed to save and John Proudfoot was unable to convert the loose ball. Liverpool kept pressing and their efforts were rewarded in the final minute when Cox dribbled past Ted Hughes and George Molyneux to set up an easy goal for Tommy Robertson.

## 23rd September 1899

First Division

**Liverpool 1**

Robertson

**Everton 2**

Taylor, Settle

*Attendance: 30,000*

**Liverpool:** *Perkins, A. Goldie, Dunlop, Howell, Raisbeck, W. Goldie, Cox, C. Wilson, Parkinson, Morgan, Robertson*

**Everton:** *Muir, Balmer, Molyneux, Wolstenholme, Boyle, Blythe, Taylor, J. Sharp, Toman, Settle, Schofield*

Everton almost took the lead within minutes of the start of this match when Jimmy Settle narrowly missed with a header from a free-kick while further efforts from Alf Schofield and Will Toman went close. The stiff breeze was helping Everton as the Liverpool players failed to adapt adequately to the conditions and the visitors were enjoying the majority of possession. After half an hour, Archie Goldie failed to clear the ball and Jack Taylor gave Bill Perkins no chance of saving his shot to put Everton into the lead although they conceded a free-kick soon after, from which Tommy Robertson levelled the match. Liverpool had the advantage of the wind behind them in the second half and had chances to put the game beyond Everton's reach, but the visitors went on to score their second when Settle dashed between the backs before unleashing an unstoppable low shot past Perkins. Indeed, Perkins was the main reason why Everton only managed to score twice although they thoroughly deserved their victory. Jack Parkinson made history when playing in this match as it turned out to be his only appearance for Liverpool between spells at Blackpool.

## 20th January 1900

First Division

**Everton 3**

Blythe, Settle 2

**Liverpool 1**

Raybould

*Attendance:* 30,000

**Everton:** *Muir, Eccles, Balmer, Wolstenholme, Blythe, Abbott, J. Sharp, Taylor, Proudfoot, Settle, Gray*

**Liverpool:** *Perkins, A. Goldie, Dunlop, Howell, Raisbeck, W. Goldie, Raybould, Satterthwaite, Walker, Morgan, Robertson*

Many thought that Liverpool had as much of the play in this match as their opponents in blue and deserved a point, but Everton took the chances that came their way and claimed victory on a sunny January Saturday afternoon. Liverpool got the game off to a cracking start within the first minute when Willie Muir in the Everton goal fumbled an Alex Raisbeck long-range shot and Sam Raybould was first to the lose ball. Perhaps somewhat overconfident, Liverpool failed to press in search of a second goal – instead preferring to show off their passing game – and this proved to be their undoing, despite the Everton forwards having few chances in the first half. Having led the match for more than an hour, this danger became a reality when Robert Gray forced a corner from which Joe Blythe scored the equalizer. Unbelievably, Settle scored twice in the space of three minutes – both chances created by Gray – to put Everton 3-1 in front with 17 minutes to go.

# Chapter Two

# The Early 20<sup>th</sup> Century

The new century saw Liverpool claim the First Division crown for the first time in 1900–01 with Everton having to be content with runners-up position the following season. Liverpool were relegated in 1903–04 but bounced back at the first time of asking as Second Division champions and went on to repeat that feat the following season in the top flight. Everton, meanwhile, won another First Division title in 1914–15 before the First World War put a halt to League football. In the FA Cup Everton reached the Final on two occasions, winning the trophy for the first time in their history with a 1-0 victory over Newcastle United in 1906 and losing to The Wednesday the following year. Liverpool made their first Final appearance in 1914 but ended up losing 1-0 against Burnley.

## Record in the Early 20<sup>th</sup> Century

**Everton**

| Season | League | P | W | D | L | F | A | Pts | Pos |
|--------|--------|---|---|---|---|---|---|-----|-----|
| 1900–01 | Div 1 | 34 | 16 | 5 | 13 | 55 | 42 | 37 | 7 |
| 1901–02 | Div 1 | 34 | 17 | 7 | 10 | 53 | 35 | 41 | 2 |
| 1902–03 | Div 1 | 34 | 13 | 6 | 15 | 45 | 47 | 32 | 12 |
| 1903–04 | Div 1 | 34 | 19 | 5 | 10 | 59 | 32 | 43 | 3 |
| 1904–05 | Div 1 | 34 | 21 | 5 | 8 | 63 | 36 | 47 | 2 |
| 1905–06 | Div 1 | 38 | 15 | 7 | 16 | 70 | 66 | 37 | 11 |
| 1906–07 | Div 1 | 38 | 20 | 5 | 13 | 70 | 46 | 45 | 3 |
| 1907–08 | Div 1 | 38 | 15 | 6 | 17 | 58 | 64 | 36 | 11 |
| 1908–09 | Div 1 | 38 | 18 | 10 | 10 | 82 | 57 | 46 | 2 |
| 1909–10 | Div 1 | 38 | 16 | 8 | 14 | 51 | 56 | 40 | 10 |
| 1910–11 | Div 1 | 38 | 19 | 7 | 12 | 50 | 36 | 45 | 4 |

| 1911–12 | Div 1 | 38 | 20 | 6 | 12 | 46 | 42 | 46 | 2 |
| 1912–13 | Div 1 | 38 | 15 | 7 | 16 | 48 | 54 | 37 | 11 |
| 1913–14 | Div 1 | 38 | 12 | 11 | 15 | 46 | 55 | 35 | 15 |
| 1914–15 | Div 1 | 38 | 19 | 8 | 11 | 76 | 47 | 46 | 1 |
| 1919–20 | Div 1 | 42 | 12 | 14 | 16 | 69 | 68 | 38 | 16 |

## FA Cup

| 1900–01 | 0-2 v Sheffield United (Second Round) |
| 1901–02 | 2-2, 0-2 v Liverpool (First Round) |
| 1902–03 | 0-1 v Millwall (Third Round) |
| 1903–04 | 1-2 v Tottenham Hotspur (First Round) |
| 1904–05 | 1-1, 1-2 v Aston Villa (Semi-final) |
| 1905–06 | 1-0 v Newcastle United (Final) |
| 1906–07 | 1-2 v The Wednesday (Final) |
| 1907–08 | 0-0, 2-3 v Southampton (Fourth Round) |
| 1908–09 | 0-1 v Manchester United (Second Round) |
| 1909–10 | 0-0, 0-3 v Barnsley (Semi-final) |
| 1910–11 | 0-5 v Derby County (Third Round) |
| 1911–12 | 1-2 v Swindon Town (Fourth Round) |
| 1912–13 | 0-1 v Oldham Athletic (Fourth Round) |
| 1913–14 | 1-2 v Glossop North End (First Round) |
| 1914–15 | 0-2 v Chelsea (Semi-final) |
| 1919–20 | 0-2 v Birmingham (First Round) |

## Liverpool

| Season | League | P | W | D | L | F | A | Pts | Pos |
| --- | --- | --- | --- | --- | --- | --- | --- | --- | --- |
| 1900–01 | Div 1 | 34 | 19 | 7 | 8 | 59 | 35 | 45 | 1 |
| 1901–02 | Div 1 | 34 | 10 | 12 | 12 | 42 | 38 | 32 | 11 |
| 1902–03 | Div 1 | 34 | 17 | 4 | 13 | 68 | 49 | 38 | 5 |
| 1903–04 | Div 1 | 34 | 9 | 8 | 17 | 49 | 62 | 26 | 17 |
| 1904–05 | Div 2 | 34 | 27 | 4 | 3 | 93 | 25 | 58 | 1 |
| 1905–06 | Div 1 | 38 | 23 | 5 | 10 | 79 | 46 | 51 | 1 |
| 1906–07 | Div 1 | 38 | 13 | 7 | 18 | 64 | 65 | 33 | 15 |
| 1907–08 | Div 1 | 38 | 16 | 6 | 16 | 68 | 61 | 38 | 8 |
| 1908–09 | Div 1 | 38 | 15 | 6 | 17 | 57 | 65 | 36 | 16 |
| 1909–10 | Div 1 | 38 | 21 | 6 | 11 | 78 | 57 | 48 | 2 |

| 1910–11 | Div 1 | 38 | 15 | 7 | 16 | 53 | 51 | 37 | 13 |
| 1911–12 | Div 1 | 38 | 12 | 10 | 16 | 49 | 55 | 34 | 17 |
| 1912–13 | Div 1 | 38 | 16 | 5 | 17 | 61 | 71 | 37 | 12 |
| 1913–14 | Div 1 | 38 | 14 | 7 | 17 | 46 | 62 | 35 | 16 |
| 1914–15 | Div 1 | 38 | 14 | 9 | 15 | 65 | 75 | 37 | 13 |
| 1919–20 | Div 1 | 42 | 19 | 10 | 13 | 59 | 44 | 48 | 4 |

## FA Cup

| 1900–01 | 0-2 v Notts County (First Round) |
| 1901–02 | 1-4 v Southampton (Second Round) |
| 1902–03 | 1-2 v Manchester United (First Round) |
| 1903–04 | 1-3 v Blackburn Rovers (First Round) |
| 1904–05 | 1-1, 1-2 v Everton (First Round) |
| 1905–06 | 0-2 v Everton (Semi-final) |
| 1906–07 | 0-1 v The Wednesday (Fourth Round) |
| 1907–08 | 1-3 v Newcastle United (Third Round) |
| 1908–09 | 2-3 v Norwich City (Second Round) |
| 1909–10 | 0-2 v Bristol City (First Round) |
| 1910–11 | 1-2 v Everton (Second Round) |
| 1911–12 | 0-3 v Fulham (Second Round) |
| 1912–13 | 1-1, 0-1 v Newcastle United (Third Round) |
| 1913–14 | 0-1 v Burnley (Final) |
| 1914–15 | 0-1 v Sheffield United (Second Round) |
| 1919–20 | 1-2 v Huddersfield Town (Fourth Round) |

## The Matches

## 22nd September 1900

First Division

**Everton 1**

McDonald

**Liverpool 1**

Raybould

*Attendance:* **50,000**

**Everton:** *Muir, Balmer, Watson, Wolstenholme, Booth, Abbott, J. Sharp, McDonald, Proudfoot, Settle, Turner*

**Liverpool:** *Perkins, J. Robertson, Dunlop, Wilson, Raisbeck, W. Goldie, Cox, Walker, Raybould, Satterthwaite, T. Robertson*

After Everton won the toss, they launched an attack on the Liverpool defence that almost brought a goal when Jimmy Settle's shot was just wide of the post. It wasn't long before the Liverpool goal was in danger again, this time when an Alex Raisbeck free-kick provided Jack Sharp with an opportunity that Bill Perkins was equal to. Liverpool rallied but the defences held firm and it was a while before either keeper was called into action. Jack Cox and Charlie Satterthwaite both had chances for the visitors before Everton took the lead after half an hour when Raisbeck conceded a corner from which Alex McDonald headed in the first goal of the game. Immediately after the interval, Liverpool levelled in spectacular fashion when Cox lifted the ball over Sam Wolstenholme for the advancing Sam Raybould to finish the move off. It sparked both sides into action but the safe hands of Perkins and Willie Muir ensured that the game ended one apiece.

## 19th January 1901

First Division

**Liverpool 1**

Cox

**Everton 2**

Taylor 2

*Attendance:* **18,000**

**Liverpool:** *Perkins, J. Robertson, Dunlop, Wilson, Raisbeck, W. Goldie, Cox, Walker, Raybould, McGuigan, T. Robertson*

**Everton:** *Muir, Eccles, Crelley, Wolstenholme, Booth, Abbott, J. Sharp, Taylor, Proudfoot, Settle, Turner*

Few would have guessed, after they had witnessed Liverpool lose this derby match, that they had been watching the team that would go on to win the First Division that season. Indeed, even the League table failed to point in that direction with Liverpool in eighth position, seven points behind leaders Nottingham Forest albeit with two games in hand. The match had been in serious doubt due to the recent bad weather that had left the pitch waterlogged but, once the whistle blew, Everton adapted better to the conditions and began sending in long passes that the Liverpool defence found difficult to deal with. Jack Taylor opened the scoring after 18 minutes and Liverpool chances were few and far between until sloppy defending allowed Jack Cox to equalize in the 37th minute. After the interval, the frantic action continued with Willie Muir producing a fine save to deny Sam Raybould while Alex Raisbeck and John Walker also had chances to put the home side in front. Shortly after the hour mark, Taylor managed to get on the end of one of a string of crossed shots to drive the ball home past Bill Perkins to give Everton the victory.

## 14th September 1901

First Division

**Liverpool 2**

White, Raybould

**Everton 2**

J. Sharp, Settle

*Attendance: 30,000*

**Liverpool:** *Perkins, Glover, Dunlop, Wilson, Raisbeck, Goldie, Bowen, White, Raybould, McGuigan, Cox*

**Everton:** *Muir, Balmer, Watson, Boyle, Booth, Abbott, J. Sharp, Taylor, Proudfoot, Settle, J. Bell*

The First Division champions had begun the defence of their title with a draw and a defeat, without scoring a goal, as Everton arrived for the third fixture of the 1901–02 season. An enjoyable match was played out over the 90 minutes and press reports later praised the two sets of players for "concentrating their energies on the ball rather than the player". Bill White had a dream start to his Anfield career when he scored after combining with fellow Liverpool debutant George Bowen within the first five minutes. The home side's lead, however, would last just three minutes as Bill Perkins parried Walter Abbott's shot and Jack Sharp thundered the ball into the back of the net. Liverpool were soon having the better of the match in terms of possession and territory, with Andy McGuigan having chances that included a disallowed goal.

Everton's forays into the Liverpool half were less frequent although Jimmy Settle and Jack Taylor both sent efforts over the bar. Settle eventually gave the visitors the lead three minutes before half-time but Sam Raybould restored parity three minutes into the second half and neither side could find a winner.

## 11ᵗʰ January 1902

First Division

**Everton 4**

J. Bell, Young, Settle 2

**Liverpool 0**

*Attendance:* **25,000**

**Everton:** *Kitchen, Balmer, B. Sharp, Wolstenholme, Booth, Abbott, J. Sharp, Taylor, Young, Settle, J. Bell*

**Liverpool:** *Marshall, Glover, Dunlop, Fleming, Raisbeck, Goldie, Cox, Walker, Raybould, McGuigan, T. Robertson*

Liverpool gave a debut to goalkeeper William Marshall with first-choice custodian Bill Perkins unavailable for this derby fixture and the 22-year-old Liverpudlian was to have a nightmare introduction. Press reports later criticized his positioning but the majority were sympathetic towards the youngster who never played for the Liverpool first team again. Everton began the brightest, creating chances from the outset, and Jack Bell scored from close range after 10 minutes. Just five minutes later and Alex "Sandy" Young was presented with his side's second goal when the Liverpool halves failed to deal with a ball forward and Young ran on to easily beat the advancing Marshall. Liverpool responded with some good attacking football but a lack of accuracy meant that George Kitchen was rarely troubled in the Everton goal. After the interval, sleet began to fall and the quality of football somewhat succumbed to the conditions. Bert Sharp launched the ball into the Liverpool goalmouth and, while the visiting defenders desperately tried to clear the danger, Jimmy Settle pounced to score Everton's third goal. The England forward notched his second in the final minutes to give Everton the biggest win to date in the Merseyside derby.

## 25th January 1902

FA Cup First Round

**Liverpool 2**

T. Robertson (pen), Hunter

**Everton 2**

Taylor, J. Sharp

*Attendance: 25,000*

**Liverpool:** *Perkins, J.T. Robertson, Dunlop, Wilson, Raisbeck, Goldie,*
*T. Robertson, Hunter, McGuigan, Fleming, Cox*

**Everton:** *Kitchen, Balmer, Eccles, Wolstenholme, Booth, Abbott, J. Sharp,*
*Taylor, Young, Bowman, J. Bell*

Just a fortnight after Everton's emphatic 4-0 win, they travelled to Anfield for the first FA Cup encounter between the Merseyside clubs. Anyone who was anticipating a repeat of the rout was mistaken as Liverpool gave the visitors a stern test. The home side had the better of the first half with Andy McGuigan having a couple of chances but failing to find a way past George Kitchen. They did, however, take the lead just before half-time after Alex Raisbeck was fouled in the area. Kitchen saved Tommy Robertson's first effort but the outside-left made no mistake with the rebound. Everton became more aggressive as the second half kicked off and soon equalized through Jack Taylor. That energized Liverpool and Billy Dunlop dispossessed Jack Sharp before passing to John 'Sailor' Hunter who let fly with an unstoppable shot to regain the lead. Such was the pressure on the Everton defence that it seemed most likely that it would be Liverpool adding to their tally but, when Raisbeck conceded a free-kick, George Eccles put the ball into the box and Sharp buried the ball in the net to earn his side a replay.

## 30th January 1902

FA Cup First Round replay

**Everton 0**

**Liverpool 2**

Balmer (og), Hunter

*Attendance: 20,000*

**Everton:** *Kitchen, Balmer, B. Sharp, Wolstenholme, Booth, Abbott, J. Sharp, Taylor, Young, Bowman, J. Bell*
**Liverpool:** *Perkins, Dunlop, J.T. Robertson, Wilson, Raisbeck, Goldie, T. Robertson, Hunter, McGuigan, Davies, Cox*

With Everton still missing Jimmy Settle, George Eccles was another casualty who failed to take to the pitch for this FA Cup replay. As in the original fixture, Liverpool looked by far the better side and Everton were soon repelling waves of attacking football while trying to make chances of their own. Four minutes before the interval, a Liverpool free-kick was sent into the box by Alex Raisbeck and Billy Balmer misdirected his header to put the ball into his own net. Everton were effectively a man down once Jack Bell injured his arm and soon found themselves two goals down as well. Liverpool's second came from another Raisbeck free-kick when John Hunter latched onto the ball to drive past George Kitchen and decide the tie.

## 27th September 1902

First Division
**Everton 3**
Brearley, Young, Abbott
**Liverpool 1**
Raybould (pen)
*Attendance:* **40,000**
**Everton:** *Kitchen, Henderson, W. Balmer, Taylor, Booth, Abbott, J. Sharp, Brearley, Young, Sheridan, J. Bell*
**Liverpool:** *Perkins, Glover, Dunlop, Parry, Raisbeck, Goldie, Goddard, Livingstone, Raybould, Morris, Cox*

While Liverpool had the better of the opening exchanges, it was Everton who set the match alight with three goals in five first-half minutes. John Brearley notched their first in the 18th minute with a thunderous shot that gave Bill Perkins no chance. Two minutes later, Sandy Young doubled the home side's advantage from Jack Sharp's cross and Walter Abbott notched Everton's third with a decisive strike from a defensive clearance. Although Liverpool did pull one back through a Sam Raybould penalty on 35 minutes after George Livingstone had been pushed in the area, they paid the price for not taking more of the numerous chances they created. Many felt that a draw would have been a fair reflection of the match, but it was Everton who claimed all the points.

## 10th April 1903

First Division
**Liverpool 0**
**Everton 0**
*Attendance: 28,000*
**Liverpool:** *Platt, Glover, Dunlop, Parry, Raisbeck, Goldie, Goddard, Livingstone, Raybould, Chadwick, Cox*
**Everton:** *Kitchen, W. Balmer, Crelley, Wolstenholme, Booth, Abbott, J. Sharp, Taylor, Young, Settle, J. Bell*

This end-of-season derby fixture took place on Good Friday in brilliant sunshine and, while the defences played well, the goalless scoreline at the end of 90 minutes was as the result of poor finishing. Jimmy Settle saw his early shot saved by Peter Platt in the Liverpool goal with the help of the post, and both Jack Sharp and Sam Raybould failed to score when the opportunity arose. Although Sharp again tested Platt after the interval, it was Liverpool who were playing the better football and an Arthur Goddard shot was claimed to be over the line but the goal wasn't given. Tensions rose as the match progressed with free-kicks frequently being conceded and the best chance of a goal went begging as Raybould missed from close range.

## 10th October 1903

First Division
**Liverpool 2**
Morris 2
**Everton 2**
Sheridan 2
*Attendance: 30,000*
**Liverpool:** *Platt, J. McLean, Fleming, Parry, Raisbeck, Hughes, Goddard, Buck, Parkinson, Morris, Cox*

**Everton:** *Kitchen, Henderson, Crelley, Wolstenholme, Booth, Abbott, Taylor, McDermott, Young, Sheridan, Hardman*

Liverpool were again guilty of squandering their chances and should have been at least two goals up by half-time with both Jack Parkinson and Fred Buck wasting glorious opportunities to open the scoring. Everton's Jim Sheridan was not suffering from the same ailment, however, and notched his side's first after 20 minutes with a shot that went in off the crossbar. Sheridan got his second five minutes later and the visitors found themselves two goals in front against the run of play. Liverpool pulled one back almost immediately when Jack Cox eluded Sam Wolstenholme and Bill Henderson to cross to Parkinson. This time, the half-back made better use of the ball and headed back to Dickie Morris who drove the ball into the net to reduce the deficit. Morris was again on the scoresheet when his header brought about a Liverpool equalizer. The four goals had come in little more than 15 minutes of a frantic first half. While the second period threatened further scoring, neither side managed to find the winner and both had to be satisfied with a draw.

## 1<sup>st</sup> April 1904

First Division
**Everton 5**
Wolstenholme, Young 4
**Liverpool 2**
Robinson, Parry
*Attendance:* **40,000**
**Everton:** *Kitchen, W. Balmer, Crelley, Wolstenholme, Booth, Abbott, J. Sharp, Taylor, Young, McDermott, Hardman*
**Liverpool:** *Cotton, West, Dunlop, Parry, Raisbeck, Hughes, Goddard, Robinson, Raybould, J. Hewitt, Cox*

In spite of the numerous objections to Good Friday football, the attendances were almost up to record proportions. The splendid weather, no doubt, accounted for this, and a crowd of 40,000 witnessed the biggest win to date in the Merseyside derby and the first hat-trick. After Liverpool had threatened the Everton goal, Sam Wolstenholme finished off a counter-attack with a long shot that Charles Cotton should have saved in the third minute. But it wasn't long before Liverpool were on level terms as clever skill from Joe Hewitt took him away from the Everton backs and gave him room to pass to Jack Cox who centred for Bobby Robinson to head home. The home side again took the lead shortly before half-time when Sandy Young shot past Cotton following a breakaway by Harold Hardman. Young added his second when Cotton caught his header behind the line and a goal was awarded but Liverpool pulled one back after a goalmouth scramble in which Maurice Parry seemed to get the final touch. With the game finely balanced at 3-2, Liverpool went in search of an equalizer but it was Everton who scored the next goal when a weak clearance by Alf West presented Young with an open goal which he did not miss. Young added his fourth, and his side's fifth, late in the game before Sam Raybould missed a penalty for the visitors. Liverpool's misery was compounded when they were relegated at the end of the season.

## 4th February 1905

FA Cup First Round

**Liverpool 1**

Parkinson

**Everton 1**

Makepeace (pen)

*Attendance:* **28,000**

**Liverpool:** Doig, West, Dunlop, Parry, Raisbeck, Fleming, Goddard, Robinson, Parkinson, Raybould, Cox

**Everton:** Roose, R. Balmer, Crelley, Makepeace, Taylor, Abbott, J. Sharp, McDermott, Young, Settle, Hardman

All previous form would have pointed to an easy victory for Everton, and, as a matter of fact, they were the better team throughout. But the forwards hung on the ball too much, and against the vigorous, dashing defence of Liverpool, this fatal fault nearly cost them the game. As it was, however, the very vigour which had saved Liverpool on many occasions during the course of the game in the end was their undoing. Sandy Young was fouled by Alex Raisbeck, and Harry

Makepeace scored from a penalty kick and saved the situation to the extent that Liverpool and Everton would have to meet again during the week. It was a desperate game to watch and Liverpool were not too particular in the methods they adopted to stop the combination of the Everton players. Referee Mr Lewis, however, was not one of those officials who ever allow players to get out of hand. Still, on more than one occasion, he had to administer words of advice to the excited players. Jack Parkinson, Sam Raybould and Bobby Robinson – the three Liverpool inside-forwards – all played in fine, dashing style with Parkinson scoring for the home side. Raisbeck was the best half-back on the field, and Billy Dunlop the best of the backs. For Everton, Dick Roose gave a magnificent display in goal, Jimmy Settle was the only one of the forwards to play up to form while Makepeace, Jack Crelley and Robert Balmer – although worked hard in defence – came out of the ordeal with flying colours.

## 8th February 1905

FA Cup First Round replay

**Everton 2**

McDermott, Hardman

**Liverpool 1**

Goddard

*Attendance:* **40,000**

**Everton:** Roose, R. Balmer, Crelley, Makepeace, Taylor, Abbott, J. Sharp, McDermott, Young, Settle, Hardman

**Liverpool:** Doig, West, Dunlop, Parry, Raisbeck, Fleming, Goddard, Carlin, Parkinson, Raybould, Cox

With the weather fine, the replayed Cup tie between the local rivals proved a big attraction. Everton attacked from the start and the match had only been in progress for three minutes when Thomas McDermott scored. From this point to the interval, however, there was little or nothing to choose between the two sides. Liverpool played a strong game, but Dick Roose was in fine form and made several smart saves. The visitors began the second half strongly and within four minutes Arthur Goddard put in a beautiful shot which beat Roose, the ball going into the corner of the net. Contested with great keenness, the play was full of interest. The sides were very evenly matched but, five minutes from the end, Harold Hardman scored the winning goal for Everton.

## 30th September 1905

First Division

**Everton 4**

Settle, Abbott, Hardman, J. Sharp

**Liverpool 2**

Hewitt 2

*Attendance:* **40,000**

**Everton:** *Scott, R. Balmer, Crelley, Makepeace, Taylor, Abbott, J. Sharp, McDermott, Young, Settle, Hardman*

**Liverpool:** *Doig, West, Murray, Parry, Raisbeck, Bradley, Goddard, Robinson, Hewitt, Raybould, Cox*

The absence of Billy Dunlop weakened the Liverpool defence as his replacement, David Murray, was found wanting but the game was not as one-sided as the scoreline might suggest. Liverpool had the ball in the net first but Arthur Goddard's goal was disallowed for offside and it wasn't long before Jimmy Settle had notched his seventh Merseyside derby goal. A dodgy back-pass by Murray forced keeper Ted Doig to concede a corner and, from the resulting kick, Walter Abbott extended Everton's lead although Joe Hewitt did manage to net one for the visitors before half-time with a well-placed shot past Billy Scott. The second half continued in the same vein with Liverpool producing the better football but Everton reaping the results of the chances they had. Harold Hardman scored Everton's third before a long run by Jack Sharp ended with the ball in the back of the net. Hewitt scored a second for the visitors although there were heated claims that he had been in an offside position when the ball deflected off him and past Scott, but the goal stood and gave a final score of 4-2 in favour of the home side.

# 31ˢᵗ March 1906

FA Cup Semi-final (at Villa Park)
**Everton 2**
Abbott, Hardman
**Liverpool 0**
*Attendance:* **37,000**
**Everton:** *Scott, R. Balmer, Crelley, Makepeace, Taylor, Abbott, J. Sharp, Bolton, Young, Settle, Hardman*
**Liverpool:** *Hardy, West, Dunlop, Parry, Raisbeck, Bradley, Goddard, Robinson, Parkinson, Carlin, Hewitt*

Everton's victory over Liverpool was a case of science beating force, superior tactics overcoming vigour, and it was one of the most exciting games seen in a while. Never a dull moment and desperately fast-paced, it would have been a cold-blooded spectator who did not find their pulse quicken as they looked on at the stirring incidents of the momentous struggle. Half of the second half had elapsed before a goal was scored, but in that hour and a quarter there had been enough thrilling incidents for half a dozen matches. Everton scored after Liverpool had been attacking in most resolute style for a long time. There was a dash on Liverpool's goal and Walter Abbott, one of the half-backs, sent in a ground shot. Billy Dunlop, Liverpool's left-back, tried to kick the ball away but failed to get hold of it and, slithering off his toe, it rolled softly over the line, well out of reach of Sam Hardy. Then was a scene equalling pandemonium: blue favours were waved; hats, sticks and caps flew wildly up into the air; and a mighty roar burst from that section of the crowd whose pent-up enthusiasm had waited so long for a chance to let itself loose in a shriek of triumph. It was a rather lucky goal but, in less than a minute, Everton were swarming around the Liverpool goal again with Harold Hardman getting his head to a fine centre from Jack Sharp. This time, there was nothing lucky about the goal and Everton secured the win. The other 89 minutes of the match had always promised goals but the defence was the primary feature and for the most part prevailed. One man on each side stood out above his fellows and, curiously enough, they both filled the same position: Alex Raisbeck (Liverpool's flaxen-haired centre half-back) and Jack Taylor (Everton). Raisbeck was ubiquitous, always in the right place, defending valiantly one minute and sending his forwards away in a fierce attack on the Everton goal the next.

## 13th April 1906

First Division

**Liverpool 1**

West (pen)

**Everton 1**

Taylor

*Attendance:* **33,000**

**Liverpool:** *Hardy, West, Chorlton, Parry, Raisbeck, Bradley, Goddard, Carlin, Hewitt, Raybould, Parkinson*

**Everton:** *Scott, W. Balmer, R. Balmer, Black, Taylor, Abbott, J. Sharp, Bolton, Young, Cook, Hardman*

With Liverpool on course for the First Division title just 12 months after regaining their top-flight status by winning the Second Division the previous season, many were anticipating a closely fought game and that is exactly how this derby match turned out. Jack Taylor opened the scoring shortly before half-time when a speculative high shot was dropped by Sam Hardy and the Everton man followed up to slot home the loose ball. Just 10 minutes into the second half, Liverpool were awarded a penalty when Bob Balmer fouled Jack Parkinson and Alf West converted the spot-kick. Overall, the draw was a fair result because while Liverpool dominated more of the game Everton's attacking play looked far more likely to bring about a goal and Jack Sharp could well have won the game for the visitors in the dying minutes but shot wide.

## 29th September 1906

First Division

**Liverpool 1**

Parkinson

**Everton 2**

Young 2

*Attendance:* **40,000**

**Liverpool:** *Hardy, Saul, Dunlop, Robinson, Raisbeck, Bradley, Goddard, Parkinson, Hewitt, Carlin, Cox*
**Everton:** *Scott, W. Balmer, Crelley, Makepeace, Taylor, Abbott, J. Sharp, Bolton, Young, G. Wilson, Hardman*

The Merseyside derby is always a match of the season but when Liverpool – as League champions – met FA Cup holders Everton there was an added piquancy. Clever forward play by Everton won the game and Sandy Young was the hero of the day. Jack Parkinson scored the only goal of the first half while Walter Abbott missed a penalty for the visitors. In the second half, Young equalized, and some really brilliant footwork was subsequently shown by the Everton vanguard. Then, to the great excitement of the vast crowd, Young scored a second goal and Everton secured a well-deserved triumph.

## 29th March 1907

First Division

**Everton 0**

**Liverpool 0**

*Attendance:* **45,000**

**Everton:** *Scott, W. Balmer, R. Balmer, Makepeace, Taylor, Abbott, J. Sharp, Settle, Young, G. Wilson, Hardman*
**Liverpool:** *Hardy, Saul, Dunlop, Parry, Raisbeck, Bradley, Goddard, Robinson, Raybould, Hewitt, Cox*

Everton missed out on the opportunity to reel in Newcastle United with this goalless draw that left them second in the First Division, six points behind the leaders but with two games in hand. Liverpool played the better football but failed to make the most of their chances and, indeed, should have already made the game safe by half-time. Everton had Billy Scott to thank for their clean sheet, especially for saving Sam Raybould's header that should have given the visitors the lead. The half-time interval went on longer than scheduled when a large section of the crowd burst through the barriers and onto the pitch to begin an impromptu game of football of their own. Everton's performance improved in the second half and Sam Hardy was called into action, but neither side could find the back of the net.

## 5th October 1907

First Division

**Everton 2**

Settle, Makepeace

**Liverpool 4**

Raisbeck, C. Hewitt, J. Hewitt, Cox

*Attendance: 40,000*

**Everton:** *Scott, W. Balmer, R. Balmer, Makepeace, Taylor, Abbott, J. Sharp, Bolton, Young, Settle, Hardman*

**Liverpool:** *Hardy, West, Saul, Chorlton, Raisbeck, Bradley, Goddard, C. Hewitt, J. Hewitt, Robinson, Cox*

Liverpool beat Everton for the first time in a League match since January 1899 and they did it in emphatic fashion although it was the home side who opened the scoring when Jimmy Settle found the net off the post while Sam Hardy was focusing on Sandy Young. The visitors drew level courtesy of an Alex Raisbeck free-kick that navigated through a forest of legs to send the game into the interval on level terms. Charles Hewitt gave Liverpool the lead when he outfoxed Billy Scott but Everton equalized through Harry Makepeace who drove the ball home from a corner. By this point, Everton were the team on top but it was Liverpool who scored again. Joe Hewitt restored the visitors' lead while a speculative shot by Jack Cox crept in off the post to complete a Liverpool victory.

## 17th April 1908

First Division

**Liverpool 0**

**Everton 0**

*Attendance: 35,000*

**Liverpool:** *Hardy, West, Rogers, Parry, Raisbeck, Bradley, Goddard, McPherson, J. Hewitt, Orr, Cox*

**Everton:** *Scott, R. Balmer, Maconnachie, Makepeace, Taylor, Adamson, Couper, Coleman, Freeman, Young, Donnachie*

The match at Anfield provided 35,000 enthusiasts with plenty of excitement but as no goals were scored there was little disappointment although the Good Friday crowd would have loved to have seen at least one goal. The result was a fair reflection of the game, for on each side many brilliant chances came about, but both defences were great. Everton, with the wind behind them, had the best of the first half and Sam Hardy was pivotal in keeping a clean sheet with saves from George Couper, Jack Taylor and Harry Makepeace. The second period saw Liverpool with the advantage of the wind and it was Billy Scott's turn to be the busier of the two keepers. The play ranged from end to end as both teams searched for that elusive goal but to no avail.

## 3rd October 1908

First Division
**Liverpool 0**
**Everton 1**
Barlow
*Attendance: 40,000*
**Liverpool:**  *Hardy, Saul, West, Chorlton, Harrop, Bradley, Goddard, Parkinson, Hewitt, Orr, Bowyer*
**Everton:**  *William Scott, R. Balmer, Maconnachie, Harris, Taylor, Makepeace, J. Sharp, Coleman, Freeman, Young, Barlow*

Playing in broiling heat that was more akin to a summer's day, Liverpool had the unwanted distinction of being the only First Division team to lose at home on this early October Saturday. It was Liverpool's first Anfield defeat of the season as they had previously registered three home wins, scoring nine goals in the process. Everton, on the other hand, kept up their 100 per cent away record and climbed to third in the table, just one point behind Manchester United and Newcastle United. Liverpool were the better team in the first half and deserved to be in front but conceded the only goal of the game after a dangerous cross from Bertie Freeman allowed George Barlow to smash the ball home with Sam Hardy helpless in the 42nd minute. The home side's best chance of equalizing saw Joe Hewitt's thunderbolt come crashing back off the crossbar.

## 9th April 1909

First Division

**Everton 5**

Coleman, Freeman 2, White, Turner

**Liverpool 0**

*Attendance: 45,000*

**Everton:** *William Scott, R. Balmer, Maconnachie, Harris, Taylor, Makepeace, J. Sharp, Coleman, Freeman, White, Turner*

**Liverpool:** *Hardy, Crawford, Chorlton, Harrop, Raisbeck, Bradley, Goddard, Robinson, Hewitt, Orr, Uren*

Beautifully fine weather favoured this match at Goodison Park in front of 45,000 spectators. Play in the first half was very fast and compelling, but Everton were the more dangerous in front of goal. John Coleman and Bertie Freeman scored for the home side while Liverpool failed near goal. The second half was just as interesting but for a long time Liverpool held their own, with the backs doing very well. The Liverpool forwards were not able to get the better of Everton's defence, however. Everton, on the other hand, were always dangerous and Wattie White scored their third goal with a fine long shot. White later hit the post with Robert Turner scoring from the rebound. Freeman added his second as Everton registered the biggest winning margin in a Merseyside derby to date.

## 2nd October 1909

First Division

**Everton 2**

Coleman, Freeman

**Liverpool 3**

Goddard, Stewart, Parkinson

*Attendance: 45,000*

**Everton:** *William Scott, R. Balmer, Maconnachie, Harris, Clifford, Makepeace, J. Sharp, Coleman, Freeman, Young, Turner*

**Liverpool:** *Hardy, Chorlton, Crawford, Robinson, Harrop, Bradley, Goddard, Stewart, Parkinson, Orr, McDonald*

Everton had earned their position at the head of the League table through consistent excellence and they looked forward to their local derby against Liverpool with equanimity. The visitors, however, rose to the occasion and emerged victorious after a terrific match. Liverpool owed their success to their England goalkeeper Sam Hardy, who played a brilliant game throughout and made some wonderful saves. Liverpool, too, were going stronger than Everton at the close and it was that period that Jack Parkinson scored the winning goal. The match was fast and full of delightful play with the spectators never having a dull moment. Early on, John Coleman scored for the home side from a corner but Arthur Goddard equalized before the interval. Bertie Freeman scored for Everton early in the second half after a glorious run before James Stewart again levelled the scores. Then came Parkinson's goal and a fine win for Liverpool.

## 12th February 1910

First Division
**Liverpool 0**
**Everton 1**
Freeman
*Attendance:* **40,000**
**Liverpool:** *Beeby, Chorlton, Rogers, Robinson, Harrop, Bradley, Goddard, Stewart, Parkinson, Orr, McDonald*
**Everton:** *Walter Scott, Clifford, Maconnachie, Allan, Taylor, Makepeace, J. Sharp, White, Freeman, Young, Barlow*

Yet again, Liverpool were on the losing side despite being the better team for large periods of the game. It was frustrating that they created several opportunities to score but the final ball was always a let-down and the attentions of the Everton half-back line severely hampered the Liverpool forwards. The game looked to be heading for a draw when Everton counter-attacked following a Liverpool corner. Jack Sharp fed Bertie Freeman who raced between the defenders to calmly slot home his fourth goal in three consecutive derby matches.

## 1ˢᵗ October 1910

First Division
**Liverpool 0**
**Everton 2**
A. Young, Makepeace
*Attendance: 40,000*
**Liverpool:** *Beeby, Longworth, Chorlton, Robinson, Peake, McConnell, Goddard, Brough, Parkinson, Gilligan, McDonald*
**Everton:** *William Scott, R. Balmer, Maconnachie, Harris, R. Young, Makepeace, Berry, Gourlay, Freeman, A. Young, Turner*

A tremendous crowd of 40,000 turned out to see Everton beat Liverpool at Anfield. The visitors were by far the better side and their two goals – scored by Alex 'Sandy' Young and Harry Makepeace – by no means represented their actual superiority. Everton's first goal arrived after seven minutes when Arthur Berry crossed and Young pounced while the second was scored later in the first half with Makepeace heading in one of a succession of corners. Augustus Beeby, who kept goal for Liverpool instead of Sam Hardy, performed brilliantly but was unable to keep a clean sheet.

## 27ᵗʰ December 1910

First Division
**Everton 0**
**Liverpool 1**
Parkinson
*Attendance: 51,000*
**Everton:** *William Scott, Stevenson, R. Balmer, Harris, R. Young, Makepeace, Berry, Lacey, A. Young, Gourlay, Beare*
**Liverpool:** *Hardy, Longworth, Crawford, Robinson, Harrop, McConnell, Goddard, Stewart, Parkinson, Bowyer, Uren*

A crowd of more than 50,000 watched the Yuletide game at Goodison Park which ended in a rather unexpected win for Liverpool. The match itself was a tame affair with both sides seeming to be feeling the effects of previous matches. There were no goals scored in the first half but five minutes after the interval Jack Parkinson got through and won the match for the visitors. Harold Uren headed upfield following an Everton corner and passed to Jimmy Harrop who found Sam Bowyer. The striker fed the ball into the path of Parkinson who kept a cool head to ease the ball past Billy Scott for the only goal of the game.

## 4th February 1911

FA Cup Second Round

**Everton 2**

A. Young 2

**Liverpool 1**

Parkinson

*Attendance:* **50,000**

**Everton:** *William Scott, Stevenson, Maconnachie, Harris, R. Young, Makepeace, Lacey, Gourlay, Magner, A. Young, Beare*

**Liverpool:** *Hardy, Longworth, Crawford, Robinson, Harrop, McConnell, Goddard, Stewart, Parkinson, Orr, Uren*

Everton had a fright during this FA Cup tie at Goodison Park as their neighbours took a single-goal lead into the interval. Jack Parkinson had scored following a free-kick in the 23rd minute but Sandy Young equalized six minutes after the interval with a header from a corner. Everton had the best of the subsequent exchanges with Young scoring his second with a snap shot in the 77th minute to put the Toffees into the Third Round draw.

## 16th September 1911

First Division

**Everton 2**

Beare, Gourlay

**Liverpool 1**

Parkinson

*Attendance:* **40,000**

**Everton:** *William Scott, Stevenson, Holbem, Harris, R. Young, Makepeace, Beare, Jefferis, Jordan, Gourlay, Lacey*

**Liverpool:** *Hardy, Longworth, Crawford, Robinson, Lowe, McConnell, Goddard, Gilligan, Parkinson, Orr, Uren*

This derby match saw both teams depleted by injuries and Liverpool were unlucky against Everton at Goodison Park, as they lost Ronald Orr to injury early on. George Beare scored a first-half goal for the home side while Jack Parkinson equalized after the interval before James Gourlay notched the winning goal shortly before the full-time whistle. Both Parkinson and Frank Jefferis had been guilty of squandering earlier easy chances of scoring.

## 20th January 1912

First Division

**Liverpool 1**

Gilligan

**Everton 3**

T. Browell, Jefferis, Beare

*Attendance: 35,000*

**Liverpool:** *Hardy, Longworth, Pursell, Robinson, Peake, Lowe, Goddard, Bovill, Gilligan, Stewart, Uren*

**Everton:** *William Scott, Stevenson, Maconnachie, Harris, Fleetwood, Makepeace, Beare, Jefferis, T. Browell, Bradshaw, Davidson*

Everton continued their sequence of not losing at Anfield since January 1899 with a 3-1 victory over their local rivals. Tom Browell opened the scoring after half an hour when he took advantage of Sam Hardy's indecision following a cross from William Davidson. Six minutes into the second half, Frank Jefferis launched a mazy, darting run that took him almost half the length of the pitch before shooting past an unconvincing Hardy. Sam Gilligan pulled one back for the home side after 80 minutes and Liverpool pushed hard for an equalizer but Everton grabbed their third through George Beare with just three minutes to go.

## 5th October 1912

First Division

**Liverpool 0**

**Everton 2**

T. Browell, Gault

*Attendance: 46,000*

**Liverpool:** *Campbell, Longworth, Pursell, Lowe, Ferguson, McKinlay, Goddard, Stewart, Miller, Parkinson, Lacey*
**Everton:** *Caldwell, Stevenson, Holbem, Harris, Fleetwood, Makepeace, Beare, Gault, T. Browell, Bradshaw, Davidson*

Everton, as they frequently did in the first years of the 20th century, visited their neighbours at Anfield and emerged with a 2-0 victory. It could not be called a great game by any stretch of the imagination, but the play was always interesting. Everton were a trifle better than the Reds, their forwards being quicker to the ball and more resourceful, with William Gault and Frank Bradshaw doing particularly well. Harry Makepeace, at left-half, gave a capital display. The absence of John Maconnachie was not noticed with Walter Holbem, drafted into the side in his place, playing a sound and clever game. There was a lack of combination among the Liverpool forwards, but Jack Parkinson tried hard in the centre while Bill Lacey and Arthur Goddard made a good wing. Everton scored once in each half: Tom Browell heading through from a centre by George Beare; and Gault sealing the victory in the second half.

## 8th February 1913

First Division
**Everton 0**
**Liverpool 2**
Parkinson 2
*Attendance:* **40,000**
**Everton:** *Caldwell, Holbem, Maconnachie, Harris, Fleetwood, Makepeace, Beare, Jefferis, Houston, T. Browell, Davidson*
**Liverpool:** *Campbell, Longworth, Crawford, Lowe, Ferguson, Peake, Goddard, Metcalfe, Miller, Parkinson, Lacey*

Everton – who had endured a gruelling FA Cup replay against Brighton & Hove Albion during the previous week – had several reserves in their side and proved no match for Liverpool, although they did come close to scoring when Tom Browell saw his shot come back off the crossbar. The visiting forwards were in fine form and Jack Parkinson scored once in each half. Parkinson was in outstanding form and his second goal, which came in the 70th minute, was a superb piece of individual skill. He evaded Walter Holbem and beat John Maconnachie to shoot past the helpless James Caldwell in the Everton goal.

## 20th September 1913

First Division
**Everton 1**
Wareing
**Liverpool 2**
Lacey 2
*Attendance:* **40,000**
**Everton:** *Mitchell, Stevenson, Maconnachie, Harris, Wareing, Grenyer, Beare, Jefferis, T. Browell, Bradshaw, Harrison*
**Liverpool:** *Campbell, Speakman, Crawford, Fairfoul, Lowe, Ferguson, Goddard, Stewart, Miller, Gracie, Lacey*

This match saw Everton beaten for the first time during the 1913–14 campaign with Liverpool gaining their first victory of the season. There was never much to choose between the sides, but Liverpool enjoyed a one-goal advantage at the interval. Mitchell came out to claim the ball shortly after the half-hour mark but only succeeded in pushing it towards Bill Lacey who gleefully slotted into the unattended net. The 40,000 crowd saw some really exciting football and Everton equalized nine minutes into the second half when Ken Campbell was unable to prevent Billy Wareing from scoring. Seven minutes from the end, however, Liverpool were the recipients of a dubious free-kick which was taken by Lacey and his centred ball surprised everyone by curling into the net.

## 17th January 1914

First Division
**Liverpool 1**
Metcalfe
**Everton 2**
Parker 2
*Attendance:* **35,000**

**Liverpool:** *Campbell, Longworth, Crawford, Fairfoul, Lowe, Ferguson, Sheldon, Dawson, Metcalfe, Gracie, Lacey*
**Everton:** *Fern, Thompson, Maconnachie, Harris, Fleetwood, Makepeace, Palmer, Jefferis, Parker, Bradshaw, Harrison*

Liverpool had replayed their FA Cup tie with Barnsley just 48 hours before this clash so were not as fresh as Everton, who registered their sixth consecutive Anfield victory. Bill Palmer created the opportunity after half an hour but Ken Campbell allowed the ball to squirm under his prone body and Bobby Parker drove the ball into the net. The situation worsened for the home side when Parker grabbed his second before the interval with a first-time shot that left the Liverpool keeper with no chance. Arthur Metcalfe managed to pull one back in the 59th minute after sloppy goalkeeping by Tommy Fern and the home side continued in their efforts for a second goal which was ultimately not forthcoming.

## 3rd October 1914

First Division
**Liverpool 0**
**Everton 5**
Clennell 2, Parker 3
*Attendance: 32,000*
**Liverpool:** *Campbell, Longworth, Pursell, Bradley, Fairfoul, Ferguson, Sheldon, Metcalfe, Nicholl, McKinlay, Lacey*
**Everton:** *Fern, Thompson, Maconnachie, Fleetwood, Galt, Makepeace, Chedgzoy, Jefferis, Parker, Clennell, Palmer*

Everton's amazing run of success at Anfield – nine wins and five draws in 14 consecutive League games – continued with this emphatic one-sided victory. Liverpool's demise began soon after kick-off with Joe Clennell scoring after just five minutes. Bobby Parker got in on the act after 17 minutes when Campbell's attempted clearance from Clennell fell kindly for the centre-forward to drive home. Everton's third goal came after half-time when Ephraim Longworth was penalized for a foul on Bill Palmer and Parker scored from 12 yards. It really was one-way traffic and both Clennell and Parker added to their tally as the game drew to a close.

## 6th February 1915

First Division

**Everton 1**

Clennell

**Liverpool 3**

Sheldon (pen), Nicholl, Pagnam

*Attendance: 30,000*

**Everton:** *Fern, Thompson, Maconnachie, Fleetwood, Galt, Makepeace, Chedgzoy, Kirsopp, Parker, Clennell, Palmer*

**Liverpool:** *E. Scott, Longworth, Pursell, Lacey, Lowe, McKinlay, Sheldon, Banks, Pagnam, Miller, Nicholl*

Liverpool's victory at Goodison Park belied the teams' form going into this game. At the end of the season Everton were crowned First Division champions while the Reds were battling it out at the bottom of the table. The home side took the lead after 13 minutes when Joe Clennell drilled home a low shot that evaded the despairing dive of Elisha Scott and Everton looked good for both points at half-time. The second half, however, proved a very different story as Liverpool scored three unanswered goals. The first came from the penalty spot in the 56th minute after Fred Pagnam was brought down by John Maconnachie and Jackie Sheldon converted the spot-kick. Five minutes later, Jimmy Nicholl added a second for Liverpool while Pagnam rounded off the scoring with 11 minutes to go.

## 20th December 1919

First Division

**Everton 0**

**Liverpool 0**

*Attendance: 40,000*

**Everton:** *Fern, Page, Weller, Brown, Fleetwood, Grenyer, Jones, Chedgzoy, Kirsopp, Clennell, Harrison*

**Liverpool:** *Campbell, Longworth, Bamber, Bromilow, W. Wadsworth, McKinlay, Sheldon, Lacey, Chambers, Lewis, Pearson*

With Liverpool lying perilously close to the bottom of the First Division,

David Ashworth was recruited from Stockport County to manage the Anfield club. He would have been pleased with the performance displayed by his new charges as they almost scored in the opening minutes when a Bill Lacey header was desperately cleared off the line by Jack Page with Tommy Fern well beaten. Claims that the ball had crossed the line were ignored by the referee. Fern was by far the busier of the two goalkeepers – and Page again had to come to the rescue with another goal-line clearance – although Ken Campbell did well to deny Sam Chedgzoy in the closing stages.

## 27th December 1919

First Division

**Liverpool 3**

Lewis, T. Miller 2

**Everton 1**

Parker

*Attendance:* **48,000**

**Liverpool:** *Campbell, Longworth, Pursell, Bamber, W. Wadsworth, McKinlay, Sheldon, Lacey, T. Miller, Lewis, H. Wadsworth*

**Everton:** *Fern, Thompson, Weller, Brown, Wareing, Grenyer, Chedgzoy, Jefferis, Parker, Rigsby, Donnachie*

Liverpool finally rid themselves of the Everton jinx at Anfield with their first home victory over their neighbours since January 1899. The strong wind was a big factor and aided Liverpool with the first goal. A goal-kick from Tommy Fern was caught by the breeze and carried back towards the Everton keeper before Harry Lewis pounced on the loose ball to open the scoring. Tom Miller added to the home side's tally after 15 minutes when he outwitted Louis Weller and Bob Thompson to drive the ball past Fern. An injured thigh reduced Bob Pursell to the role of spectator by the second half, although Everton didn't have the same advantage as the home side due to the wind's diminishing strength. Miller added his side's third goal, while Bobby Parker scored a late consolation for Everton.

# Chapter Three

# The 1920s

The 1920s brought success in the League for both Merseyside clubs but the only time either side progressed beyond the Fourth Round of the FA Cup was when Liverpool fell to Arsenal in the Fifth Round of the 1926–27 competition. There were consecutive First Division titles for Liverpool in 1921–22 and 1922–23, while Everton topped the pile in 1927–28. The Goodison Park club flirted with relegation a number of times during the decade before finally succumbing to the reality of Second Division football in 1929–30.

## Record in the 1920s

**Everton**

| Season | League | P | W | D | L | F | A | Pts | Pos |
|--------|--------|---|---|---|---|---|---|-----|-----|
| 1920–21 | Div 1 | 42 | 17 | 13 | 12 | 66 | 55 | 47 | 7 |
| 1921–22 | Div 1 | 42 | 12 | 12 | 18 | 57 | 55 | 36 | 20 |
| 1922–23 | Div 1 | 42 | 20 | 7 | 15 | 63 | 59 | 47 | 5 |
| 1923–24 | Div 1 | 42 | 18 | 13 | 11 | 62 | 53 | 49 | 7 |
| 1924–25 | Div 1 | 42 | 12 | 11 | 19 | 40 | 60 | 35 | 17 |
| 1925–26 | Div 1 | 42 | 12 | 18 | 12 | 72 | 70 | 42 | 11 |
| 1926–27 | Div 1 | 42 | 12 | 10 | 20 | 64 | 90 | 34 | 20 |
| 1927–28 | Div 1 | 42 | 20 | 13 | 9 | 102 | 66 | 53 | 1 |
| 1928–29 | Div 1 | 42 | 17 | 4 | 21 | 63 | 75 | 38 | 18 |
| 1929–30 | Div 1 | 42 | 12 | 11 | 19 | 80 | 92 | 35 | 22 |

**FA Cup**

| | | |
|---|---|---|
| 1920–21 | 0-1 v Wolverhampton Wanderers (Fourth Round) | |
| 1921–22 | 0-6 v Crystal Palace (First Round) | |
| 1922–23 | 1-1, 0-1 v Bradford City (First Round) | |
| 1923–24 | 2-5 v Brighton & Hove Albion (Second Round) | |

1924–25    0-1 v Sheffield United (Third Round)
1925–26    1-1, 0-1 v Fulham (Third Round)
1926–27    1-1, 2-2, 2-3 v Hull City (Fourth Round)
1927–28    3-4 v Arsenal (Fourth Round)
1928–29    0-2 v Chelsea (Third Round)
1929–30    1-4 v Blackburn Rovers (Fourth Round)

## Liverpool

| Season | League | P | W | D | L | F | A | Pts | Pos |
|--------|--------|---|---|---|---|---|---|-----|-----|
| 1920–21 | Div 1 | 42 | 18 | 15 | 9 | 63 | 35 | 51 | 4 |
| 1921–22 | Div 1 | 42 | 22 | 13 | 7 | 63 | 36 | 57 | 1 |
| 1922–23 | Div 1 | 42 | 26 | 8 | 8 | 70 | 31 | 60 | 1 |
| 1923–24 | Div 1 | 42 | 15 | 11 | 16 | 49 | 48 | 41 | 12 |
| 1924–25 | Div 1 | 42 | 20 | 10 | 12 | 63 | 55 | 50 | 4 |
| 1925–26 | Div 1 | 42 | 14 | 16 | 12 | 70 | 63 | 44 | 7 |
| 1926–27 | Div 1 | 42 | 18 | 7 | 17 | 69 | 61 | 43 | 9 |
| 1927–28 | Div 1 | 42 | 13 | 13 | 16 | 84 | 87 | 39 | 16 |
| 1928–29 | Div 1 | 42 | 17 | 12 | 13 | 90 | 64 | 46 | 5 |
| 1929–30 | Div 1 | 42 | 16 | 9 | 17 | 63 | 79 | 41 | 12 |

## FA Cup

1920–21    0-1 v Newcastle United (Second Round)
1921–22    0-1 v West Bromwich Albion (Second Round)
1922–23    1-2 v Sheffield United (Third Round)
1923–24    0-1 v Newcastle United (Fourth Round)
1924–25    0-1 v Southampton (Fourth Round)
1925–26    1-3 v Fulham (Fourth Round)
1926–27    0-2 v Arsenal (Fifth Round)
1927–28    1-2 v Cardiff City (Fourth Round)
1928–29    0-0, 2-5 v Bolton Wanderers (Fourth Round)
1929–30    1-2 v Cardiff City (Third Round)

## The Matches

### 23rd October 1920

First Division

**Liverpool 1**

Forshaw

**Everton 0**

*Attendance: 50,000*

**Liverpool:** McNaughton, Lucas, McKinlay, Bamber, W. Wadsworth, Bromilow, Sheldon, Forshaw, Johnson, Chambers, H. Wadsworth

**Everton:** Fern, Thompson, McDonald, Fleetwood, Brewster, Grenyer, Jones, Kirsopp, Peacock, Reid, Harrison

This win lifted Liverpool above their rivals into third place in the First Division table, level on 16 points but having played two games fewer. Both sides were deprived of some of their star players who were away on international duty but the 22 who took the field gave the 50,000 crowd an entertaining match. The home side made the most of their first-half superiority and Tommy Fern was called upon to keep them at bay on more than one occasion. He was beaten, however, after 35 minutes when Dick Forshaw got on the end of Harold Wadsworth's cross to ram the ball into the net. A concerted period of Everton pressure after the interval failed to bring about an equalizer and the closest that the visitors came to scoring was when George Harrison's shot beat Harry McNaughton, but not the crossbar.

### 30th October 1920

First Division

**Everton 0**

**Liverpool 3**

Johnson, Chambers 2

*Attendance: 55,000*

**Everton:** Fern, Downs, McDonald, Fleetwood, Brewster, Grenyer, Chedgzoy, Crossley, Peacock, Reid, Harrison

**Liverpool:** Scott, Longworth, McKinlay, Lacey, W. Wadsworth, Bromilow, Sheldon, Forshaw, Johnson, Chambers, H. Wadsworth

Everton experienced their first home defeat of the season with Liverpool halting their unbeaten run. Smarter on the ball and faster all round, Liverpool were two up at the interval with Dick Johnson and Harry Chambers having scored. The game was more even after the break, but Chambers scored again after having a goal disallowed for offside.

## 5th November 1921

First Division

**Everton 1**

Brewster

**Liverpool 1**

Shone

*Attendance:* **52,000**

**Everton:** *Fern, Downs, McDonald, Fleetwood, Brewster, Grenyer, Chedgzoy, Fazackerley, Davies, Crossley, Harrison*

**Liverpool:** *Scott, Longworth, McKinlay, McNab, W. Wadsworth, Bromilow, Lacey, Forshaw, Shone, Lewis, Hopkin*

Liverpool had the best of the game but had to be content with a draw and one point from this Goodison Park encounter. Everton started the brightest but temporarily lost the services of Dickie Downs when the right-back was knocked out heading away a fast-paced ball. By the time he had returned to the field of play, Liverpool were in the ascendancy and Danny Shone scored the opening goal of the game on 38 minutes after Tommy Fern had failed to hold Tom Bromilow's stinging shot. A second Liverpool goal was disallowed early in the second half as Dick Forshaw was offside when he rammed the ball into the net, before George Brewster equalized from a corner. The remaining half an hour was less frantic, as both sides seemed content to play out the draw.

## 12th November 1921

First Division

**Liverpool 1**

Forshaw

**Everton 1**

Chedgzoy

*Attendance:* **50,000**

**Liverpool:** *Scott, Longworth, McKinlay, McNab, W. Wadsworth, Bromilow, Lacey, Forshaw, Shone, Lewis, Hopkin*

**Everton:** *Fern, Downs, McDonald, Fleetwood, Brewster, Peacock, Chedgzoy, Fazackerley, Irvine, Crossley, Harrison*

This November day turned out to be so foggy that matches were called off around the country with England's match against Ireland at Leicester postponed and Coventry's clash with Derby abandoned after half an hour. The conditions in Liverpool at least allowed for this match to proceed and the home side took the lead shortly before half-time with a superb strike from Dick Forshaw. Many thought that Everton were fortunate to claim a point for their afternoon's work as they created little in the way of chances and their equalizer came courtesy of a refereeing mistake. Mr Howcroft blew for offside against Bobby Irvine but realized his mistake and ordered a drop-ball literally on the penalty line. Suffice to say, Sam Chedgzoy took full advantage of the situation to send the ball past Elisha Scott. Luckily for Liverpool they were not left ruing their two drawn encounters with Everton – they were crowned champions at the end of the season, claiming their third Fist Division title with a six-point advantage over second-placed Spurs. Everton finished just one place above the relegation zone, albeit with four points to spare.

## 7th October 1922

First Division

**Liverpool 5**

Chambers 3, McNab, Bromilow

**Everton 1**

Williams

*Attendance:* **54,368**

**Liverpool:** *Scott, Longworth, McKinlay, McNab, W. Wadsworth, Bromilow, Lacey, Forshaw, Johnson, Chambers, Hopkin*

**Everton:** *Fern, Raitt, McDonald, Peacock, Fleetwood, Hart, Chedgzoy, Irvine, Forbes, Williams, Harrison*

When Liverpool went into the interval a goal down at Anfield, few could have predicted the turnaround that the second half produced. William Williams pounced when Elisha Scott failed to hold a back-pass from Donald McKinlay to give the visitors the lead on 17 minutes. Liverpool came out a different team for the second half and pressed themselves on their opponents' goal. Harry Chambers grabbed a hat-trick, Jock McNab scored once with a glorious shot and Tom Bromilow gained his side's fifth in the softest fashion when he beat Tommy Fern with a long-range effort. The result put Liverpool on top of the First Division with Everton down in lowly 19th place.

## 14th October 1922

First Division
**Everton 0**
**Liverpool 1**
Johnson
*Attendance:* **52,000**
**Everton:** *Fern, Raitt, McDonald, Peacock, Fleetwood, Hart, Chedgzoy, Irvine, Chadwick, Williams, Harrison*
**Liverpool:** *Scott, Longworth, McKinlay, McNab, W. Wadsworth, Bromilow, Lacey, Forshaw, Johnson, Chambers, Hopkin*

Liverpool maintained their position at the top of the First Division by virtue of this 1-0 victory over Everton that ensured they remained one point ahead of Middlesbrough, Chelsea and Sunderland. There were more than 50,000 people at Goodison Park and around half of them were disappointed with the result. Everton had the best of the midfield play but could not score, whereas Dick Johnson seized an opening before the interval to score for Liverpool who ended up lucky winners.

## 6th October 1923

First Division
**Everton 1**
Chadwick
**Liverpool 0**
*Attendance:* **51,000**

**Everton:** *Fern, McDonald, Livingstone, Brown, McBain, Hart, Chedgzoy, Irvine, Cock, Chadwick, Troup*
**Liverpool:** *Scott, Parry, McKinlay, McNab, W. Wadsworth, Pratt, Lacey, Forshaw, Walsh, Chambers, Hopkin*

Everton beat Liverpool by the only goal of the game but the previous season's champions would have lost by a much bigger margin if the Goodison inside men – Jack Cock in particular – had been less anxious. The only goal of the game came after 30 minutes when Neil McBain passed the ball up the centre of the field to Wilf Chadwick who took the ball in his stride and unleashed an unstoppable shot past Elisha Scott. Both sides played well and created chances with Scott and Tommy Fern being called upon to prevent goalscoring opportunities. As it was, Everton registered their first Merseyside derby victory since October 1914.

## 13th October 1923

First Division
**Liverpool 1**
Walsh
**Everton 2**
Chedgzoy, Cock
*Attendance:* **50,000**
**Liverpool:** *Scott, Lucas, McKinlay, McNab, W. Wadsworth, Pratt, H. Wadsworth, Forshaw, Walsh, Chambers, Hopkin*
**Everton:** *Fern, McDonald, Livingstone, Brown, McBain, Hart, Chedgzoy, Irvine, Cock, Chadwick, Troup*

With Everton having had to wait for nine years – albeit including four seasons of wartime football – for a victory over Liverpool, it was ironic that two should come in the space of eight days. Again, the Blues were deserving of their win, although it was Liverpool who opened the scoring when Jimmy Walsh struck a deflected shot past Tommy Fern and into the net after 11 minutes. That lead lasted just 12 minutes as Sam Chedgzoy dispossessed David Pratt and drove the ball past Elisha Scott from a narrow angle. Chedgzoy turned provider for Everton's winning goal when he beat the offside trap and launched a shot towards goal.

Scott managed to parry but Jack Cock was on hand to put the ball into the net. While Liverpool had had their chances to add to their tally, the remainder of the match belonged to the visitors.

## 4th October 1924

First Division
**Everton 0**
**Liverpool 1**
Rawlings
*Attendance:* **53,000**
**Everton:** Harland, Raitt, Livingstone, Brown, McBain, Hart, Chedgzoy, Irvine, Cock, Chadwick, Troup
**Liverpool:** E. Scott, Lucas, McKinlay, McNab, W. Wadsworth, Bromilow, Rawlings, Forshaw, Johnson, Shone, Lawson

This match took place when the season was not even a quarter of the way through and both sides were languishing near the foot of the table having lost three games apiece. The two teams had one of their old-time duels at Goodison Park, but Everton – praised by many as being the best footballing side in the country at that time – were struggling to use the ball constructively in the final third of the field and Elisha Scott only had to deal with three potentially dangerous shots all game. This was a frantic contest after Archie Rawlings had opened the scoring in the fourth minute. Tom Bromilow took a throw-in and lofted the return pass towards the Everton goal area, but Alf Harland misjudged the flight of the ball. Having committed himself, the keeper was out of position when Dick Forshaw nodded the ball back to Rawlings who had the simplest of tasks to knock the ball into the empty net.

## 7th February 1925

First Division
**Liverpool 3**
Shone, Hopkin, Chambers
**Everton 1**
Chadwick
*Attendance:* **56,000**

**Liverpool:** *E. Scott, Lucas, McKinlay, McNab, W. Wadsworth, Pratt, Rawlings, Chambers, Johnson, Shone, Hopkin*
**Everton:** *Harland, Raitt, McDonald, Brown, McBain, Reid, Chedgzoy, Irvine, Cock, Chadwick, Troup*

This match showed the difference in class between Liverpool – fourth in the table – and Everton, desperately trying to move away from the relegation zone. Liverpool were more dangerous and had several opportunities to open the scoring before Danny Shone beat Alf Harland shortly after the half-hour. Archie Rawlings wasted three glorious chances but redeemed himself by setting up the first goal. Rawlings was also involved in the second goal with a neat pass to Dick Johnson who had the chance to shoot but instead squared the ball for the unmarked Fred Hopkin to drill home six minutes after the interval. Just four minutes later and Everton realized they were in deep trouble when Harry Chambers held firm to steer a left-footed shot past the advancing Harland to make it three. The visitors netted a consolation goal through Wilf Chadwick, but Jack Cock was guilty of missing an open goal on two occasions as Liverpool claimed the victory.

## 26th September 1925

First Division
**Liverpool 5**
Forshaw 3, Walsh, Chambers
**Everton 1**
Kennedy
*Attendance:* **55,000**
**Liverpool:** *E. Scott, Lucas, McKinlay, McNab, Cockburn, Bromilow, Rawlings, Chambers, Forshaw, Walsh, Hopkin*
**Everton:** *Harland, Raitt, O'Donnell, Peacock, McBain, Hart, Chedgzoy, Irvine, Dean, Kennedy, Troup*

While there might not have been much in general to choose between the two teams at the end of the derby fixture, what was apparent was the superior ability of the Liverpool players to take the chances that they had created. Both Sam Chedgzoy and Fred Kennedy were guilty of glaring misses for the visitors but the Reds soon built themselves an unassailable lead. Dick Forshaw notched the first with a header from a corner after six minutes while Jimmy Walsh and Harry Chambers made it 3-0 by half-time. Forshaw added two more in the second half, though Everton, in scoring a late goal through Kennedy, took some consolation in becoming the first team to score at Anfield that season.

## 6th February 1926

First Division

**Everton 3**

Irvine, Chedgzoy, Dean

**Liverpool 3**

Oxley, Forshaw 2

*Attendance: 45,793*

**Everton:** *Hardy, Livingstone, McDonald, Peacock, Bain, Virr, Chedgzoy, Irvine, Dean, O'Donnell, Troup*

**Liverpool:** *E. Scott, Lucas, McKinlay, McNab, Cockburn, Bromilow, Oxley, Forshaw, Walsh, Chambers, Hopkin*

For the second time in the season, the Merseyside derby match threw up a six-goal thriller but – unlike its predecessor – this time the goals were shared evenly between the two sides at Goodison Park. Everton couldn't have got off to a better start when Bobby Irvine scored from close range in the first minute although the lead lasted about a quarter of an hour as Dick Forshaw and Cyril Oxley both tried to get on the end of a Fred Hopkin cross with Oxley being the one to drive the ball into the net. Liverpool added their second five minutes later through Forshaw while Sam Chedgzoy levelled just before the interval. Everton restored their advantage on the hour when Dixie Dean headed past Elisha Scott, but Liverpool were again back on level terms five minutes later when Forshaw grabbed his second.

## 25th September 1926

First Division

**Everton 1**

O'Donnell

**Liverpool 0**

*Attendance: 43,973*

**Everton:** *Baker, McDonald, Kerr, Brown, Hart, Virr, Parker, Irvine, Bain, O'Donnell, Troup*

**Liverpool:** *Riley, Lucas, Longworth, Shears, Cockburn, Bromilow, Edmed, Hodgson, Forshaw, Chambers, Hopkin*

Everton defeated Liverpool on their merits and this recorded their first victory of the season. They were still propping up the First Division table with just three points from their opening nine games but, having got off the mark, Everton were now expected to make steady progress up the table. The only goal of the game was scored in the 55th minute by Jack O'Donnell, whom the Goodison club had signed from Darlington for £3,000 – a pretty big sum for a defender – as a left-back. O'Donnell was not a polished forward according to the high tradition of the Evertonians, but he certainly applied thrust to the attack and he knew how to hit the ball true and hard when near goal.

## 12th February 1927

First Division

**Liverpool 1**

Chambers

**Everton 0**

*Attendance: 52,677*

**Liverpool:** *E. Scott, Lucas, McKinlay, McNab, Pratt, Bromilow, Edmed, Hodgson, Reid, Chambers, Hopkin*

**Everton:** *Taylor, Cresswell, O'Donnell, Kelly, Hart, Virr, Critchley, Dominy, Irvine, Kennedy, Troup*

Everton, who during the previous week had signed right-back Warney Cresswell from Sunderland, were hoping to strengthen their defence by securing the transfers of internationals in order to cement their place in the First Division for the following season. There was about a month in which clubs struggling to avoid relegation could strengthen their ranks and they seemed to be getting busy earlier than usual. Everton fielded two new players against Liverpool – goalkeeper Ted Taylor (previously of Huddersfield) and right-half Jeremiah Kelly (formerly of Ayr) – and still lost to their neighbours across the park. It was only a single-goal defeat, but it meant the loss of valuable points which were crucial to the Everton cause. Liverpool deserved their win with Harry Chambers scoring the all-important goal just a minute into the second half. The defeat left Everton one place off the bottom of the table, two points ahead of West Bromwich Albion, but having played two games more.

## 15th October 1927

First Division

**Everton 1**

Troup

**Liverpool 1**

Edmed

*Attendance:* **65,729**

**Everton:** *Taylor, Cresswell, O'Donnell, Kelly, Hart, Virr, Critchley, Forshaw, Dean, Weldon, Troup*

**Liverpool:** *Riley, Lucas, McKinlay, McMullan, Jackson, Bromilow, Edmed, Hodgson, Devlin, Reid, Pither*

Everton had not been beaten since the second game of the season and were expected to be at full strength for this clash. They started as favourites with Liverpool missing their superb goalkeeper Elisha Scott, but with Tommy Lucas and Donald McKinlay in the back line, a point was easily attainable if they could restrain the exuberant Dixie Dean. As it turned out, the Everton striker had a subdued game, owing to the close attention of James Jackson, and Dean's attempt to score in every match of the campaign was quashed. His team-mate Alec Troup managed to break the deadlock three minutes into the second half, but the home side were pegged back when Dick Edmed equalized after 62 minutes.

## 25th February 1928

First Division

**Liverpool 3**

Hopkin, Bromilow, Hodgson

**Everton 3**

Dean 3

*Attendance: 56,447*
**Liverpool:** *Riley, Lucas, McKinlay, Morrison, Jackson, Bromilow, Edmed, Hodgson, Race, Chambers, Hopkin*
**Everton:** *Hardy, Cresswell, O'Donnell, Kelly, Hart, Virr, Critchley, Forshaw, Dean, Weldon, Troup*

Everton's leadership of the First Division was being seriously challenged, and they now only headed Huddersfield on goal average, having played a match more. They had Dixie Dean to thank for the fact that they got a point at Liverpool as he scored all three of his side's goals. He first equalized a fifth-minute goal netted by Fred Hopkin and then gave Everton a 2-1 half-time lead. In the second half he extended Everton's advantage to 3-1 but Tom Bromilow and George Hodgson took their chances to bring the scores level. Apart from losing twice in the space of four days in March, Everton would register six wins and five draws by the end of the season to claim the First Division crown for the third time in their history with a two-point advantage over the Yorkshire club.

# 29th September 1928

First Division
**Everton 1**
Troup
**Liverpool 0**
*Attendance: 55,415*
**Everton:** *Davies, Cresswell, O'Donnell, Kelly, Hart, Virr, Ritchie, Dunn, Dean, Weldon, Troup*
**Liverpool:** *Scott, Jackson, Done, Morrison, Davidson, Bromilow, Edmed, Hodgson, Whitehurst, McDougall, Hopkin*

Everton's defence of their title was faltering by the time they played this, their eighth match of the season, and they had already lost three times. It was another game of missed opportunities with both Albert Whitehurst and Jimmy McDougall being unable to make the most of the chances created by their Liverpool team-mates. Everton took a little while to get into their stride but almost scored when Jimmy Dunn headed past Elisha Scott only to have Bob Done make a goal-line clearance. Scottish international Alex Troup scored the only goal of the match in the second half when he collected a pinpoint pass from Dunn and placed his shot perfectly past Scott. The Liverpool keeper was instrumental in restricting Everton to just one goal and was more than aware of the danger posed in the air by Dixie Dean.

## 9th February 1929

First Division
**Liverpool 1**
Race
**Everton 2**
Griffiths, White
*Attendance: 55,000*
**Liverpool:** *Riley, Jackson, Done, Morrison, Davidson, Bromilow, Edmed, Clark, McFarlane, Race, Salisbury*
**Everton:** *Davies, Common, O'Donnell, Kelly, Griffiths, Hart, Ritchie, Dunn, White, Easton, Troup*

Everton completed the double over Liverpool with a competitive and clinical display at Anfield. John McFarlane made his debut for the home side in the absence of George Hodgson and gave a good account of himself, but the 17-year-old would only make one more appearance during his Anfield career. The visitors took a first-half lead when Tom Griffiths headed home Alec Troup's corner, but Harry Race equalized after 62 minutes. Within two minutes of the restart, however, Everton regained their advantage when Jerry Kelly lobbed the ball goalwards for Tommy White to smash in the winner.

## 7th September 1929

First Division
**Liverpool 0**
**Everton 3**
Dean 2, Martin
*Attendance: 45,600*
**Liverpool:** *Riley, Jackson, Done, Morrison, McDougall, Davidson, Edmed, Clark, Hodgson, Race, Hopkin*

**Everton:** *Davies, Cresswell, O'Donnell, Kelly, White, Hart, Ritchie, Dunn, Dean, Martin, Stein*

Liverpool had their chances in the first half and frittered them away while Dixie Dean netted twice before the break with goalkeeper Arthur Riley being at fault in one case. The Everton striker's first came after 16 minutes when he volleyed the ball speculatively over his head and Riley was not in a position to do anything to prevent the goal. The second, four minutes before the interval, saw Riley fumble Harry Ritchie's cross under a challenge from Dean who was quickest to react. In the second half, Liverpool lost forward Bob Clark to injury and George Martin netted the visitors' third following a corner seven minutes from time.

## 4ᵗʰ January 1930

First Division

**Everton 3**

Critchley, Dean 2

**Liverpool 3**

Edmed, McPherson, McDougall

*Attendance:* **52,600**

**Everton:** *Davies, Cresswell, O'Donnell, Robson, Hart, McPherson, Critchley, Dunn, Dean, Rigby, Stein*

**Liverpool:** *Riley, Jackson, Lucas, Morrison, McDougall, Bromilow, Edmed, Hodgson, Smith, McPherson, Hopkin*

Everton came into this derby match on the back of four straight League defeats and were in dire straits near the foot of the First Division table. After 10 minutes it looked like things were going to get worse for the Evertonians when Jimmy Smith put the ball in the back of the net but the Liverpool striker was adjudged to be offside. Four minutes later, the home side went in front through Ted Critchley but the match really came to life five minutes into the second half when three goals were scored in the space of just four minutes. Dixie Dean extended Everton's lead before Dick Edmed scored for Liverpool, only for Dean then to net his second to restore the two-goal advantage. Everton looked to be heading for both points but Liverpool were not finished. Goals from

Archie McPherson and Jimmy McDougall, just two minutes apart, gave the visitors a share of the points. Everton's poor form continued and the Goodison Park club would go on to lose six consecutive League matches in March and April. The season's end saw them propping up the table and coming to terms with a drop into the Second Division.

# Chapter Four

# The 1930s

The blue half of the city headed the silverware table during the 1930s as Everton emulated their rivals' feat of the previous decade with back-to-back Second and First Division titles in 1930–31 and 1931–32. In a repeat of history, Everton also won the final campaign before League football was once more suspended due to a second global conflict. They also added another FA Cup win to their trophy cabinet with a convincing 3-0 victory over Manchester City in 1933. The Reds, on the other hand, had very little to celebrate with a seventh-place finish in 1934–35 being their best showing in the League, while the furthest they progressed in the FA Cup was to the Quarter-final in 1931–32 where they lost 2-0 to Chelsea.

## Record in the 1930s

**Everton**

| Season | League | P | W | D | L | F | A | Pts | Pos |
|--------|--------|---|---|---|---|---|---|-----|-----|
| 1930–31 | Div 2 | 42 | 28 | 5 | 9 | 121 | 66 | 61 | 1 |
| 1931–32 | Div 1 | 42 | 26 | 4 | 12 | 116 | 64 | 56 | 1 |
| 1932–33 | Div 1 | 42 | 16 | 9 | 17 | 81 | 74 | 41 | 11 |
| 1933–34 | Div 1 | 42 | 12 | 16 | 14 | 62 | 63 | 40 | 14 |
| 1934–35 | Div 1 | 42 | 16 | 12 | 14 | 89 | 88 | 44 | 8 |
| 1935–36 | Div 1 | 42 | 13 | 13 | 16 | 89 | 89 | 39 | 16 |
| 1936–37 | Div 1 | 42 | 14 | 9 | 19 | 81 | 78 | 37 | 17 |
| 1937–38 | Div 1 | 42 | 16 | 7 | 19 | 79 | 75 | 39 | 14 |
| 1938–39 | Div 1 | 42 | 27 | 5 | 10 | 88 | 52 | 59 | 1 |

**FA Cup**

| 1930–31 | 0-1 v West Bromwich Albion (Semi-final) |
| 1931–32 | 1-2 v Liverpool (Third Round) |

# EVERTON vs LIVERPOOL

| 1932–33 | 3-0 v Manchester City (Final) |
| 1933–34 | 0-3 v Tottenham Hotspur (Third Round) |
| 1934–35 | 1-2 v Bolton Wanderers (Quarter-final) |
| 1935–36 | 1-3 v Preston North End (Third Round) |
| 1936–37 | 1-1, 3-4 v Tottenham Hotspur (Fifth Round) |
| 1937–38 | 0-1 v Sunderland (Fourth Round) |
| 1938–39 | 0-2 v Wolverhampton Wanderers (Quarter-final) |

## Liverpool

| Season | League | P | W | D | L | F | A | Pts | Pos |
|---|---|---|---|---|---|---|---|---|---|
| 1930–31 | Div 1 | 42 | 15 | 12 | 15 | 86 | 85 | 42 | 9 |
| 1931–32 | Div 1 | 42 | 19 | 6 | 17 | 81 | 83 | 44 | 10 |
| 1932–33 | Div 1 | 42 | 14 | 11 | 17 | 79 | 84 | 39 | 14 |
| 1933–34 | Div 1 | 42 | 14 | 10 | 18 | 79 | 87 | 38 | 18 |
| 1934–35 | Div 1 | 42 | 19 | 7 | 16 | 85 | 88 | 45 | 7 |
| 1935–36 | Div 1 | 42 | 13 | 12 | 17 | 60 | 64 | 38 | 19 |
| 1936–37 | Div 1 | 42 | 12 | 11 | 19 | 62 | 84 | 35 | 18 |
| 1937–38 | Div 1 | 42 | 15 | 11 | 16 | 65 | 71 | 41 | 11 |
| 1938–39 | Div 1 | 42 | 14 | 14 | 14 | 62 | 63 | 42 | 11 |

## FA Cup

| 1930–31 | 0-2 v Birmingham (Third Round) |
| 1931–32 | 0-2 v Chelsea (Quarter-final) |
| 1932–33 | 0-2 v West Bromwich Albion (Third Round) |
| 1933–34 | 0-3 v Bolton Wanderers (Fifth Round) |
| 1934–35 | 0-1 v Blackburn Rovers (Fourth Round) |
| 1935–36 | 0-2 v Arsenal (Fourth Round) |
| 1936–37 | 0-3 v Norwich City (Third Round) |
| 1937–38 | 0-1 v Huddersfield Town (Fifth Round) |
| 1938–39 | 1-4 v Wolverhampton Wanderers (Fifth Round) |

## The Matches

### 19th September 1931

First Division
**Liverpool 1**
Wright
**Everton 3**
Dean 3
*Attendance:* **55,000**
**Liverpool:** *Scott, Done, Jackson, Morrison, Bradshaw, McDougall, Barton, Hodgson, Smith, Wright, Gunson*
**Everton:** *Sagar, Bocking, Cresswell, McClure, Gee, McPherson, Critchley, Dunn, Dean, Johnson, Stein*

With Everton having been crowned champions of the Second Division at the first time of asking, the Merseyside derby hiatus had lasted just one season and both sets of fans looked forward to this meeting. Liverpool's confidence was at a high following their 7-2 thrashing of Middlesbrough in the previous match, so the stage was set for a classic. The speed at which the goals went in was astounding. Dixie Dean grabbed the first within a minute of kick-off when he headed in Ted Critchley's cross, but Dave Wright equalized for the home side just two minutes later. Dean notched his second after a quarter of an hour and completed his hat-trick six minutes later to sew the game up for the visitors. Liverpool were unable to deal with the threat of the Everton striker and some of their players put on a woeful performance that left the Blues deserved winners.

### 9th January 1932

FA Cup Third Round
**Everton 1**
Dean
**Liverpool 2**
Gunson, Hodgson
*Attendance:* **57,090**
**Everton:** *Sagar, Williams, Bocking, Clark, Gee, Thomson, Critchley, White, Dean, Johnson, Stein*

**Liverpool:** *Scott, Steel, Jackson, Morrison, Bradshaw, McDougall, McRorie, Hodgson, Barton, Wright, Gunson*

This first FA Cup meeting between the Merseysiders since February 1911 got off to a spectacular start when Dixie Dean beat Elisha Scott with a low drive in the first minute. After that, however, the Liverpool half-backs – ably assisted by Jimmy Jackson – completely upset the Everton forwards. From a free-kick, winger Gordon Gunson levelled the scores and in the second half put over a cross from which Gordon Hodgson headed the winning goal. The deciding factor of the game had been accuracy – while Everton had had more shots on the Liverpool goal, the visitors made the ones they had count.

## 30th January 1932

First Division

**Everton 2**

White, Critchley

**Liverpool 1**

Wright

*Attendance:* **46,537**

**Everton:** *Sagar, Williams, Bocking, Clark, McClure, Thomson, Critchley, White, Dean, Johnson, Rigby*

**Liverpool:** *Scott, Done, Steel, Morrison, Bradshaw, McDougall, Barton, Hodgson, Wright, McPherson, Gunson*

This was the third meeting of the 1931–32 season and Everton were out to avenge the FA Cup defeat inflicted by their neighbours earlier in the month. They were also looking to do the double over them in the League. Harold Barton took the place of Danny McRorie on the wing for the visitors who installed Dave Wright as centre-forward, although they sorely missed the determination and skill of Jimmy Jackson in defence. The game kicked off at a frenetic pace with chances at both ends, but it was Liverpool who opened the scoring through Wright after 29 minutes. Dixie Dean turned provider for Tommy White to equalize before Ted Critchley grabbed the winner after an hour. Everton maintained their lead over Sheffield United at the top of the table with this victory and would only lose another four games on their way to claiming the First Division title for a fourth time.

## 1ˢᵗ October 1932

First Division
**Everton 3**
Critchley, Dean 2
**Liverpool 1**
Gunson
*Attendance: 44,214*
**Everton:** *Sagar, Williams, Cresswell, Britton, White, Thomson, Critchley, McGourty, Dean, Johnson, Stein*
**Liverpool:** *Scott, Steel, Jackson, Morrison, Bradshaw, McDougall, Barton, Hodgson, Wright, McPherson, Gunson*

Everton kept up their impressive record against Liverpool with this decisive victory that left the visitors still looking for a first League win over their neighbours since February 1927. For a long time it looked like Liverpool could get something out of this game after they had taken the lead through Gordon Gunson after 23 minutes, but three Everton goals in 13 second-half minutes dashed their dreams. Ted Critchley equalized after 61 minutes and Dixie Dean grabbed two goals in as many minutes to make the game safe.

## 11ᵗʰ February 1933

First Division
**Liverpool 7**
Barton 3, Hanson, Morrison, Taylor, Roberts
**Everton 4**
Dean 2, Johnson, Stein
*Attendance: 50,000*
**Liverpool:** *Scott, Steel, Jackson, Morrison, Bradshaw, Taylor, Barton, Roberts, Wright, McPherson, Hanson*
**Everton:** *Sagar, Cook, Cresswell, Britton, White, Thomson, Geldard, Dunn, Dean, Johnson, Stein*

In this clash at Anfield, Everton's defence was so poor that many believed it was impossible for them to play so badly ever again. They were slow, uncertain and relied on offside appeals that were never answered by the referee. Liverpool's half-backs were the main cause of the runaway win and could do nothing wrong with centre-forward Henry Barton helping himself to a hat-trick. It was Liverpool's first League victory at Anfield for six years and still stands today as the highest scoring derby game. It had all started so well for the visitors with Dixie Dean netting after eight minutes, but they failed to take their chances and Liverpool equalized when Barton glided the ball over Ted Sagar's head and Alf Hanson soon added a second. Tom Morrison extended the home side's lead but Tommy Johnson reduced the deficit and the half-time score was 3-2. The second half saw Liverpool running rampant with Harry Taylor and Barton both scoring before Dean nodded one in past Elisha Scott for his second after 75 minutes. A minute later, and Liverpool had restored their three-goal advantage with Syd Roberts scoring while Barton completed his hat-trick after 85 minutes. The action wasn't over though, as Jimmy Stein registered Everton's fourth goal with just three minutes to go. There wouldn't have been many Evertonians who would have believed that their side could score four goals yet still be on the receiving end of such an impressive attacking display of football.

## 30<sup>th</sup> September 1933

First Division

**Liverpool 3**

Nieuwenhuys, Hanson, English

**Everton 2**

Johnson, White

*Attendance:* **54,800**

**Liverpool:** *Riley, Steel, Tennant, Morrison, Bradshaw, McDougall, Nieuwenhuys, Hodgson, English, D. Wright, Hanson*

**Everton:** *Sagar, Cook, Cresswell, Britton, Gee, Thomson, Geldard, Dunn, White, Johnson, Stein*

Even without the talismanic Dixie Dean, Everton started this match by showing their clear intentions, but were unable to take the chances they created. Despite the fact that five goals were eventually scored, the talking points of the game revolved around those that could have been . . . Berry 'Nivvy' Nieuwenhuys opened the scoring in the 32nd minute in only his second game for Liverpool before Tommy White equalized four minutes later. Alf Hanson restored Liverpool's lead on the hour and Sam English added a third 20 minutes later. For all their promise, all Everton could do was to close the gap through Tommy Johnson with two minutes to go and an equalizer proved to be elusive.

## 10th February 1934

First Division
**Everton 0**
**Liverpool 0**
*Attendance: 52,088*
**Everton:** *Coggins, Williams, Cook, Britton, Gee, Thomson, Critchley, Cunliffe, Johnson, Stevenson, Stein*
**Liverpool:** *E. Scott, Tennant, Done, Morrison, Bradshaw, McDougall, Nieuwenhuys, Hodgson, English, Taylor, Hanson*

Hampered by the loss of Alf Hanson in the first half, Liverpool did well to force a goalless draw at Goodison Park, but the display from both sides was poor. Everton dictated the game for long stretches in the first half, and Elisha Scott made saves from Alex Stevenson and Jim Cunliffe to save the game for his side. Tom Bradshaw joined him in the day's honours list with a perfect display of heading and control. Liverpool improved as soon as Berry Nieuwenhuys took a more active and confident role in the game. The South African had been nervy and unsettled, but later became a force to be reckoned with and came close to winning the game off his own bat.

## 15th September 1934

First Division
**Everton 1**
Dean
**Liverpool 0**
*Attendance: 43,001*

**Everton:** *Sagar, Cresswell, Cook, Britton, Gee, Thomson, Leyfield, Cunliffe, Dean, Stevenson, Stein*

**Liverpool:** *Riley, Steel, Blenkinsop, Morrison, Low, McDougall, E.V. Wright, Hodgson, English, Taylor, Hanson*

Everton were unchanged from their previous match and were still without their hefty pivot up front, Tommy White. Liverpool had brought in Vic Wright and Harry Taylor in place of Tosh Johnson and Berry Nieuwenhuys. The pundits were predicting an easy Everton victory as the home side had won each of their Goodison Park matches while Liverpool had lost each of their away engagements. Norman Low deputized for the injured Thomas 'Tiny' Bradshaw and the youngster managed to keep Dixie Dean quiet for the majority of the match. Many of the crowd had started to leave Goodison Park, believing the match was going to end in stalemate, and so missed Dean's headed goal from a Charlie Leyfield cross one minute before the final whistle.

## 20ᵗʰ March 1935

First Division
**Liverpool 2**
Hodgson 2 (1 pen)
**Everton 1**
Dean (pen)
*Attendance:* **32,000**
**Liverpool:** *Kane, Cooper, Tennant, Savage, Bradshaw, McDougall, Nieuwenhuys, E.V. Wright, Hodgson, Johnson, Hanson*
**Everton:** *Sagar, Jackson, Jones, Britton, Gee, Thomson, Geldard, Cunliffe, Dean, Coulter, Stein*

Liverpool took to the field with Stanley Kane deputizing for the injured Arthur Riley between the goalposts and making his debut for the Anfield club. The Liverpool defenders were well aware of Dixie Dean's tendency to shoulder-charge opposing goalkeepers so positioned themselves to protect their keeper when they saw it coming. Early in the first half, Jack Tennant was penalized for impeding the Everton striker in such circumstances, and Dean scored from the resultant penalty despite

Kane getting his hand to the ball. This cancelled-out Gordon Hodgson's penalty on five minutes after Jackie Coulter had handled the ball. Hodgson scored his second on the stroke of half-time with a swerving shot that evaded the dive of Ted Sagar to give the home side victory.

## 7th September 1935

First Division

**Liverpool 6**

Howe 4, Hodgson 2

**Everton 0**

*Attendance:* 48,000

**Liverpool:** *Riley, Cooper, Blenkinsop, Savage, Bradshaw, McDougall, Nieuwenhuys, Hodgson, Wright, Howe, Carr*

**Everton:** *Sagar, Williams, Cresswell, Britton, White, Thomson, Geldard, Miller, Dean, Stevenson, Leyfield*

Everton's form on the road had been severely lacking the previous season and this 6-0 rout at Anfield suggested that their issues away from home may still have been with them. Although Everton began in fine form, it wasn't long before Liverpool began to find the back of the Blues' net with regularity. Once Fred Howe notched the home side's first goal, it was more a question of how many Liverpool would score rather than whether Everton would get any. Lance Carr provided the cross from which Howe headed home and Gordon Hodgson soon added two more with ferocious drives that Ted Sagar could do nothing about. Howe grabbed his second shortly before half-time and any hopes Everton had in the second half of rescuing the situation were dashed by injuries to Dixie Dean and Ben Williams that effectively left them playing with nine men. Howe scored twice in the final four minutes to give Liverpool a massive margin of victory.

# 4th January 1936

First Division

**Everton 0**

**Liverpool 0**

*Attendance: 52,282*

**Everton:** *King, Cook, Jones, Britton, White, Mercer, Geldard, Bentham, Cunliffe, Miller, Gillick*

**Liverpool:** *Riley, Cooper, Dabbs, Savage, Bradshaw, McDougall, Nieuwenhuys, Wright, Howe, Glassey, Carr*

This match was played in a sporting spirit before an appreciative crowd. From start to finish a fast pace was maintained, which indicated not only superb physical condition, but admirable keenness. There were, however, two of those examples of lack of self-control which should never occur in any game between grown men, whether it is football or any other sport. In the second half, for instance, Everton's Joe Mercer considered that a wrong line decision deprived his side of a throw-in and he threw the ball away in a huff. Shortly after, Lance Carr – one of Liverpool's three South Africans – kicked the ball away after having a decision given against him. Everton's indefatigable right-back, Billy Cook, was prone to making rash challenges and several times he missed an opponent more by luck than judgment. The outstanding incident of this goalless match saw Berry Nieuwenhuys, the Liverpool outside-right, receive the ball in an offside position. Without hesitation referee Mr Thompson blew his whistle. Most of the players stopped, but Nivvy presumably did not hear and went on at full speed towards goal. The linesman, who had been right on the spot, made no attempt to flag. Instead he ran down the line beside Nieuwenhuys and the Liverpool man – naturally supposing he was to be allowed to go on – surged forward until he collided with Francis King, the Everton goalkeeper, who was hurt and had to receive attention. Meanwhile, the ball went to Fred Howe, who calmly put it into the net. Since he had blown for offside, Mr Thompson was firm in his decision and Tom Cooper was later slated for arguing with the referee, even taking him by the arm in his eagerness to claim that Liverpool should be allowed a goal. This incident could have caused serious trouble, and matters were not improved when another wrong line decision was given a minute later. The stoppage count at the end of 90 minutes recorded no fewer than 86 throw-ins, 23 goal-kicks and nine corners. There were also 22 free-kicks for fouls and 12 for offside, a fact the press labelled "a terrible indictment of the forwards". Jim Cunliffe, Everton's centre-forward, was penalized for offside on six occasions and it was suggested that he "owed it to his club to study methods of circumventing the wiles of full-backs while using his doubtless intelligence in the business of positioning himself".

## 19th September 1936

First Division

**Everton 2**

Stevenson, Dean

**Liverpool 0**

*Attendance: 55,835*

**Everton:** *Sagar, Jackson, Cook, Britton, Gee, Mercer, Gillick, Cunliffe, Dean, Stevenson, Coulter*

**Liverpool:** *Hobson, Dabbs, Blenkinsop, Busby, Bradshaw, McDougall, Nieuwenhuys, P. Taylor, Howe, Wright, Hanson*

Liverpool rushed out of the starting blocks and could have taken the lead within the first minute when Phil Taylor sent in a perfect cross that Ted Sagar tried to cut out. The onrushing Alf Hanson missed the ball though, and ended up in the back of the net himself. Indeed, Sagar would have a busy afternoon and was largely responsible for the home side keeping a clean sheet. Both Taylor and Hanson had further chances to score and when Fred Howe did manage to get the ball in the back of the net it was ruled out for offside. With Liverpool having had the majority of chances, it was ironic that the first goal of the game was scored by Alex Stevenson after 64 minutes to give Everton the lead. Nine minutes later and Dixie Dean took a back-heel from Torry Gillick, dribbled towards the six-yard box and broke Liverpool's resolve with Everton's second goal.

## 23rd January 1937

First Division

**Liverpool 3**

Howe, Taylor, Balmer

**Everton 2**

Stevenson 2

*Attendance:* **37,632**

**Liverpool:** *Riley, Cooper, Dabbs, Busby, Bradshaw, McDougall, Nieuwenhuys, P. Taylor, Balmer, Howe, Hanson*

**Everton:** *Sagar, Cook, Jones, Britton, Gee, Mercer, Gillick, Cunliffe, Dean, Stevenson, Coulter*

Liverpool's mid-season form had been severely lacking – their lowest League position was 19th following a 4-0 Christmas Day mauling at the hands of Huddersfield Town that started a run of six games without victory. Because of this, many were expecting Everton to claim at least a share of the points in this Anfield clash. Three goals in little more than quarter of an hour set this match alight and gave the crowd plenty to cheer about. The first went to the home side when Fred Howe headed home a corner after eight minutes before Phil Taylor extended their lead just four minutes later with a sluggish long-range effort that Ted Sagar allowed to slip under his body. Everton reduced the deficit on 16 minutes when Dixie Dean slipped the ball to Alex Stevenson who unleashed a fierce drive into the right-hand side of the goal. Jack Balmer restored Liverpool's two-goal cushion on the hour with a shot that flashed in off the post, while Dean and Stevenson again combined for the latter to score 11 minutes from time and set up a nail-biting finale.

## 2nd October 1937

First Division

**Liverpool 1**

Nieuwenhuys

**Everton 2**

Trentham, Lawton (pen)

*Attendance:* **45,000**

**Liverpool:** *Kemp, Harley, Dabbs, Busby, Rogers, McDougall, Nieuwenhuys, Eastham, Howe, P. Taylor, Hanson*
**Everton:** *Sagar, Cook, J.E. Jones, Mercer, Gee, Watson, Geldard, Stevenson, Lawton, Dougal, Trentham*

Neither club had made a particularly great start to the season and by the time this game had reached its conclusion both Everton and Liverpool had succumbed to five defeats within the first nine games of the League campaign. Liverpool played a lot of good football, but were beaten by Everton's speed and first-time passing. Both teams seemed to be erratic at times but one deciding factor was Charlie Gee's mastery of Fred Howe, Liverpool's leader. Fred Rogers responded to this by keeping Tommy Lawton quiet as much as he could and the Everton striker was restricted to one goal. That came from the penalty spot shortly before the half-hour mark to add to the opener scored by Douglas Trentham on 15 minutes. Liverpool pulled one back through Berry Nieuwenhuys five minutes from time, but the majority of the spectators would have agreed that the better team won on the day.

## 16th February 1938

First Division
**Everton 1**
Lawton
**Liverpool 3**
Balmer, Shafto 2
*Attendance: 33,465*
**Everton:** *Morton, Cook, J.E. Jones, Britton, T.G. Jones, Mercer, Geldard, Cunliffe, Lawton, Stevenson, Gillick*
**Liverpool:** *Riley, Cooper, Ramsden, P. Taylor, Rogers, Bush, Nieuwenhuys, Balmer, Shafto, Fagan, Van Den Berg*

The spectators who had managed to get to their seats by the time this match kicked off were treated to the fastest goal in the history of the Merseyside derby (reports of the exact timing of the goal varied between five and 15 seconds). Liverpool began a move from the kick-off that soon moved towards the Everton goal and when Tommy Jones dispossessed John Shafto it seemed that any chance of a goal had slipped away. Jack Balmer was not one to give up on a loose ball, however, and he pounded on the feeble clearance, beat Jones and struck the ball into the net to shock the home side. Everton were level within minutes when Tommy Lawton headed an Albert Geldard cross past Arthur Riley and for much of the match it seemed that a draw was on the cards. Liverpool, though, were determined to earn their first League win at Goodison Park since October 1924 and this became a reality with two goals from Shafto in the final nine minutes.

## 1st October 1938

First Division
**Everton 2**
Bentham, Boyes
**Liverpool 1**
Fagan (pen)
*Attendance:* **64,977**
**Everton:** *Sagar, Cook, Greenhalgh, Mercer, T.G. Jones, Thomson, Gillick, Bentham, Lawton, Stevenson, Boyes*
**Liverpool:** *Riley, Cooper, Bush, Busby, Rogers, McInnes, Nieuwenhuys, Taylor, Fagan, Balmer, Van Den Berg*

Everton began the 1938–39 season in fine form with six straight wins and only succumbed to their first defeat the previous week with a 3-0 loss at Huddersfield. Stan Bentham got the home side off to the perfect start with the opening goal after 14 minutes when he headed home a Walter Boyes corner at the far post. Boyes added to Everton's tally after 39 minutes when he took advantage of Arthur Riley's inability to hold an Alex Stevenson shot to slot home the rebound. That was not the final action of the first half, however, as Ted Sagar was adjudged to have pushed Harman Van Den Berg in the back while making a save and a penalty was awarded, much to the consternation of the Everton players. Willie Fagan stepped up and smashed the spot-kick into the roof of the net just two minutes from the interval. Neither side managed to convert any of the numerous chances the second half produced, and it would be December before Everton dropped any points at Goodison.

## 4th February 1939

First Division
**Liverpool 0**
**Everton 3**
Bentham, Lawton 2
*Attendance: 55,994*
**Liverpool:** *Kemp, Cooper, Harley, Busby, Mush, McInnes, Nieuwenhuys, Taylor, Fagan, Balmer, Eastham*
**Everton:** *Sagar, Cook, Greenhalgh, Mercer, T.G. Jones, Thomson, Gillick, Bentham, Lawton, Stevenson, Boyes*

A rampant Everton side took advantage of a shot-shy Liverpool to win the final Merseyside derby before the Second World War. Stan Bentham opened the scoring after 14 minutes with Tommy Lawton adding two more in the final 17 minutes. After the match, Liverpool chairman Will Harrop presented Berry Nieuwenhuys with a cheque for £650 as a reward for his five years' distinguished service. Nivvy had been waiting for the presentation of his benefit cheque so that he could prepare a home for the pretty Liverpool hairdresser he intended to wed shortly. Everton, meanwhile, stayed on course for the title and by the end of the season had claimed their fifth First Division Championship.

# Chapter Five

# The 1940s and 1950s

Apart from a First Division crown for Liverpool in 1946–47, the post-war years were a barren spell on Merseyside in terms of silverware. Both clubs endured relegation to the Second Division – Everton in 1950–51 and Liverpool in 1953–54 – but by a strange quirk of fate there has never been a Merseyside derby fixture at that level as Everton bounced back the same season that Liverpool went down. The FA Cup Semi-final of 1949–50 did, however, stage a Merseyside derby with Liverpool emerging 2-0 winners but they lost the Wembley showpiece by the same margin against Arsenal.

## Record in the 1940s and 1950s

**Everton**

| Season | League | P | W | D | L | F | A | Pts | Pos |
|--------|--------|---|---|---|---|---|---|-----|-----|
| 1946–47 | Div 1 | 42 | 17 | 9 | 16 | 62 | 67 | 43 | 10 |
| 1947–48 | Div 1 | 42 | 17 | 6 | 19 | 52 | 66 | 40 | 14 |
| 1948–49 | Div 1 | 42 | 13 | 11 | 18 | 41 | 63 | 37 | 18 |
| 1949–50 | Div 1 | 42 | 10 | 14 | 18 | 42 | 66 | 34 | 18 |
| 1950–51 | Div 1 | 42 | 12 | 8 | 22 | 48 | 86 | 32 | 22 |
| 1951–52 | Div 2 | 42 | 17 | 10 | 15 | 64 | 58 | 44 | 7 |
| 1952–53 | Div 2 | 42 | 12 | 14 | 16 | 71 | 75 | 38 | 16 |
| 1953–54 | Div 2 | 42 | 20 | 16 | 6 | 92 | 58 | 56 | 2 |
| 1954–55 | Div 1 | 42 | 16 | 10 | 16 | 62 | 68 | 42 | 11 |
| 1955–56 | Div 1 | 42 | 15 | 10 | 17 | 55 | 69 | 40 | 15 |
| 1956–57 | Div 1 | 42 | 14 | 10 | 18 | 61 | 79 | 38 | 15 |
| 1957–58 | Div 1 | 42 | 13 | 11 | 18 | 65 | 75 | 37 | 16 |
| 1958–59 | Div 1 | 42 | 17 | 4 | 21 | 71 | 87 | 38 | 16 |
| 1959–60 | Div 1 | 42 | 13 | 11 | 18 | 73 | 78 | 37 | 15 |

## FA Cup

|  |  |
|---|---|
| 1945–46 | 1-2, 2-2 v Preston North End (Third Round, over two legs) |
| 1946–47 | 1-2 v Sheffield Wednesday (Fourth Round) |
| 1947–48 | 1-1, 0-1 v Fulham (Fifth Round) |
| 1948–49 | 0-2 v Chelsea (Fourth Round) |
| 1949–50 | 0-2 v Liverpool (Semi-final) |
| 1950–51 | 0-2 v Hull City (Third Round) |
| 1951–52 | 0-0, 1-3 v Leyton Orient (Third Round) |
| 1952–53 | 3-4 v Bolton Wanderers (Semi-final) |
| 1953–54 | 1-3 v Sheffield Wednesday (Fifth Round) |
| 1954–55 | 0-4 v Liverpool (Fourth Round) |
| 1955–56 | 1-2 v Manchester City (Quarter-final) |
| 1956–57 | 0-1 v Manchester United (Fifth Round) |
| 1957–58 | 1-2 v Blackburn Rovers (Fourth Round) |
| 1958–59 | 1-4 v Aston Villa (Fifth Round) |
| 1959–60 | 0-3 v Bradford City (Third Round) |

## Liverpool

| Season | League | P | W | D | L | F | A | Pts | Pos |
|---|---|---|---|---|---|---|---|---|---|
| 1946–47 | Div 1 | 42 | 25 | 7 | 10 | 84 | 52 | 57 | 1 |
| 1947–48 | Div 1 | 42 | 16 | 10 | 16 | 65 | 61 | 42 | 11 |
| 1948–49 | Div 1 | 42 | 13 | 14 | 15 | 53 | 43 | 40 | 12 |
| 1949–50 | Div 1 | 42 | 17 | 14 | 11 | 64 | 54 | 48 | 8 |
| 1950–51 | Div 1 | 42 | 16 | 11 | 15 | 53 | 59 | 43 | 9 |
| 1951–52 | Div 1 | 42 | 12 | 19 | 11 | 57 | 61 | 43 | 11 |
| 1952–53 | Div 1 | 42 | 14 | 8 | 20 | 61 | 82 | 36 | 17 |
| 1953–54 | Div 1 | 42 | 9 | 10 | 23 | 68 | 97 | 28 | 22 |
| 1954–55 | Div 2 | 42 | 16 | 10 | 16 | 93 | 96 | 42 | 11 |
| 1955–56 | Div 2 | 42 | 21 | 6 | 15 | 85 | 63 | 48 | 3 |
| 1956–57 | Div 2 | 42 | 21 | 11 | 10 | 82 | 54 | 53 | 3 |
| 1957–58 | Div 2 | 42 | 22 | 10 | 10 | 79 | 54 | 54 | 4 |
| 1958–59 | Div 2 | 42 | 24 | 5 | 13 | 87 | 62 | 53 | 4 |
| 1959–60 | Div 2 | 42 | 20 | 10 | 12 | 90 | 66 | 50 | 3 |

## FA Cup

| | |
|---|---|
| 1945–46 | 0-5, 2-0 v Bolton Wanderers (Fourth Round, over two legs) |
| 1946–47 | 0-0, 0-01 v Burnley (Semi-final) |
| 1947–48 | 0-3 v Manchester United (Fourth Round) |
| 1948–49 | 1-3 v Wolverhampton Wanderers (Fifth Round) |
| 1949–50 | 0-2 v Arsenal (Final) |
| 1950–51 | 1-3 v Norwich City (Third Round) |
| 1951–52 | 0-2 v Burnley (Fifth Round) |
| 1952–53 | 0-1 v Gateshead (Third Round) |
| 1953–54 | 0-1 v Bolton Wanderers (Third Round) |
| 1954–55 | 0-2 v Huddersfield Town (Fifth Round) |
| 1955–56 | 0-0, 1-2 v Manchester City (Fifth Round) |
| 1956–57 | 1-2 v Southend United (Third Round) |
| 1957–58 | 1-2 v Blackburn Rovers (Quarter-final) |
| 1958–59 | 1-2 v Worcester City (Third Round) |
| 1959–60 | 1-3 v Manchester United (Fourth Round) |

## The Matches

## 21st September 1946

First Division

**Liverpool 0**

**Everton 0**

*Attendance: 49,838*

**Liverpool:** *Sidlow, Lambert, Ramsden, Taylor, Hughes, Paisley, Nieuwenhuys, Balmer, Stubbins, Jones, Liddell*

**Everton:** *Burnett, Saunders, Greenhalgh, Mercer, T.G. Jones, Bentham, McIlhatton, Fielding, Higgins, Stevenson, Eglington*

With the resumption of League football following the Second World War, the contrast between the two Merseyside clubs was startling. Liverpool would finish the season as First Division champions while Everton had been stagnant with manager Theo Kelly preferring not to dabble in the transfer market. It was a decision that would cost the Goodison Park club dearly within a few years. Kelly had stepped up from being the club's secretary in May 1939 and had angered fans by selling Tommy

Lawton to Chelsea in the previous year, despite the striker's incredible record of 65 goals in 87 League appearances. Lawton's absence was far too obvious in this goalless draw.

## 29th January 1947

First Division

**Everton 1**

Wainwright

**Liverpool 0**

*Attendance: 30,612*

**Everton:** *Sagar, Jackson, Greenhalgh, Bentham, Humphreys, Farrell, McIlhatton, Stevenson, Wainwright, Fielding, Eglington*

**Liverpool:** *Sidlow, Harley, Lambert, Taylor, Jones, Paisley, Eastham, Balmer, Stubbins, Done, Liddell*

Despite signing for Everton in 1939, Eddie Wainwright had to wait until the 1946–47 season to make his debut for the club and would go on to make more than 220 appearances, scoring 76 goals. This was his first Merseyside derby and he scored the only goal of the game to give the Blues a home win. Everton managed to finish the season in a respectable 10th position while Liverpool used this result as a watershed. The Anfield club upped their game and only lost one more League match (3-2 at home to Blackpool) to end the first post-war campaign as First Division champions, their first title since 1923.

## 27th September 1947

First Division

**Everton 0**

**Liverpool 3**

Balmer, Stubbins, Fagan

*Attendance: 66,776*

**Everton:** *Sagar, Saunders, Greenhalgh, Watson, T.G. Jones, Farrell, Fielding, Wainwright, Catterick, Stevenson, Eglington*

**Liverpool:** *Sidlow, Lambert, Hughes, Taylor, Jones, Paisley, Priday, Fagan, Stubbins, Balmer, Liddell*

Although Tommy Jones ended up on the losing side in this derby match, the Everton centre-half – making his first appearance of the season – put in such a display that many thought it would probably earn him a Welsh cap. Jones kept a tight hold on Albert Stubbins while Liverpool wingers Billy Liddell and Bob Priday were the danger men. Liddell, normally an outside-left, was tried at outside-right with great success. Jack Balmer opened the scoring in the 50th minute with Stubbins adding the visitors' second just a minute later. By the time Willie Fagan had the ball in the net in the 80th minute, Liverpool had the game well and truly sewn up. Both Balmer and Fagan had the distinction of scoring in Merseyside derbies before and after the Second World War.

## 21st April 1948

First Division

**Liverpool 4**

Stubbins, Liddell, Brierley, Balmer

**Everton 0**

*Attendance: 55,035*

**Liverpool:** *Sidlow, Jones, Lambert, Taylor, Hughes, Paisley, Liddell, Balmer, Stubbins, Fagan, Brierley*

**Everton:** *Sagar, Saunders, Hedley, Lindley, T.G. Jones, Farrell, Higgins, Wainwright, Lello, Stevenson, Eglington*

With both Liverpool and Everton safe in mid-table there was little to play for in this derby match – apart from local pride – and it was the red half of the city who gained most enjoyment. Albert Stubbins opened the scoring for the home side in the 14th minute but the majority of the match was a closely fought affair. Indeed, it wasn't until three goal-laden minutes late on that the floodgates opened. Billy Liddell doubled his side's advantage in the 80th minute while outside-left Ken Brierley scored his first Liverpool goal (and his only Merseyside derby goal) a minute later. Jack Balmer completed the rout in the 83rd minute as Liverpool ensured they stayed ahead of Everton in the First Division table.

## 18th September 1948

First Division

**Everton 1**

Dodds (pen)

**Liverpool 1**

Fagan

*Attendance:* **78,299**

**Everton:** *Sagar, Saunders, Hedley, Bentham, T.G. Jones, Watson, Powell, Fielding, Dodds, Stevenson, Boyes*

**Liverpool:** *Sidlow, Shepherd, Lambert, Taylor, Jones, Paisley, Payne, Balmer, Shannon, Fagan, Liddell*

The 1948–49 season had not begun well for Everton with just one victory and one draw from their opening eight matches, costing manager Theo Kelly his job. Their failure to get more than a point from this game left them rooted to the bottom of the First Division table, below Aston Villa on goal difference. It was a sign of the times that the public were overjoyed that life was returning to normal following the horrors of the Second World War that this post-war Merseyside derby drew in a record crowd of over 78,000. They witnessed heroics in both goals from Cyril Sidlow and Ted Sagar and the match sprung to life when Everton's Welsh centre-half Tommy Jones had to go off with an injury 10 minutes from the end. Willie Fagan took advantage of the extra man to put Liverpool in front but they conceded a penalty when Bill Shepherd was guilty of handling the ball in the area. Jock Dodds' penalty was not particularly well struck but the ball crept over the line to give the home side a share of the points.

## 5th February 1949

First Division

**Liverpool 0**

**Everton 0**

*Attendance:* **50,132**

**Liverpool:** *Sidlow, Shepherd, Lambert, Taylor, Jones, Paisley, Payne, Balmer, Stubbins, Done, Liddell*

**Everton:** *Sagar, Saunders, Hedley, Farrell, T.G. Jones, Lello, Powell, Wainwright, Catterick, Fielding, Eglington*

While goals were absent from this match, Everton's Tommy Jones was again the standout player with the centre-half being cheered by both sets of supporters for his defensive performance at Anfield. Everton's form had improved enough in the second half of the season to ensure their top-flight survival but scoring goals had been an issue throughout the campaign with a total of just 41 from their 42 games. Indeed, only Eddie Wainwright reached double figures for the season (with 10) as manager Cliff Britton struggled with the side he had inherited from Theo Kelly. For Liverpool, even such scoring stars as Jack Balmer, Albert Stubbins and Billy Liddell were unable to break down the visitors' defence and find that elusive winning goal.

## 27th August 1949

First Division

**Everton 0**

**Liverpool 0**

*Attendance:* **70,812**

**Everton:** *Burnett, Saunders, Dugdale, Farrell, T.G. Jones, Lello, Corr, Wainwright, McIntosh, Fielding, Eglington*

**Liverpool:** *Sidlow, Shepherd, Lambert, Taylor, Hughes, Paisley, Payne, Baron, Stubbins, Balmer, Liddell*

Creative genius was the only thing missing from this match, which was the epitome of good sportsmanship. The game missed the skill of Alex Stevenson (Everton) and Willie Fagan (Liverpool), stars of previous encounters who were watching this time. Jack Balmer tried to fill the double role for Liverpool of opening maker and taker, but individual ability could not overcome the supremacy of the strong-tackling half-backs. There was sheer joy in the work of Liverpool's Phil Taylor and Peter Farrell of Everton but a goalless draw was the perfect result to another game lacking masterminds in attack.

## 24th December 1949

First Division

**Liverpool 3**

Baron, Fagan 2

**Everton 1**
Farrell
*Attendance:* **50,485**
**Liverpool:** *Sidlow, Lambert, Spicer, Taylor, Jones, Hughes, Payne, Baron, Done, Fagan, Liddell*
**Everton:** *Burnett, Moore, Saunders, Grant, T.G. Jones, Lello, Buckle, Farrell, Wainwright, Powell, Eglington*

The pre-match gossip was that Everton were likely to follow the lead of Eire for their derby game against Liverpool by playing Peter Farrell, their half-back, at inside-right – his international position. Liverpool's Ken Brierley was injured, so Jimmy Payne returned to outside-right with Billy Liddell moving to the other wing. Eddie Spicer had recovered from injury and resumed at left-back for Ray Lambert, who crossed over to right-back. It seemed that Everton's ploy had worked when Farrell scored the opening goal of the game but Kevin Baron equalized and two goals from Willie Fagan allowed Liverpool to reap the dividends of their tactical reshuffle.

## 25th March 1950

FA Cup Semi-final (at Maine Road)
**Everton 0**
**Liverpool 2**
Paisley, Liddell
*Attendance:* **72,000**
**Everton:** *Burnett, Moore, Hedley, Grant, Falder, Farrell, Buckle, Wainwright, Catterick, Fielding, Eglington*
**Liverpool:** *Sidlow, Lambert, Spicer, Taylor, Jones, Paisley, Payne, Baron, Stubbins, Fagan, Liddell*

No one was more surprised at the ease with which they reached Wembley than the Liverpool players. After beating Everton 2-0, they felt like a tug-o'-war team who had taken the strain and simply walked backwards, although Liverpool appreciated that the Final against Arsenal would be a much more awkward proposition. The Maine Road canter was not likely to make them over-confident; they kept a sense of proportion and were soberly methodical both in their play and their attitude towards the adventure of trying to win the FA Cup for the first time in the club's history. Everton had reached the Semi-final the hard way – with tough visits to Queens Park Rangers, West Ham and Derby – and Liverpool thought that such worthy opponents would heavily barricade the door to the Final. They were not put out when it swung open with a touch: the lob from Bob Paisley which opened the scoring in the 30th minute. After that, Liverpool, although comfortably on top, showed their true character. There was no hint that they believed, as they had every right to, that the game was in the bag. Everton's defence wilted under the surging, concerted pressure which followed and there was no doubt who would win. Yet for that first half-hour, Everton had not played badly. They kept the ball on the ground and used it well in raids which were deservedly successful until they reached the Liverpool penalty area. Then they either fell apart through overelaboration or were broken down by Bill Jones, on this form the finest centre-half in Britain. Liverpool thought they had got another goal when Albert Stubbins was under the impression that the ball had crossed the line after he had headed it. The referee was in no doubt, however, and waved for the game to continue. The second half was a one-horse race. Liverpool scored again when Eddie Wainwright – trying to prevent a corner – accidentally gave the ball to Billy Liddell and the Scottish winger calmly tapped it into the net. Liddell was never ruffled but he finished the game with respect for Eric Moore. The young Everton back had kept on top of him and tackled splendidly.

## 16th September 1950

First Division

**Everton 1**

Eglington

**Liverpool 3**

Stubbins, Balmer 2

*Attendance:* **71,150**

**Everton:** *O'Neill, Moore, Clinton, Grant, Humphreys, Farrell, Buckle, Wainwright, Hold, Fielding, Eglington*

**Liverpool:** *Sidlow, Lambert, Spicer, Jones, Hughes, Paisley, Payne, Taylor, Stubbins, Balmer, Liddell*

Jack Humphreys, Everton's Welsh international, was recalled at centre-half and was the fourth player chosen for that position up to this point in the 1950–51 campaign. It would prove to be the last of his 61 games for the club before the 37-year-old returned to Llandudno Town. The Toffees' other switch brought the return of Eric Moore at right-back with Tommy Clinton moving to the left as his partner. Three first-half goals killed off Everton's challenge though, with Albert Stubbins scoring just before the half-hour and Jack Balmer adding two more just before the interval. Tommy Eglington did manage to pull one back for the home side, but it was simply a consolation as Everton remained 19th in the First Division table.

## 20th January 1951

First Division
**Liverpool 0**
**Everton 2**
McIntosh 2
*Attendance:* **48,688**
**Liverpool:** *Crossley, Shepherd, Spicer, Heydon, Jones, Paisley, Woan, Haigh, Stubbins, Balmer, Liddell*
**Everton:** *Sagar, Moore, Rankin, Grant, Jones, Farrell, Fielding, Hold, McIntosh, Potts, Eglington*

Everton clawed their way up to 16th in the League with this gutsy 2-0 win at Anfield courtesy of a goal in each half from their Scottish forward Jimmy McIntosh. Sadly, they could not sustain the improvement and the end of the season saw them propping up the First Division table with the prospect of Second Division football now a reality for only the second time in their history. This game marked the end of Don Woan's Liverpool career after just two League appearances. The locally born outside-right found himself being transferred to Leyton Orient later that year as part of an exchange deal for 18-year-old Brian Jackson.

## 29th January 1955

FA Cup Fourth Round

**Everton 0**

**Liverpool 4**

Liddell, A'Court, Evans 2

*Attendance:* **72,000**

**Everton:** *O'Neill, Moore, Rankin, Farrell, Jones, Lello, Wainwright, Fielding, Hickson, Potts, Eglington*

**Liverpool:** *Rudham, Lambert, Moran, Saunders, Hughes, Twentyman, Jackson, Anderson, Liddell, Evans, A'Court*

In a bizarre twist of fate that would temporarily deprive fans of both clubs the thrills of a Merseyside derby, the 1953–54 season had seen Liverpool relegated from the First Division while a resurgent Everton had finished runners-up in the second tier to regain their top-flight status. This FA Cup fixture – the only meeting of the two sides between January 1951 and September 1962 – therefore pitted Second Division Liverpool against Everton of the First Division, and is the only time they have contested a competitive match while not being at the same level of professional football. Liverpool stalwart Billy Liddell scored the visitors' first in the 18th minute after being picked out by Brian Jackson following Geoff Twentyman's free-kick. A little more than 10 minutes later and Liverpool turned the form book completely upside down when Alan A'Court doubled their lead from another Twentyman free-kick. Jackson was involved in the Reds' two other goals as well: it was his shot that Jimmy O'Neill failed to hold to give John Evans the chance to notch Liverpool's third; and Evans scored his second from Jackson's cross after 75 minutes.

# Chapter Six

# The 1960s

Liverpool started the decade as they had finished the 1950s, stuck in the Second Division until they claimed their fourth – and last to date – Championship in 1961–62. The 1960s saw a long period of stability and success with long-serving managers steadying the ship: Harry Catterick at Everton and Bill Shankly at Liverpool. The First Division trophy almost took up permanent residence on Merseyside with each club winning the title on two occasions (Liverpool 1963–64 and 1965–66 and Everton 1962–63 and 1969–70). Liverpool also won their first FA Cup with a 2-1 victory over Leeds United in 1965 while Everton repeated that feat the following year, beating Sheffield Wednesday 3-2, and fell at the last hurdle to West Bromwich Albion in 1968. The 1960s were also notable in that they saw the introduction of the Football League Cup (which has since gone through many guises in terms of its sponsor) and European competition.

## Record in the 1960s

**Everton**

| Season | League | P | W | D | L | F | A | Pts | Pos |
|---|---|---|---|---|---|---|---|---|---|
| 1960–61 | Div 1 | 42 | 22 | 6 | 14 | 87 | 69 | 50 | 5 |
| 1961–62 | Div 1 | 42 | 20 | 11 | 11 | 88 | 54 | 51 | 4 |
| 1962–63 | Div 1 | 42 | 25 | 11 | 6 | 84 | 42 | 61 | 1 |
| 1963–64 | Div 1 | 42 | 21 | 10 | 11 | 84 | 64 | 52 | 3 |
| 1964–65 | Div 1 | 42 | 17 | 15 | 10 | 69 | 60 | 49 | 4 |
| 1965–66 | Div 1 | 42 | 15 | 11 | 16 | 56 | 62 | 41 | 11 |
| 1966–67 | Div 1 | 42 | 19 | 10 | 13 | 65 | 46 | 48 | 6 |
| 1967–68 | Div 1 | 42 | 23 | 6 | 13 | 67 | 40 | 52 | 5 |
| 1968–69 | Div 1 | 42 | 21 | 15 | 6 | 77 | 36 | 57 | 3 |
| 1969–70 | Div 1 | 42 | 29 | 8 | 5 | 72 | 34 | 66 | 1 |

## FA Cup

| | |
|---|---|
| 1960–61 | 0-1 v Sheffield United (Third Round) |
| 1961–62 | 1-3 v Burnley (Fifth Round) |
| 1962–63 | 0-1 v West Ham United (Fifth Round) |
| 1963–64 | 1-3 v Sunderland (Fifth Round) |
| 1964–65 | 1-1, 1-2 v Leeds United (Fourth Round) |
| 1965–66 | 3-2 v Sheffield Wednesday (Final) |
| 1966–67 | 2-3 v Nottingham Forest (Quarter-final) |
| 1967–68 | 0-1 v West Bromwich Albion (Final) |
| 1968–69 | 0-1 v Manchester City (Semi-final) |
| 1969–70 | 1-2 v Sheffield United (Third Round) |

## League Cup

| | |
|---|---|
| 1960–61 | 1-2 v Shrewsbury Town (Quarter-final) |
| 1961–62 | Did not enter |
| 1962–63 | Did not enter |
| 1963–64 | Did not enter |
| 1964–65 | Did not enter |
| 1965–66 | Did not enter |
| 1966–67 | Did not enter |
| 1967–68 | 2-3 v Sunderland (Third Round) |
| 1968–69 | 0-0, 0-1 v Derby County (Fourth Round) |
| 1969–70 | 0-2 v Manchester City (Fourth Round) |

## Europe

| | |
|---|---|
| 1960–61 | Did not qualify |
| 1961–62 | Did not qualify |
| 1962–63 | Fairs Cup: 1-0, 0-2 v Dunfermline Athletic (First Round) |
| 1963–64 | European Cup: 0-0, 0-1 v Inter Milan (First Round) |
| 1964–65 | Fairs Cup: 1-1, 1-2 v Manchester United (Third Round) |
| 1965–66 | Fairs Cup: 0-3, 2-1 v Újpesti Dózsa (Second Round) |
| 1966–67 | European Cup Winners' Cup: 0-2, 1-0 v Real Zaragoza (Second Round) |
| 1967–68 | Did not qualify |
| 1968–69 | Did not qualify |
| 1969–70 | Did not qualify |

## Liverpool

| Season | League | P | W | D | L | F | A | Pts | Pos |
|--------|--------|----|----|----|----|----|----|-----|-----|
| 1960–61 | Div 2 | 42 | 21 | 10 | 11 | 87 | 58 | 52 | 3 |
| 1961–62 | Div 2 | 42 | 27 | 8 | 7 | 99 | 43 | 62 | 1 |
| 1962–63 | Div 1 | 42 | 17 | 10 | 15 | 71 | 59 | 44 | 8 |
| 1963–64 | Div 1 | 42 | 26 | 5 | 11 | 92 | 45 | 57 | 1 |
| 1964–65 | Div 1 | 42 | 17 | 10 | 15 | 67 | 73 | 44 | 7 |
| 1965–66 | Div 1 | 42 | 26 | 9 | 7 | 79 | 34 | 61 | 1 |
| 1966–67 | Div 1 | 42 | 19 | 13 | 10 | 64 | 47 | 51 | 5 |
| 1967–68 | Div 1 | 42 | 22 | 11 | 9 | 71 | 40 | 55 | 3 |
| 1968–69 | Div 1 | 42 | 25 | 11 | 6 | 63 | 24 | 61 | 2 |
| 1969–70 | Div 1 | 42 | 20 | 11 | 11 | 65 | 42 | 51 | 5 |

## FA Cup

| | |
|--|--|
| 1960–61 | 0-2 v Sunderland (Fourth Round) |
| 1961–62 | 0-0, 0-0, 0-1 v Preston North End (Fifth Round) |
| 1962–63 | 0-1 v Leicester City (Semi-final) |
| 1963–64 | 1-2 v Swansea Town (Quarter-final) |
| 1964–65 | 2-1 v Leeds United (Final) |
| 1965–66 | 1-2 v Chelsea (Third Round) |
| 1966–67 | 0-1 v Everton (Fifth Round) |
| 1967–68 | 0-0, 1-1, 1-2 v West Bromwich Albion (Quarter-final) |
| 1968–69 | 0-0, 0-1 v Leicester City (Fifth Round) |
| 1969–70 | 0-1 v Watford (Quarter-final) |

## League Cup

| | |
|--|--|
| 1960–61 | 1-2 v Southampton (Third Round) |
| 1961–62 | Did not enter |
| 1962–63 | Did not enter |
| 1963–64 | Did not enter |
| 1964–65 | Did not enter |
| 1965–66 | Did not enter |
| 1966–67 | Did not enter |
| 1967–68 | 1-1, 2-3 v Bolton Wanderers (Second Round) |
| 1968–69 | 1-2 v Arsenal (Fourth Round) |
| 1969–70 | 2-3 v Manchester City (Third Round) |

## Europe

| | |
|---|---|
| 1960–61 | Did not qualify |
| 1961–62 | Did not qualify |
| 1962–63 | Did not qualify |
| 1963–64 | Did not qualify |
| 1964–65 | European Cup: 3-1, 0-3 v Inter Milan (Semi-final) |
| 1965–66 | European Cup Winners' Cup: 1-2 v Borussia Dortmund (Final) |
| 1966–67 | European Cup: 1-5, 2-2 v Ajax (Second Round) |
| 1967–68 | Fairs Cup: 0-1, 0-1 v Ferencváros (Third Round) |
| 1968–69 | Fairs Cup: 1-2, 2-1 (lost on coin flip) v Athletic Bilbao (First Round) |
| 1969–70 | Fairs Cup: 0-1, 3-2 (away goals) v Vitória Setúbal (Second Round) |

## The Matches

## 22nd September 1962

First Division

**Everton 2**

Vernon (pen), Morrissey

**Liverpool 2**

Lewis, Hunt

*Attendance:* **72,488**

**Everton:** *West, Meagan, Thomson, Gabriel, Labone, Harris, Bingham, Stevens, Young, Vernon, Morrissey*

**Liverpool:** *Furnell, Byrne, Moran, Milne, Yeats, Leishman, Callaghan, Hunt, Lewis, Melia, A'Court*

The first Merseyside derby in seven years ended with honours even at Goodison Park but Liverpool left it late to level the match. Roger Hunt broke Evertonian hearts with a last-gasp goal after Kevin Lewis had knocked down an Alan A'Court cross. The home side had taken the lead shortly before the half-hour mark when Roy Vernon slotted home a penalty given after Gerry Byrne had been judged to have handled the ball. Winger Kevin Lewis equalized just six minutes later but Johnny Morrissey – who had recently joined Everton from Liverpool

89

for £10,000 – restored the Blues' lead on 62 minutes with a goal on his Everton debut.

## 8th April 1963

First Division

**Liverpool 0**

**Everton 0**

*Attendance:* **56,060**

**Liverpool:** *Lawrence, Byrne, Moran, Milne, Yeats, Stevenson, Callaghan, Hunt, Arrowsmith, Melia, Lewis*

**Everton:** *West, Parker, Meagan, Gabriel, Labone, Kay, Scott, Stevens, Young, Vernon, Morrissey*

Everton left Anfield in third position in the League, just three points behind leaders Leicester City but with a game in hand, and a point was a welcome boost to their season that had suffered a hiccup the previous month with back-to-back defeats at the hands of Arsenal and Sheffield United. Their neighbours were safe in sixth place but were a massive nine points behind and would suffer a humiliating 7-2 reverse at White Hart Lane the following week. The Toffees, however, remained unbeaten until the end of the season with a run of seven wins and two draws to claim the First Division crown for the first time since 1939.

## 28th September 1963

First Division

**Liverpool 2**

Callaghan 2

**Everton 1**

Vernon

*Attendance:* **51,973**

**Liverpool:** *Lawrence, Byrne, Ferns, Milne, Yeats, Stevenson, Callaghan, Hunt, St John, Melia, Thompson*

**Everton:** *West, Parker, Brown, Kay, Labone, Harris, Scott, Stevens, Temple, Vernon, Morrissey*

Everton's defence of their First Division title didn't get off to a brilliant start in the summer of 1963 with a 5-1 defeat at Manchester United being closely followed by a 4-3 reverse at home to Burnley. The week prior to this fixture had also seen them knocked out of the European Cup by Inter Milan by an aggregate score of 1-0, so manager Harry Catterick would not have been at all pleased to lose this derby match as well. Ian Callaghan set the home side on the way to victory with goals either side of half-time and, while Roy Vernon pulled one back for Everton in the 74th minute, they were unable to get back on level terms.

## 8th February 1964

First Division
**Everton 3**
Vernon 2, Gabriel
**Liverpool 1**
St John
*Attendance: 66,515*
**Everton:** *West, Brown, Meagan, Harris, Labone, Kay, Scott, Stevens, Gabriel, Vernon, Temple*
**Liverpool:** *Lawrence, Byrne, Moran, Milne, Yeats, Stevenson, Callaghan, Hunt, St John, Melia, Thompson*

Everton manager Harry Catterick was asked if he considered choosing wing-half Jimmy Gabriel – who had scored three goals in three games playing as centre-forward – as a stop-gap in that position to which he replied: "All my players are stop-gaps until we can get someone better . . . and that goes for the manager, too!" The strategy paid off with Gabriel adding to Roy Vernon's ninth-minute goal to send the home side in 2-0 up at half-time. Ian St John reduced the deficit after 80 minutes but Vernon got his second and Everton's third just three minutes later in what turned out to be Jimmy Melia's final appearance for Liverpool before a transfer to Wolves.

## 19<sup>th</sup> September 1964

First Division
**Liverpool 0**
**Everton 4**
Temple, Pickering, Harvey, Morrissey
*Attendance: 52,619*
**Liverpool:** *Lawrence, Byrne, Moran, Milne, Yeats, Stevenson, Callaghan, Hunt, St John, Wallace, Thompson*
**Everton:** *Rankin, Harris, Brown, Gabriel, Labone, Stevens, Scott, Harvey, Pickering, Temple, Morrissey*

Just two seasons after winning the Second Division and promotion back to the top flight, Liverpool had won the First Division title and much was expected of them as they prepared to defend their crown. The reality, however, was not to the fans' expectations as the Reds suffered four defeats in their first seven games. Everton, in comparison, had lost twice – away to Nottingham Forest and Manchester United – and began the match with a first-minute goal when Derek Temple shot past Tommy Lawrence. Fred Pickering added a second with a deflected shot that wrong-footed the Liverpool keeper before Colin Harvey added a third just before half-time. Johnny Morrissey rounded off the scoring with a long-range shot from outside the area to send the blue half of the city ecstatic with their first Anfield win since 1951.

## 12<sup>th</sup> April 1965

First Division
**Everton 2**
Temple, Morrissey
**Liverpool 1**
Stevenson (pen)
*Attendance: 65,402*
**Everton:** *West, Wright, Brown, Gabriel, Labone, Harris, Scott, Harvey, Pickering, Temple, Morrissey*
**Liverpool:** *Lawrence, Lawler, Byrne, Milne, Yeats, Stevenson, Callaghan, Hunt, St John, Smith, Thompson*

Having already booked their place in the FA Cup Final, Liverpool crashed to their third consecutive defeat with a 2-1 loss at Everton. The Blues had not had a particularly successful run of late either, with only two draws to show from their previous five matches. By the end of 90 minutes, however, Willie Stevenson's penalty proved insufficient as Derek Temple and Johnny Morrissey scored for the home side to ensure Everton did the double over their neighbours and earned the bragging rights for the season.

## 25th September 1965

First Division

**Liverpool 5**

Smith, Hunt 2, Stevenson, St John

**Everton 0**

*Attendance: 53,557*

**Liverpool:** *Lawrence, Strong (Arrowsmith), Byrne, Milne, Yeats, Stevenson, Callaghan, Hunt, St John, Smith, Thompson*

**Everton:** *West, Wright, Wilson, Gabriel, Labone (Glover), Harris, Scott, Young, Pickering, Harvey, Morrissey*

Buoyed by the previous season's results against Liverpool, Everton left Anfield shell-shocked, although the avalanche didn't begin until the 34th minute when Tommy Smith headed past Gordon West. The floodgates opened in the second half as Liverpool ran rampant with Roger Hunt and Willie Stevenson adding to the home side's tally within seven minutes of the restart. Stevenson and Hunt combined on 73 minutes to give the latter his second and Ian St John completed the rout with a minute to go.

## 19th March 1966

First Division

**Everton 0**

**Liverpool 0**

*Attendance: 62,337*

**Everton:** *West, Brown, Wilson, Gabriel, Labone, Harris, Scott, Young, Pickering (Wright), Harvey, Temple*

**Liverpool:** *Lawrence, Lawler, Byrne, Smith, Yeats, Stevenson, Callaghan, Hunt, St John, Arrowsmith, Thompson*

A goalless draw was not anticipated before this match as Liverpool topped the League table – with 68 goals for, compared to Everton's 53 – but that was how the 90 minutes played out. The visitors had only lost twice since the turn of the year;: a 2-1 defeat to Chelsea in the Third Round of the FA Cup and a 2-0 loss at Craven Cottage in the First Division. Everton had been unbeaten since the middle of January, but neither side was able to provide the breakthrough moment.

## 13th August 1966
First Division
FA Charity Shield
**Everton 0**
**Liverpool 1**
Hunt
*Attendance:* **63,329**
**Everton:** *West, Wright, Wilson, Gabriel, Labone, Glover, Scott, Young, Trebilcock, Harvey, Temple*
**Liverpool:** *Lawrence, Lawler, Byrne, Smith, Yeats, Stevenson, Callaghan, Hunt, St John, Strong, Thompson*

The year of 1966 would prove an emphatic one for both Merseyside clubs and the England national team. Liverpool qualified for this Charity Shield match as League champions while Everton had won the FA Cup. England stars Roger Hunt, Alan Ball and Ray Wilson paraded the World Cup trophy – won with an exciting 4-2 extra-time victory over West Germany at Wembley the previous month – around Goodison Park before the match. The game itself was decided by a Roger Hunt goal in the ninth minute in front of a crowd of more than 63,000.

## 27th August 1966
First Division
**Everton 3**
Ball 2, Brown

**Liverpool 1**
Smith
*Attendance: 64,318*
**Everton:** *West, Wright, Wilson, Gabriel, Labone, Harvey, Temple, Ball,*
*Pickering (Brown), Young, Morrissey*
**Liverpool:** *Lawrence, Lawler, Milne, Smith, Yeats, Stevenson, Callaghan,*
*Hunt, St John, Strong, Thompson*

Two weeks after Liverpool drew the first blood of the 1966–67 campaign with their Charity Shield victory, the two sides returned to Goodison Park for the first League game of the season. The Blues were out for revenge and got off to a fantastic start when World Cup-winner Alan Ball notched two goals within the first 17 minutes to stun the visitors. Tommy Smith reduced the deficit just before half-time but Sandy Brown put the result beyond doubt with Everton's third just seven minutes from time.

# 31ˢᵗ December 1966

First Division
**Liverpool 0**
**Everton 0**
*Attendance: 53,744*
**Liverpool:** *Lawrence, Lawler, Milne, Smith, Yeats, Stevenson, Callaghan,*
*Hunt, St John, Strong, Thompson*
**Everton:** *West, Wright, Brown, Gabriel, Labone, Harvey, Hurst, Ball, Young,*
*Temple, Morrissey*

With one win apiece and a draw in the preceding three matches, the fourth Merseyside derby meeting in a single calendar year proved to be a nail-biting affair as both sides sought the goal that would give them the advantage over their city rivals for another season. Like their first encounter of 1966, though, neither team was able to successfully penetrate their opponents' defence, and the game ended without any goals.

## 11th March 1967

FA Cup Fifth Round

**Everton 1**

Ball

**Liverpool 0**

*Attendance: 64,851*

**Everton:** *West, Wright, Wilson, Hurst, Labone, Harvey, Young, Ball, Temple, Husband, Morrissey*

**Liverpool:** *Lawrence, Lawler, Milne, Byrne, Yeats, Stevenson, Callaghan, Hunt, St John, Smith, Thompson*

Once more anticipation of a great meeting – a derby clash between the FA Cup holders and the League champions – proved more satisfying than the reality. That mood of effervescent expectation was soon blown away. The wind was indeed one of the villains; it swirled, it gusted and blew swathes of lavatory paper so that the Everton goal area in the first half resembled a municipal rubbish dump. It swept dirty smoke over the field and much of the play in the first half matched the tumultuous atmosphere. The climate of excitement soon gave way to a climate of violence, with many crunching and vicious tackles coming from both sides. The only goal of the game came as a result of a disastrous mistake by Gordon Milne, a superb piece of opportunism by Jimmy Husband and a rapier thrust to the vitals by Alan Ball less than 30 seconds before the half-time whistle. That goal was alleged to have saved bookmakers more than £250,000 because if this tie had ended in a draw, fixed-odds bookies would have had their heaviest loss of the season. They already faced a massive pay-out because there were 18 draws on the coupons from the afternoon matches. With Everton v Liverpool the most popular choice for a draw, thousands of punters were hoping that the evening match's result would complete their winning lines.

## 23rd September 1967

First Division

**Liverpool 1**

Hunt

**Everton 0**

*Attendance: 54,189*

**Liverpool:** *Lawrence, Lawler, Byrne, Smith, Yeats, Hughes, Callaghan, Hunt, Hateley, St John, Thompson*

**Everton:** *West, Wright, Brown, Kendall, Labone, Harvey, Ball, Hunt, Young, Hurst, Morrissey*

This result kept Liverpool on top of the First Division, level on points with Arsenal and Sheffield Wednesday, and each of the three clubs had identical statistics for the first nine games of the new season: six wins, one draw and two defeats. Everton, meanwhile, were languishing in 15th position with just three wins and a draw to show for their efforts in the same period. This match was notable in that it was the last time that Roger Hunt scored in a Merseyside derby. Less than two months later, the striker became Liverpool's record scorer when he netted his 242nd goal for the club and his final tally of 286 (reached in 1969) would stand until beaten by Ian Rush 23 years later.

## 3rd February 1968

First Division

**Everton 1**

Kendall

**Liverpool 0**

*Attendance: 64,482*

**Everton:** *West, Wright, Wilson, Kendall, Labone, Harvey, Hurst, Ball (Brown), Royle, Hunt, Husband*

**Liverpool:** *Lawrence, Lawler, Smith, Strong, Yeats, Hughes, Callaghan, Hunt, Hateley, St John, Thompson*

Playing in only his second Merseyside derby, Howard Kendall scored the only goal of the game to secure the points for Everton. The result also avenged Liverpool's victory by the same scoreline at Anfield the previous September. Not a prolific goalscorer by nature, this would prove to be Kendall's only strike in the derby fixture between his £85,000 transfer from Preston North End in March 1967 and his departure for Birmingham City in August 1977.

## 27ᵗʰ August 1968

First Division
**Everton 0**
**Liverpool 0**
*Attendance: 63,998*
**Everton:** *West, Wright, Brown, Kendall, Labone, Harvey, Husband, Ball,
Royle, Hurst, Morrissey*
**Liverpool:** *Lawrence, Lawler, Wall, Smith, Yeats, Hughes, Callaghan, Hunt,
Hateley, St John, Thompson*

This Goodison Park clash, watched by almost 64,000, ended with
honours even as the Everton and Liverpool defences dominated in a 0-0
thriller. The home side had kicked off the season in disappointing style
with two defeats in their first three outings (against Manchester United
and Spurs) but would go on to be undefeated in the League until losing
to Leeds United in November. For Tommy Lawrence and the rest of his
Liverpool team-mates, however, this match represented the first clean
sheet they had managed thus far in the 1968–69 campaign.

## 8ᵗʰ October 1968

First Division
**Liverpool 1**
Smith
**Everton 1**
Ball
*Attendance: 54,496*
**Liverpool:** *Lawrence, Lawler, Wall, Smith, Yeats, Hughes, Callaghan, Hunt,
Evans, St John, Thompson*
**Everton:** *West, Wright, Brown, Kendall, Labone, Harvey, Husband, Ball,
Royle, Hurst, Morrissey*

There was only one change for Liverpool from the previous encounter
just six weeks earlier, with Alun Evans replacing Tony Hateley (who had
recently joined Coventry City) in attack, while Everton fielded the same 11
who had fought out the goalless draw at Goodison Park. It was perhaps
no surprise then that the two sides cancelled each other out and again

had to settle for a share of the points. Alan Ball had given Everton a 65th-minute lead but Tommy Smith equalized 10 minutes later.

## 6th December 1969

First Division

**Everton 0**

**Liverpool 3**

Hughes, Brown (og), Graham

*Attendance: 57,370*

**Everton:** *West, Wright, Brown, Kendall, Labone, Jackson, Whittle, Ball, Royle, Hurst, Morrissey*

**Liverpool:** *Lawrence, Lawler, Wall, Strong, Yeats, Hughes, Callaghan, Ross, Thompson, St John, Graham*

Everton suffered only their third home defeat of the season as they fell 3-0 to a rampant Liverpool side in third position in the First Division, hot on the heels of their table-topping city rivals. Alan Ball was guilty of an inexcusable challenge on Ian St John that was one of the major talking points after the match. The real story of the game, however, was the three goals scored for Liverpool – the first time the Reds had managed to score more than one at Goodison Park since September 1962. Emlyn Hughes opened the scoring shortly after the interval with Sandy Brown scoring an own goal seven minutes later. Bobby Graham notched the visitors' third in the 74th minute and Everton's misery was complete.

## 21st March 1970

First Division

**Liverpool 0**

**Everton 2**

Royle, Whittle

*Attendance: 54,496*

**Liverpool:** *Clemence, Lawler, Strong, Smith, Yeats, Hughes, Thompson (A. Evans), Livermore, St John, Callaghan, Graham*

**Everton:** *West, Wright, Brown, Kendall, Kenyon, Harvey, Whittle, Ball, Royle, Hurst, Morrissey*

Everton gained revenge for their home Merseyside derby defeat earlier in the season with a convincing 2-0 win at Anfield. Everton had arrived on the back of an eight-match unbeaten run of four wins and four draws and would go on to claim the First Division title. They continued their form and registered four wins and a draw in their final five games to leave them an untouchable nine points clear of their nearest rival Leeds United. Joe Royle and Alan Whittle scored the goals that gave Everton their first win at Anfield since September 1964 while Liverpool left-back Geoff Strong was making his final appearance for the club before a summer move to Coventry City.

# Chapter Seven

# The 1970s

Much as Everton lorded it over their city rivals in the 1930s, so Liverpool dominated the 1970s on Merseyside. The Anfield club won five First Division titles and an FA Cup as the transition from Bill Shankly to Bob Paisley progressed seamlessly. Everton twice lost out to the Reds at the Semi-final stage of the FA Cup (1971 and 1977) and spent almost equal portions of the decade in both the top and bottom halves of the First Division. It was in Europe, however, that Liverpool truly trounced Everton in terms of success with two European Cups (1977 and 1978) and two UEFA Cups (1973 and 1976).

## Record in the 1970s

**Everton**

| Season | League | P | W | D | L | F | A | Pts | Pos |
|--------|--------|---|---|---|---|---|---|-----|-----|
| 1970–71 | Div 1 | 42 | 12 | 13 | 17 | 54 | 60 | 37 | 14 |
| 1971–72 | Div 1 | 42 | 9 | 18 | 15 | 37 | 48 | 36 | 15 |
| 1972–73 | Div 1 | 42 | 13 | 11 | 18 | 41 | 49 | 37 | 17 |
| 1973–74 | Div 1 | 42 | 16 | 12 | 14 | 50 | 48 | 44 | 7 |
| 1974–75 | Div 1 | 42 | 16 | 18 | 8 | 56 | 42 | 50 | 4 |
| 1975–76 | Div 1 | 42 | 15 | 12 | 15 | 60 | 66 | 42 | 11 |
| 1976–77 | Div 1 | 42 | 14 | 14 | 14 | 62 | 64 | 42 | 9 |
| 1977–78 | Div 1 | 42 | 22 | 11 | 9 | 76 | 45 | 55 | 3 |
| 1978–79 | Div 1 | 42 | 17 | 17 | 8 | 52 | 40 | 51 | 4 |
| 1979–80 | Div 1 | 42 | 9 | 17 | 16 | 43 | 51 | 35 | 19 |

### FA Cup

| 1970–71 | 1-2 v Liverpool (Semi-final) |
| 1971–72 | 0-2 v Tottenham Hotspur (Fifth Round) |
| 1972–73 | 0-2 v Millwall (Fourth Round) |

| 1973–74 | 0-0, 0-1 v West Bromwich Albion (Fourth Round) |
| 1974–75 | 1-2 v Fulham (Fifth Round) |
| 1975–76 | 1-2 v Derby County (Third Round) |
| 1976–77 | 2-2, 0-3 v Liverpool (Semi-final) |
| 1977–78 | 2-3 v Middlesbrough (Fourth Round) |
| 1978–79 | 1-2 v Sunderland (Third Round) |
| 1979–80 | 1-1, 1-2 v West Ham United (Semi-final) |

## League Cup

| 1970–71 | Did not enter |
| 1971–72 | 1-2 v Southampton (Second Round) |
| 1972–73 | 0-1 v Arsenal (Second Round) |
| 1973–74 | 0-1 v Norwich City (Third Round) |
| 1974–75 | 1-1, 0-3 v Aston Villa (Second Round) |
| 1975–76 | 2-2, 0-2 v Notts County (Fourth Round) |
| 1976–77 | 0-0, 1-1, 2-3 v Aston Villa (Final) |
| 1977–78 | 1-4 v Leeds United (Quarter-final) |
| 1978–79 | 2-3 v Nottingham Forest (Fourth Round) |
| 1979–80 | 1-2 v Grimsby Town (Fourth Round) |

## Europe

| 1970–71 | European Cup: 1-1, 0-0 (away goals) v Panathinaikos (Quarter- final) |
| 1971–72 | Did not qualify |
| 1972–73 | Did not qualify |
| 1973–74 | Did not qualify |
| 1974–75 | Did not qualify |
| 1975–76 | UEFA Cup: 0-0, 0-1 v AC Milan (First Round) |
| 1976–77 | Did not qualify |
| 1977–78 | Did not qualify |
| 1978–79 | UEFA Cup: 2-1, 0-1 (lost on away goals) v Dukla Prague (Second Round) |
| 1979–80 | UEFA Cup: 0-1, 0-1 v Feyenoord (First Round) |

## Liverpool

| Season | League | P | W | D | L | F | A | Pts | Pos |
|--------|--------|---|---|---|---|---|---|-----|-----|
| 1970–71 | Div 1 | 42 | 17 | 17 | 8 | 42 | 24 | 51 | 5 |
| 1971–72 | Div 1 | 42 | 24 | 9 | 9 | 64 | 30 | 57 | 3 |
| 1972–73 | Div 1 | 42 | 25 | 10 | 7 | 72 | 42 | 60 | 1 |
| 1973–74 | Div 1 | 42 | 22 | 13 | 7 | 52 | 31 | 57 | 2 |
| 1974–75 | Div 1 | 42 | 20 | 11 | 11 | 60 | 39 | 51 | 2 |
| 1975–76 | Div 1 | 42 | 23 | 14 | 5 | 66 | 31 | 60 | 1 |
| 1976–77 | Div 1 | 42 | 23 | 11 | 8 | 62 | 33 | 57 | 1 |
| 1977–78 | Div 1 | 42 | 24 | 9 | 9 | 65 | 34 | 57 | 2 |
| 1978–79 | Div 1 | 42 | 30 | 8 | 4 | 85 | 16 | 68 | 1 |
| 1979–80 | Div 1 | 42 | 25 | 10 | 7 | 81 | 30 | 60 | 1 |

## *FA Cup*

| | |
|---|---|
| 1970–71 | 1-2 v Arsenal (Final) |
| 1971–72 | 0-0, 0-2 v Leeds United (Fourth Round) |
| 1972–73 | 0-0, 0-2 v Manchester City (Fourth Round) |
| 1973–74 | 3-0 v Newcastle United (Final) |
| 1974–75 | 0-1 v Ipswich Town (Fourth Round) |
| 1975–76 | 0-1 v Derby County (Fourth Round) |
| 1976–77 | 1-2 v Manchester United (Final) |
| 1977–78 | 2-4 v Chelsea (Third Round) |
| 1978–79 | 2-2, 0-1 v Manchester United (Semi-final) |
| 1979–80 | 1-1, 0-1 v Arsenal (Semi-final) |

## *League Cup*

| | |
|---|---|
| 1970–71 | 0-2 v Swindon Town (Third Round) |
| 1971–72 | 1-2 v West Ham United (Fourth Round) |
| 1972–73 | 1-1, 1-3 v Tottenham Hotspur (Quarter-final) |
| 1973–74 | 0-1 v Wolverhampton Wanderers (Quarter-final) |
| 1974–75 | 0-1 v Middlesbrough (Fourth Round) |
| 1975–76 | 1-1, 0-1 v Burnley (Third Round) |
| 1976–77 | 1-1, 0-1 v West Bromwich Albion (Second Round) |
| 1977–78 | 0-0, 0-1 v Nottingham Forest (Final) |
| 1978–79 | 0-1 v Sheffield United (Second Round) |
| 1979–80 | 0-1, 1-1 v Nottingham Forest (Semi-final) |

### Europe

| | |
|---|---|
| 1970–71 | Fairs Cup: 0-1, 0-0 v Leeds United (Semi-final) |
| 1971–72 | European Cup Winners' Cup: 0-0, 1-3 v Bayern Munich (Second Round) |
| 1972–73 | UEFA Cup: 3-0, 0-2 v Borussia Mönchengladbach (Final) |
| 1973–74 | European Cup: 1-2, 1-2 v Red Star Belgrade (Second Round) |
| 1974–75 | European Cup Winners' Cup: 1-1, 0-0 (away goals) v Ferencváros (Second Round) |
| 1975–76 | UEFA Cup: 3-2, 1-1 v FC Bruges (Final) |
| 1976–77 | European Cup: 3-1 v Borussia Mönchengladbach (Final) |
| 1977–78 | European Cup: 1-0 v FC Bruges (Final) |
| 1978–79 | European Cup 0-2, 0-0 v Nottingham Forest (First Round) |
| 1979–80 | European Cup: 2-1, 0-3 v Dinamo Tblisi (First Round) |

## The Matches

### 21ˢᵗ November 1970

First Division

**Liverpool 3**

Heighway, Toshack, Lawler

**Everton 2**

Whittle, Royle

*Attendance: 53,777*

**Liverpool:** *Clemence, Lawler, Lindsay, Smith, Lloyd, Hughes, Hall, McLaughlin, Heighway, Toshack, Ross*

**Everton:** *Rankin, Wright, H. Newton, Kendall (K. Newton), Labone, Harvey, Whittle, Ball, Royle, Hurst, Morrissey*

Sir Alf Ramsey shared a five-goal second-half thriller with 53,777 fans . . . and then went home reflecting on the star that got away. The man in question was Liverpool's Steve Heighway, who scored the first goal to spark a 3-2 triumph over Everton. The England team manager told Liverpool officials after the match that Heighway's goal was one of the best he'd seen that season. Heighway could have played for England; though born in Dublin, his parents were English and the family returned to England when he was only five. But the talent-starved Eire selectors beat Sir Alf to it and snapped Heighway up even before he joined Liverpool. "This boy is a touch of genius," extolled Liverpool manager Bill Shankly. "It is fantastic to think that only last season he was playing amateur football with Skelmersdale."

## 20th February 1971

First Division
**Everton 0**
**Liverpool 0**
*Attendance: 56,846*
**Everton:** *West, Wright, H. Newton, Kendall, Kenyon, Harvey, Husband, Ball, Royle, Hurst, Morrissey*
**Liverpool:** *Clemence, Lawler, Yeats, Smith, Lloyd, Hughes, Boersma, McLaughlin, Heighway, Toshack, Hall*

Liverpool were one of two sides to end the 1970–71 season with an unbeaten home record, the other team – Arsenal – finished as First Division champions and the Anfield club could well have challenged them more strongly had they not drawn so many matches. This goalless stalemate was one of 17 games that they drew during the campaign as the tactics decided upon by opposing managers Bill Shankly and Harry Catterick cancelled each other out.

## 27th March 1971

FA Cup Semi-final (at Old Trafford)
**Everton 1**
Ball
**Liverpool 2**
Evans, Hall
*Attendance: 62,144*
**Everton:** *Rankin, Wright, K. Newton, Kendall, Labone (Brown), Harvey, Whittle, Ball, Royle, Hurst, Morrissey*
**Liverpool:** *Clemence, Lawler, Lindsay, Smith, Lloyd, Hughes, Callaghan, Evans, Heighway, Toshack, Hall*

The record would show that Bill Shankly did it his way and as Merseyside prepared to march on Wembley for the FA Cup Final, his way merited nomination as the managerial feat of the season. Shankly was a man whose enthusiasm never wilted, whose faith in his Liverpool players never wavered. He ripped apart one successful team and put together another – ready and able to dominate football for the next five years. Shankly kicked off what became a memorable campaign by dropping Tommy Lawrence, Ron Yeats and Ian St John. By the turn of the year, injuries had robbed him of Alun Evans, Alec Lindsay, Bobby Graham, Ian Callaghan and Peter Thompson. But the side who so superbly beat Everton at Old Trafford bore testimony to the success of Shankly's transplant of new talent. Shankly paid tribute to the part the educated feet of university graduates Steve Heighway and Brian Hall played in that triumph: "I would be wrong if I didn't say that Tommy Smith has had a lot to do with our success. He has knitted this young team together." Everton led through an Alan Ball goal at half-time, then lost hope, and finally heart, as Brian Labone limped off in the 50th minute. Evans, who had a marvellous match, scored a 60th-minute equalizer that was followed 14 minutes later by Hall's winner . . . his first goal in 36 senior games.

## 13th November 1971

First Division

**Everton 1**

Johnson

**Liverpool 0**

*Attendance:* **56,293**

**Everton:** *West, H. Newton, McLaughlin, Kendall, Kenyon, Harvey, Johnson, Ball, Husband, Hurst, Jones*

**Liverpool:** *Clemence, Lawler, Lindsay, Smith, Lloyd (Graham), Hughes, Ross, A. Evans, Heighway, Toshack, Callaghan*

David Johnson marked his first ever Merseyside derby appearance with the winning goal when Ray Clemence failed to hold his downward header and the Everton striker made no mistake with the rebound. The 20-year-old had made his debut for the Goodison Park club the previous January and quickly established a reputation as a goalscorer. Such was his talent that Bill Shankly was desperate to bring him to the Reds . . . a plan that eventually worked out after a four-year spell with Ipswich Town.

## 4th March 1972

First Division
**Liverpool 4**
T. Wright (og), McLaughlin (og), Lawler, Hughes
**Everton 0**
*Attendance: 53,922*
**Liverpool:** *Clemence, Lawler, Lindsay, Smith, Lloyd, Hughes, Keegan, Hall, Heighway, Toshack, Callaghan*
**Everton:** *West, T. Wright, McLaughlin, Kendall, Kenyon, Harvey, Husband, Darracott, Johnson (B. Wright), Lyons, Whittle*

Bernie Wright made his debut for Everton following his transfer from Walsall after impressing during an FA Cup tie between the two clubs. The young striker was unable to make an impression on this game, but his namesake Tommy Wright had the unwanted privilege – along with John McLaughlin – of scoring an own goal as Liverpool ran rampant. Further Reds goals from defenders Chris Lawler and Emlyn Hughes completed the scoreline and Bernie Wright's Everton career would last just 11 months following a training ground altercation with coach Stewart Imlach.

## 7th October 1972

First Division
**Liverpool 1**
Cormack
**Everton 0**
*Attendance: 55,975*
**Liverpool:** *Clemence, Lawler, Lindsay, Storton, Lloyd, Hughes, Keegan, Cormack, Heighway, Boersma, Callaghan*
**Everton:** *Lawson, T. Wright, Newton, Kendall (Lyons), Kenyon, Hurst, Johnson, Bernard, Royle, Harvey, Connolly*

This was Howard Kendall's final appearance in a Merseyside derby because he had been sold to Birmingham City by the time of the return fixture in March 1973, but even the Everton captain was unable to lead his side to a clean sheet at Anfield. Scottish midfielder Peter Cormack – who had joined Liverpool from Nottingham Forest the previous July for a fee of £110,000 – left it late to get his name on the scoresheet, but netted the only goal of the game after 77 minutes.

## 3rd March 1973

First Division

**Everton 0**

**Liverpool 2**

Hughes 2

*Attendance: 54,856*

**Everton:** *Lawson, T. Wright, Styles, Hurst, Kenyon, Darracott, Jones, Kendall, Harper, Lyons, Connolly*

**Liverpool:** *Clemence, Lawler, Lindsay, Smith, Lloyd, Hughes, Keegan, Hall, Boersma, Heighway, Callaghan*

Everton had failed to build upon their First Division title success and it was now the red half of the city's turn to celebrate their team being crowned champions. The Toffees' 1972–73 campaign had begun well enough with an unbeaten run of eight matches, but things turned sour for the Goodison Park club as they then only won eight more times in the League. Liverpool, on the other hand, were riding high when the two sides met in this Merseyside derby and a late brace from defender Emlyn Hughes secured the points.

## 8th December 1973

First Division

**Everton 0**

**Liverpool 1**

Waddle

*Attendance: 56,098*

**Everton:** *Lawson, Darracott, McLaughlin, Clements, Lyons, Hurst, Bernard, Harper, Royle, Buckley, Connolly*

**Liverpool:** *Clemence, Smith, Lindsay, P.B. Thompson, Lloyd, Hughes, Keegan (Hall), Cormack, Waddle, Boersma, Callaghan*

This tense derby match was decided eventually by 19-year-old striker Alan Waddle and fellow Geordie David Lawson. A well-hit cross-cum-centre from Ian Callaghan was sailing comfortably into Lawson's arms in the 69th minute when six-footer Waddle snaked his left leg. For a split second, Lawson must have felt the ball . . . then he didn't. Waddle's boot made contact despite the leech-like marking of Mick Lyons and the ball bounced over the line. Liverpool had struggled to find composure and the rare chances which came along had fallen Everton's way. Everton boss Billy Bingham looked fed-up after the final whistle and he had reasonable complaint. Lyons looked to have sneaked his side ahead in the 56th minute only to be ruled offside. Joe Harper, who made the cross, received a booking for his vigorous protest. There was also a flash of fisticuffs between Harper and Emlyn Hughes which earned them a stern lecture from the referee.

## 20th April 1974

First Division
**Liverpool 0**
**Everton 0**
*Attendance:* **55,858**
**Liverpool:** *Clemence, Smith, Lindsay, P.B. Thompson, Cormack, Hughes, Keegan, Hall, Heighway, Boersma, Callaghan*
**Everton:** *Lawson, Bernard, Seargeant, Clements, Kenyon, Hurst, Harvey, Jones, Latchford, Lyons, Telfer*

Bill Shankly was still optimistic about Liverpool's title aspirations even after this goalless draw at Anfield. The Reds were neck-and-neck with Leeds United in the race for the Championship but would ultimately surrender their League crown to their Yorkshire rivals. That this game ended without any goals was somewhat bizarre because as early as the third minute Steve Heighway miskicked when it seemed simpler to score. A goal would have completely changed the pattern of the game. Instead, Everton played it cool and withstood enormous Liverpool pressure without any great difficulty.

## 16th November 1974

First Division
**Everton 0**
**Liverpool 0**
*Attendance: 57,190*
**Everton:** *Davies, Bernard, Seargeant, Clements, Kenyon, Hurst, Buckley (Pearson), Dobson, Lyons, Jones, Connolly*
**Liverpool:** *Clemence, Smith, Neal, McDermott, Lawler, Hughes, Keegan, Cormack, Boersma, Kennedy, Callaghan*

Everton went into this match with all the signs and portents justifying their optimism that this was their greatest opportunity for years to elbow aside and overtake their rivals. Liverpool's reputation for resilience had been badly dented by three setbacks which put them out of the European Cup Winners' Cup, out of the League Cup and dumped them from the top of the table. They were disorganized by the inclusion of two new players – Phil Neal at left-back and Terry McDermott in midfield – and, for the whole of the first half, Everton showed every indication of dismantling them. In the crowded midfield, they had the more effective combination of Martin Dobson and Dave Clements, but as the game wore on Everton became increasingly conscious that their superiority had failed to win the match.

## 22nd February 1975

First Division
**Liverpool 0**
**Everton 0**
*Attendance: 55,583*
**Liverpool:** *Clemence, Smith, Neal, Thompson, Cormack, Hughes, Keegan, Hall, Heighway, Toshack, Callaghan*
**Everton:** *Davies, Bernard, Seargeant, Clements, Kenyon, Hurst, Jones, Dobson, Latchford, Lyons, Telfer (Pearson)*

Everton's reputation for killing away games stone-dead by concentrating on containing opponents lulled Liverpool almost into losing this match. Bob Latchford broke through with only Ray Clemence to beat in the last attack of the game, but lobbed into the keeper's arms. Indeed, Everton set about attacking as often as they could and the result was a thrilling game. When Liverpool did set the pace, they came up against Everton goalkeeper Dai Davies in great form.

## 27th September 1975

First Division

**Everton 0**

**Liverpool 0**

*Attendance:* 55,769

**Everton:** *Davies, McLaughlin, Seargeant, Pearson, Kenyon, Lyons, Buckley, Dobson, Latchford, Smallman, G. Jones*

**Liverpool:** *Clemence, Neal, Lindsay, Thompson, Cormack, Hughes, Keegan, Hall, Heighway, Toshack, Callaghan*

The goal drought that had blighted the previous three derby matches continued in this game with both sides unable to score, despite the inclusion of such deadly marksmen as Kevin Keegan, John Toshack and Bob Latchford. In fact, Everton had failed to score against their rivals since November 1971 but both clubs were safely ensconced in mid-table as the season approached its second quarter.

## 3rd April 1976

First Division

**Liverpool 1**

Fairclough

**Everton 0**

*Attendance:* 54,632

**Liverpool:** *Clemence, Smith, Neal, Thompson, Kennedy, Hughes, Keegan, Case, Heighway, Toshack (Fairclough), Callaghan*

**Everton:** *Davies, Bernard, D. Jones, Lyons, McNaught (Kenyon), Buckley, Hamilton, Dobson, Latchford, Connolly, Telfer*

A goal at last . . . and what a goal! The kick-off time of this match had been brought forward to 11.00 a.m. to avoid clashing with the Grand National at Aintree and Mersey football fans were finally treated to a goal after four scoreless draws. With three minutes to play, Everton won a throw-in on the halfway line and turned their attention towards the Liverpool goal, but a stray pass from Roger Kenyon gave the Reds possession. David Fairclough – on as a 65th-minute sub for John Toshack – picked the ball up and set off towards the Everton penalty area. He managed to shake off his opponents' challenges to squeeze a shot past Dai Davies at the near post to earn himself legendary status.

## 16th October 1976

First Division

**Liverpool 3**

Heighway, Neal (pen), Toshack

**Everton 1**

Dobson

*Attendance: 55,141*

**Liverpool:** *Clemence, Neal (Fairclough), Jones, Thompson, Kennedy, Hughes, Keegan, McDermott, Heighway, Toshack, Callaghan*

**Everton:** *Davies, Darracott, Jones, Lyons, McNaught, Bernard (Pearson), King, Dobson, Latchford, Goodlass, Telfer*

While Everton finally managed to score their first goal in 10 derby matches, it was not enough to earn them any points at Anfield. Indeed, by the time that Martin Dobson netted three minutes into the second half, Liverpool were already three goals up. Steve Heighway made the most of John Toshack's nod-down from a Terry McDermott corner to open the scoring while Phil Neal converted a penalty won by Kevin Keegan within the first 12 minutes. Welshman Toshack got in on the act shortly before half-time and Everton knew it wasn't going to be their day when Phil Neal appeared to handle the ball in the Liverpool penalty area and their claims for a penalty were dismissed.

## 22nd March 1977

First Division

**Everton 0**

**Liverpool 0**

*Attendance: 56,562*

**Everton:** *Lawson, Darracott, Pejic, Lyons, McNaught, King, Kenyon (Telfer), Dobson, Latchford, Rioch, Pearson*
**Liverpool:** *Clemence, Neal, Jones, Smith, Kennedy, Hughes, Keegan, Case, Heighway, Fairclough, McDermott*

Liverpool's goalless draw with Everton lost them the First Division leadership but won them the first round in the FA Cup battle of nerves. In front of more than 56,000 spectators, Liverpool again proved the masters of Merseyside and gained a well-timed psychological advantage for the following month's Semi-final. But Everton boss Gordon Lee was unperturbed by the result. "I feel all right about the Semi-final," he said. "I know we can play better over 90 minutes than we did tonight, particularly in the second half when we were handicapped by an injury to Roger Kenyon."

## 23rd April 1977

FA Cup Semi-final (at Maine Road)
**Everton 2**
McKenzie, Rioch
**Liverpool 2**
McDermott, Case
*Attendance: 52,637*
**Everton:** *Lawson, Darracott, Pejic, Lyons, McNaught, Rioch, Buckley, Dobson (Hamilton), Pearson, McKenzie, Goodlass*
**Liverpool:** *Clemence, Neal, Jones, Smith, Kennedy, Hughes, Keegan, Case, Heighway, Fairclough (Johnson), McDermott*

Gordon Lee stated that he was more disappointed with this draw than when they lost to Aston Villa in the League Cup. He felt that they had played well enough in the first half to have had the game finished and deserved to win. Everton would have won if the goal scored by substitute Bryan Hamilton just before the final whistle hadn't been ruled out for offside by referee Clive Thomas. Television replays didn't really give any conviction to the decision that Hamilton was offside. Liverpool scored first, superbly through Terry McDermott, but were lucky not to lose. Duncan McKenzie had an outstanding match and cheekily equalized. He continued to be at the heart of all Everton's best moves, even after Jimmy Case had headed Liverpool back in front. It was McKenzie's marvellously judged pass that left Bruce Rioch clear to earn Everton their replay eight minutes from the end. Everton and Liverpool were both racing against the clock to get key men fit for the following Wednesday's replay at Maine Road. Centre-forward Bob Latchford was given a 50/50 chance of being fit for Everton with an injured ankle while Liverpool's experienced defender Tommy Smith was struggling with a thigh injury. The Anfield club were already without England international Phil Thompson and had no experienced deputy for Smith.

## 27th April 1977

FA Cup Semi-final replay (at Maine Road)

**Liverpool 3**

Neal (pen), Case, Kennedy

**Everton 0**

*Attendance: 52,579*

**Liverpool:** *Clemence, Neal, Jones, Smith, Kennedy, Hughes, Keegan, Case, Johnson, Fairclough, McDermott*

**Everton:** *Lawson, Darracott, Pejic, Lyons, McNaught, Rioch, Buckley, Dobson (King), Pearson, McKenzie, Goodlass*

Liverpool earned the right to meet Manchester United at Wembley as they piled on the goals late in the Semi-final replay, but Gordon Lee showed his disgust by bouncing angrily out of his touchline dugout several times in protest at decisions by referee Clive Thomas. Many officials might not have been firm enough to award the penalty from which Phil Neal put Liverpool ahead in the 30th minute, but Liverpool striker David Johnson was quite clearly shoved in the back a yard inside the box. Lee was not happy on the two occasions that Thomas blew his whistle – apparently for serious fouls by Liverpool in the penalty area – and then awarded only indirect free-kicks. There was trouble at the end with Everton striker Jim Pearson clashing with Liverpool coach Ronnie Moran, as Tommy Smith and Mick Lyons lay stretched out unconscious after a crushing collision in the closing seconds. There could, however, be no doubt about Liverpool's overall superiority. The machine which had spluttered uncharacteristically in the previous meeting was back in top gear . . . back on course for the Treble of League Championship, FA Cup and European Cup. It took them a while to settle to their job but, once they went in front, they had a near-monopoly of the most effective players on the field. Duncan McKenzie was an occasional Everton exception, but Liverpool's front three – Johnson, Keegan and Fairclough – were all equally eye-catching. In the midfield, the Liverpool trio of Jimmy Case, Terry McDermott and Ray Kennedy were totally dominant. Both sides had a reasonable quota of scoring chances but Liverpool always looked more imposing, the more dangerous and the more likely to survive shaky spells. They left it late to prove it, but did so conclusively with goals in the 86th and 89th minutes from Case and Kennedy.

## 22nd October 1977

First Division
**Liverpool 0**
**Everton 0**
*Attendance: 51,668*
**Liverpool:** *Clemence, Neal, Jones, Hansen, Kennedy, Hughes, Dalglish, Case, Heighway, Toshack, Callaghan*
**Everton:** *Wood, Jones, Pejic, Lyons, Higgins, Rioch, King, Dobson, Latchford, Pearson, Thomas*

This was George Wood's first appearance in a Merseyside derby and the young goalkeeper – signed in the summer for £150,000 from Blackpool – coped admirably with the formidable Liverpool attack. In contrast, his counterpart Ray Clemence had been a constant fixture between the Liverpool posts for the whole of the 1970s and this was a day when the defensive tactics of both teams came out on top.

## 5th April 1978

First Division
**Everton 0**
**Liverpool 1**
Johnson
*Attendance: 52,759*

**Everton:** *Wood, Jones, Pejic, Lyons, Darracott, Ross, King, Dobson, Latchford, McKenzie, Thomas*
**Liverpool:** *Clemence, Neal, Smith, Thompson, Kennedy, Hughes, Dalglish, Case, Heighway, McDermott, Johnson*

Despite this 1-0 win, Liverpool – kings of England and Europe – abdicated one of their thrones and conceded their League crown to Nottingham Forest. Following David Johnson scoring the only goal of the game in the 13th minute, Everton also admitted that the gap Forest had opened up at the top of the League was too great to bridge.

## 28th October 1978

First Division
**Everton 1**
King
**Liverpool 0**
*Attendance: 53,141*
**Everton:** *Wood, Todd, Pejic, Kenyon, Wright, Nulty, King, Dobson, Latchford, Walsh, Thomas*
**Liverpool:** *Clemence, Neal, A. Kennedy, Thompson, R. Kennedy, Hansen, Dalglish, Case (McDermott), Heighway, Johnson, Souness*

Everton's first win over Liverpool since November 1971 did the whole of football a favour at Goodison Park. They closed the gap at the top of the First Division to an attainable two points instead of a frightening six. It seemed that Liverpool had begun to believe that they could send out 10 red shirts and a green jersey and still feel complacently certain of victory against anyone, but Everton provided them with a rude awakening that showed Liverpool could be beaten in the League. It wasn't a great match and Andy King's spectacular miskick in the 58th minute deservedly won a game that Everton dominated, though it had ironically come at a time when Liverpool had at last started to play with some rhythm and style. George Wood in the Everton goal never had enough to do to impress the visiting Scotland manager Jock Stein, whereas if his England counterpart Ron Greenwood had been there he would have gone bald pulling his hair out at Ray Clemence's eccentricities in Liverpool's goal. It was fortunate for Clemence that both central defenders Phil Thompson and Alan Hansen remained so steady under pressure because right-back Phil Neal was another who had a poor game. Liverpool were so worried about Neal's limitations that they detailed Jimmy Case to stay deep in defensive support. This robbed the team of his considerable attacking ability and, incidentally, led to a caution for a wicked foul on Everton winger Dave Thomas. Thomas figured largely in the man of the match discussions because of the way his bare, bandy legs carried him at speed so many times past Case and Neal to fire in good crosses. The most eye-catching performance, however, was from Everton's 20-year-old central defender Billy Wright who superbly marshalled David Johnson and Kenny Dalglish out of the game.

## 13th March 1979

First Division

**Liverpool 1**

Dalglish

**Everton 1**

King

*Attendance: 52,352*

**Liverpool:** *Clemence, Neal, Hughes, Thompson, R. Kennedy, Hansen, Dalglish, Johnson (Fairclough), Case, McDermott, Souness*

**Everton:** *Wood, Todd, Heard, Lyons, Wright, Ross, King, Dobson, Latchford, Telfer, Thomas*

Andy King kept Everton clinging to Liverpool's coat-tails at the top of the First Division with a dramatic 77th-minute equalizer at Anfield. Despite taking their third point of the season from the European champions, Everton were still two points behind in the title race, having played three games more, with only 11 matches to play. Everton's other hero was George Wood who made a string of brilliant saves to restrict the Double-chasing Liverpool to a solitary 14th-minute goal from Kenny Dalglish, his 17th of the season. In a typically frenzied derby, six players were booked: Dalglish, Souness and Case of Liverpool; and King, Lyons and Ross of Everton.

## 20th October 1979

First Division
**Liverpool 2**
Lyons (og), R. Kennedy
**Everton 2**
Kidd, King
*Attendance: 52,201*
**Liverpool:** *Clemence, Neal, A. Kennedy, Thompson, R. Kennedy, Hansen, Dalglish, Case, Johnson, McDermott, Souness*
**Everton:** *Wood, Wright, Bailey, Lyons, Higgins, Ross, Nulty, Stanley, Latchford, Kidd, King*

It seemed that Fortress Anfield was losing some of the fear it put into visiting teams even though they hadn't lost there in nearly two years. Everton fought back twice to hold the League champions to only their eighth home draw in that time. The unfortunate Mick Lyons had opened the scoring with an own goal after eight minutes before Brian Kidd levelled the match 10 minutes later. Liverpool again took the lead with a Ray Kennedy goal 10 minutes into the second half, but were again pegged back when Andy King netted his side's second. A Garry Stanley tackle on David Johnson caused a mass brawl that resulted in the Everton midfielder being sent off along with Liverpool's Terry McDermott.

## 1st March 1980

First Division
**Everton 1**
Eastoe
**Liverpool 2**
Johnson, Neal (pen)
*Attendance: 53,108*
**Everton:** *Wood, Gidman, Bailey, Nulty (Eastoe), Lyons, Ross, Hartford, Wright, King, Kidd, McBride*
**Liverpool:** *Clemence, Neal, A. Kennedy, Thompson, R. Kennedy, Hansen, Dalglish, Case, Johnson (Fairclough), McDermott, Souness*

The biggest shock of the day was the death of Everton legend Dixie Dean. The 73-year-old – who was visiting Goodison Park for the first time in several years due to his deteriorating health – suffered a heart attack and could not be saved. On the field, goals from David Johnson and Phil Neal gave the visitors a 2-0 lead at half-time and Everton could only pull one back via substitute Peter Eastoe. The ferocity of some of the tackling was such that Liverpool manager Bob Paisley issued a "Cool it" plea for future meetings of the two clubs and it was feared that Everton defender Geoff Nulty could be ruled out for the rest of the season with knee ligaments damaged by Jimmy Case's tackle.

# Chapter Eight

# The 1980s

The First Division trophy almost took up permanent residence on Merseyside during the 1980s with Liverpool winning the title on six occasions and Everton twice. Consistency was the word of the decade at Anfield with the club only once finishing outside the top two. They also claimed two FA Cups, four League Cups and a further two European Cups. Over at Goodison Park, they were enjoying success – although not quite at the Reds' level – with an FA Cup and a European Cup Winners' Cup triumph. Howard Kendall had been the orchestrator of Everton's success while Kenny Dalglish had taken over the Liverpool managerial reins from Joe Fagan.

## Record in the 1980s

### Everton

| Season | League | P | W | D | L | F | A | Pts | Pos |
|--------|--------|---|---|---|---|---|---|-----|-----|
| 1980–81 | Div 1 | 42 | 13 | 10 | 19 | 55 | 58 | 36 | 15 |
| 1981–82 | Div 1 | 42 | 17 | 13 | 12 | 56 | 50 | 64 | 8 |
| 1982–83 | Div 1 | 42 | 18 | 10 | 14 | 66 | 48 | 64 | 7 |
| 1983–84 | Div 1 | 42 | 16 | 14 | 12 | 44 | 42 | 62 | 7 |
| 1984–85 | Div 1 | 42 | 28 | 6 | 8 | 88 | 43 | 90 | 1 |
| 1985–86 | Div 1 | 42 | 26 | 8 | 8 | 87 | 41 | 86 | 2 |
| 1986–87 | Div 1 | 42 | 26 | 8 | 8 | 76 | 31 | 86 | 1 |
| 1987–88 | Div 1 | 40 | 19 | 13 | 8 | 53 | 27 | 70 | 4 |
| 1988–89 | Div 1 | 38 | 14 | 12 | 12 | 50 | 45 | 54 | 8 |
| 1989–90 | Div 1 | 38 | 17 | 8 | 13 | 57 | 46 | 59 | 6 |

### FA Cup

| | |
|---|---|
| 1980–81 | 2-2, 1-3 v Manchester City (Semi-final) |
| 1981–82 | 1-2 v West Ham United (Third Round) |

| | |
|---|---|
| 1982–83 | 0-1 v Manchester United (Quarter-final) |
| 1983–84 | 2-0 v Watford (Final) |
| 1984–85 | 0-1 v Manchester United (Final) |
| 1985–86 | 1-3 v Liverpool (Final) |
| 1986–87 | 1-3 v Wimbledon (Fifth Round) |
| 1987–88 | 0-1 v Liverpool (Fifth Round) |
| 1988–89 | 2-3 v Liverpool (Final) |
| 1989–90 | 2-2, 1-1, 0-1 v Oldham Athletic (Fifth Round) |

## League Cup

| | |
|---|---|
| 1980–81 | 1-2 v West Bromwich Albion (Third Round) |
| 1981–82 | 2-3 v Ipswich Town (Fourth Round) |
| 1982–83 | 1-1, 0-3 v Arsenal (Third Round) |
| 1983–84 | 0-0, 0-1 v Liverpool (Final) |
| 1984–85 | 0-1 v Grimsby Town (Fourth Round) |
| 1985–86 | 2-2, 1-2 v Chelsea (Fourth Round) |
| 1986–87 | 0-1 v Liverpool (Quarter-final) |
| 1987–88 | 0-1, 1-3 v Arsenal (Semi-final) |
| 1988–89 | 1-3 v Bradford City (Fourth Round) |
| 1989–90 | 0-1 v Nottingham Forest (Fourth Round) |

## Europe

| | |
|---|---|
| 1980–81 | Did not qualify |
| 1981–82 | Did not qualify |
| 1982–83 | Did not qualify |
| 1983–84 | Did not qualify |
| 1984–85 | European Cup Winners' Cup: 3-1 v Rapid Vienna (Final) |
| 1985–86 | English clubs banned from European competition |
| 1986–87 | English clubs banned from European competition |
| 1987–88 | English clubs banned from European competition |
| 1988–89 | English clubs banned from European competition |
| 1989–90 | English clubs banned from European competition |

## Liverpool

| Season | League | P | W | D | L | F | A | Pts | Pos |
|---|---|---|---|---|---|---|---|---|---|
| 1980–81 | Div 1 | 42 | 17 | 17 | 8 | 62 | 42 | 51 | 5 |

| | | | | | | | | | |
|---|---|---|---|---|---|---|---|---|---|
| 1981–82 | Div 1 | 42 | 26 | 9 | 7 | 80 | 32 | 87 | 1 |
| 1982–83 | Div 1 | 42 | 24 | 10 | 8 | 87 | 37 | 82 | 1 |
| 1983–84 | Div 1 | 42 | 22 | 14 | 6 | 73 | 32 | 80 | 1 |
| 1984–85 | Div 1 | 42 | 22 | 11 | 9 | 68 | 35 | 77 | 2 |
| 1985–86 | Div 1 | 42 | 26 | 10 | 6 | 89 | 37 | 88 | 1 |
| 1986–87 | Div 1 | 42 | 23 | 8 | 11 | 72 | 42 | 77 | 2 |
| 1987–88 | Div 1 | 40 | 26 | 12 | 2 | 87 | 24 | 90 | 1 |
| 1988–89 | Div 1 | 38 | 22 | 10 | 6 | 65 | 28 | 76 | 2 |
| 1989–90 | Div 1 | 38 | 23 | 10 | 5 | 78 | 37 | 79 | 1 |

## *FA Cup*

| | |
|---|---|
| 1980–81 | 1-2 v Everton (Fourth Round) |
| 1981–82 | 0-2 v Chelsea (Fifth Round) |
| 1982–83 | 1-2 v Brighton & Hove Albion (Fifth Round) |
| 1983–84 | 0-2 v Brighton & Hove Albion (Fourth Round) |
| 1984–85 | 2-2, 1-2 v Manchester United (Semi-final) |
| 1985–86 | 3-1 v Everton (Final) |
| 1986–87 | 0-0, 0-3 v Luton Town (Third Round) |
| 1987–88 | 0-1 v Wimbledon (Final) |
| 1988–89 | 3-2 v Everton (Final) |
| 1989–90 | 3-4 v Crystal Palace (Semi-final) |

## *League Cup*

| | |
|---|---|
| 1980–81 | 1-1, 2-1 v West Ham United (Final) |
| 1981–82 | 3-1 v Tottenham Hotspur (Final) |
| 1982–83 | 2-1 v Manchester United (Final) |
| 1983–84 | 0-0, 1-0 v Everton (Final) |
| 1984–85 | 0-1 v Tottenham Hotspur (Third Round) |
| 1985–86 | 0-1, 2-2 v Queens Park Rangers (Semi-final) |
| 1986–87 | 1-2 v Arsenal (Final) |
| 1987–88 | 0-1 v Everton (Third Round) |
| 1988–89 | 1-4 v West Ham United (Fourth Round) |
| 1989–90 | 0-1 v Arsenal (Third Round) |

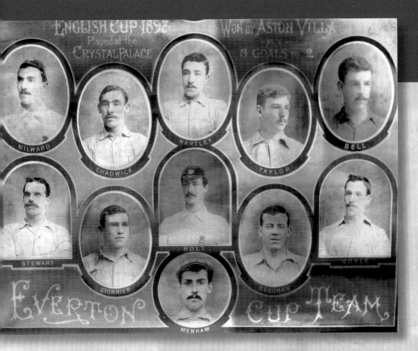

ABOVE: The Everton FA Cup Final team of 1897 who lost 3-2 to Aston Villa at the Crystal Palace.

BELOW: The Liverpool team for the 1904–05 season. Back row, left to right: Parry, Murray, Platt, Doig, Dunlop, Wilson, Evans. Second row: Connell (trainer), Fleming, Carlin, Latham, Raybould, Raisbeck (captain), Hughes, Parkinson, Chorlton, Cox, Watson (secretary). Front row: Goddard, Robinson, Morris, Hewitt, Garside.

**LEFT:** Sam Hardy was Liverpool goalkeeper from 1905 to 1912 before going on to join Aston Villa and Nottingham Forest.

**RIGHT:** Goals from Dick Forshaw (Liverpool) and Sam Chedgzoy (Everton) meant that this November 1921 Merseyside derby ended one apiece.

**ABOVE:** While Elisha Scott (right) may have been at fault for the opening goal of this October 1922 match, the Liverpool keeper more than made amends and his team emerged victorious by a massive 5-1 scoreline.

**LEFT:** Liverpool's Tom Bromilow played in 17 Merseyside derbies between the wars and scored twice.

**ABOVE:** Everton striker Dixie Dean, who set a record when he scored 60 League goals in the 1927–28 season, is pictured here during a training session at Goodison Park in April 1933.

**RIGHT:** Matt Busby was signed from Manchester City by Liverpool at a cost of £8,000 in 1936 but the Second World War brought an end to his playing days. When peacetime returned he made his name as Manchester United manager.

**ABOVE:** Everton players Cunliffe, Button and Cook in the bath after training in 1938.

**BELOW:** Everton's Tommy Lawton peruses the headlines in September 1938.

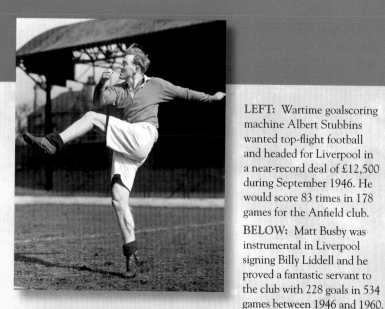

**LEFT:** Wartime goalscoring machine Albert Stubbins wanted top-flight football and headed for Liverpool in a near-record deal of £12,500 during September 1946. He would score 83 times in 178 games for the Anfield club.

**BELOW:** Matt Busby was instrumental in Liverpool signing Billy Liddell and he proved a fantastic servant to the club with 228 goals in 534 games between 1946 and 1960.

**BELOW:** Liverpool's 1948 squad. Back row, left to right: Spicer, Lambert, Hughes, Shepherd, Sidlow, Jones, Taylor, Fagan, Brierley, Shelly (trainer). Front row: Payne, Watkinson, McAvoy, Kay (manager), Cllr Williams (chairman), Balmer (captain), Done, Paisley.

**ABOVE:** Policemen on duty outside Maine Road stadium in Manchester to deal with crowds queuing for tickets for the FA Cup Semi-final match between Everton and Liverpool in March 1950.

**ABOVE:** Everton's Ted Sagar in training in 1950. The Everton keeper played in 20 Merseyside derbies between 1931 and 1951.

**BELOW:** Everton players (left to right) Moore, Jones, Lello, Fielding, Wainwright, Parker, Hickson, Eglington, Farrell, O'Neill, Rankin and Potts training at Goodison Park in preparation for the FA Cup match against Liverpool in January 1955.

**LEFT:** Everton's Colin Harvey celebrates scoring a goal on his derby debut, the third in a 4-0 win at Anfield in September 1964.

**BELOW:** The two teams are led out onto the pitch during a lap of honour at the start of the FA Charity Shield match at Goodison Park in August 1966 which the Reds won 1-0 with a goal from Roger Hunt.

**BELOW:** A fan comes onto the field during play and gives Everton keeper Gordon West a handbag with Honey West on it in September 1967.

**ABOVE:** Tommy Smith sits it out watched by Liverpool keeper Tommy Lawrence after Howard Kendall (not in picture) scores the winning goal for Everton in February 1968.

**ABOVE:** Liverpool's Ian Callaghan chases the ball in the 1971 FA Cup Semi-final. Goals from Alun Evans and Brian Hall gave the reds a 2-1 win at Old Trafford.

**LEFT:** Two Merseyside legends, Liverpool's Bill Shankly (left) and former Everton manager Harry Catterick, reminisce in October 1975.

**RIGHT:** Everton celebrate during the 2-2 draw with their Merseyside rivals in the 1977 FA Cup Semi-final. Liverpool had the last laugh though with a 3-0 win in the replay.

**LEFT:** Anfield legends Kevin Keegan and Emlyn Hughes enjoy a laugh in the post-match bath in 1977.

**RIGHT:** Everton's Bob Latchford tries out the strip which was worn by his team's predecessors 100 years earlier in 1878.

**BELOW:** A thumbs-up from Everton hero Andy King who scored the only goal in the derby match of October 1978.

**ABOVE:** Graeme Sharp celebrates his Everton equalizer at Goodison Park in March 1982.

**BELOW:** It's another goal for Liverpool as Everton are hit for five at Goodison Park in November 1982.

**BELOW:** Everton players, led by Graeme Sharp, protest a refereeing decision in November 1982.

LEFT: Bruce Grobbelaar saves a penalty from Graeme Sharp at Goodison Park in March 1984.

BELOW LEFT: Liverpool goalkeeper Bruce Grobbelaar taunts the Everton supporters during the goalless 1984 League Cup Final by pulling faces and using coins thrown on to the pitch as glasses.

BELOW: John Aldridge celebrates his Wembley goal against Everton in the FA Cup Final in May 1989.

**ABOVE:** Liverpool's Ian Rush attempts to evade the onrushing blue tide during the derby match at Anfield in February 1990.

**BELOW:** Everton keeper Neville Southall makes a save at the feet of Ian Rush as captain Kevin Ratcliffe looks on. The FA Cup Fifth Round replay at Goodison Park finished 4-4 after extra-time in February 1991 and was the last match in charge for Liverpool manager Kenny Dalglish. A single Dave Watson goal eventually won the tie for Everton in the second replay.

**ABOVE:** Roy Evans is the Carling Manager of the Month in February 1996 while Liverpool strikers Robbie Fowler and Stan Collymore share that month's player award.

**LEFT:** Robbie Fowler's infamous goal celebration during the April 1999 Premier League match with Everton at Anfield.

**ABOVE:** Liverpool manager Gérard Houllier shows how much the 3-2 victory over Everton in April 1999 means to the Anfield club.

**BELOW:** Everton manager David Moyes shows off his ball skills to the players during his first training session at Bellfield, Liverpool, March 2002.

**ABOVE:** Liverpool's faithful servant Steven Gerrard has seen lots of highs and lows since his debut in November 1998.

**BELOW:** Roberto Martínez is unveiled as the new Everton manager in June 2013.

## Europe

| | |
|---|---|
| 1980–81 | European Cup: 1-0 v Real Madrid (Final) |
| 1981–82 | European Cup: 1-0, 0-2 v CSKA Sofia (Third Round) |
| 1982–83 | 0-2, 3-2 v Widzew Łódź (Third Round) |
| 1983–84 | European Cup: 1-1 (4-2 on pens) v AS Roma (Final) |
| 1984–85 | European Cup: 0-1 v Juventus (Final) |
| 1985–86 | English clubs banned from European competition |
| 1986–87 | English clubs banned from European competition |
| 1987–88 | English clubs banned from European competition |
| 1988–89 | English clubs banned from European competition |
| 1989–90 | English clubs banned from European competition |

# The Matches

## 18th October 1980

First Division

### Everton 2

Hartford, McBride

### Liverpool 2

Lee, Dalglish

*Attendance: 52,565*

**Everton:** *McDonagh, Gidman (O'Keefe), Bailey, Wright, Lyons, Stanley, McMahon, Eastoe, Latchford, Hartford, McBride*

**Liverpool:** *Clemence, Neal, Cohen, Thompson, R. Kennedy, Hansen, Dalglish, Lee, Johnson, McDermott, Souness*

Both clubs were riding high in the First Division with just one point separating Liverpool in third from Everton in fourth after this pulsating derby match. The home side managed to eke out a 2-0 lead within the first quarter of the game thanks to goals from Asa Hartford and Joe McBride, but midfielder Sammy Lee reduced the deficit in the 23rd minute. The second half proved a tighter affair with Kenny Dalglish netting after 56 minutes to claim a share of the points for the Anfield club.

## 24ᵗʰ January 1981

FA Cup Fourth Round
**Everton 2**
Eastoe, Varadi
**Liverpool 1**
Case
*Attendance: 53,804*
**Everton:** *Hodge, Ratcliffe, Bailey, Wright, Lodge, Ross, McMahon, Eastoe, Varadi, Hartford, O'Keefe*
**Liverpool:** *Clemence, Neal, Thompson, Irwin, Cohen, R. Kennedy, Dalglish (Case), Lee, Fairclough, McDermott, Souness*

Even allowing for the tension and the passion, the total of 46 fouls and six bookings was condemned in this Mersey mayhem. Even Mick Lyons, Everton's non-playing captain, admitted that every tackle was a battle and summed up the brutality of a match that could have been a classic but instead was a pitched battle that left Liverpool counting the cost. Kenny Dalglish needed three stitches in a gashed instep and Phil Neal collected shin and eye injuries. Everton's relentless drive forward unsettled the Liverpool machine and it was no surprise when Peter Eastoe struck in the 17ᵗʰ minute. Imre Varadi got Everton's second on the hour and Jimmy Case's 77ᵗʰ-minute reply for Liverpool was no more than a token gesture.

## 21ˢᵗ March 1981

First Division
**Liverpool 1**
Bailey (og)
**Everton 0**
*Attendance: 49,743*
**Liverpool:** *Clemence, Neal, Money, Irwin, R. Kennedy, Hansen, Dalglish, Lee, Heighway, Case, Souness*
**Everton:** *McDonagh, Gidman, Bailey, Wright, Stanley, Ross, McMahon, Eastoe, Varadi (McBride), Lodge, O'Keefe*

John Bailey used to stand on the Kop as a kid and dream of scoring the winner for Liverpool in a Mersey derby. By a cruel twist of fate his dream came true . . . but not in the way he wanted. The Everton left-back's own goal after 77 minutes handed Liverpool a victory that came with a price. Kenny Dalglish suffered another knock on his injured right leg and was withdrawn from the Scotland squad along with Graeme Souness, who had damaged ankle ligaments.

## 7th November 1981

First Division

**Liverpool 3**

Dalglish 2, Rush

**Everton 1**

Ferguson

*Attendance:* **48,861**

**Liverpool:** *Grobbelaar, Neal, Lawrenson, Thompson, R. Kennedy (Johnson), Hansen, Dalglish, Whelan, Rush, McDermott, Souness*

**Everton:** *Arnold, Stevens, Bailey, Higgins, Lyons, Lodge, McMahon, O'Keefe, Ferguson, Ainscow (Biley), McBride*

Everton lost because they lost control of themselves and might have been punished for it even more heavily. They had played with mounting confidence until they went 3-0 down to goals from Kenny Dalglish (2) and Ian Rush. But once they sensed defeat, they let themselves down by hot-headed actions which resulted in Eamonn O'Keefe being sent off for fouling Ronnie Whelan.

## 27th March 1982

First Division

**Everton 1**

Sharp

**Liverpool 3**

Whelan, Souness, Johnston

*Attendance:* **51,847**

**Everton:** *Southall, Borrows, Ratcliffe, Higgins, Wright, Richardson, Irvine, Heath, Sharp, McMahon, Ross*

**Liverpool:** *Grobbelaar, Neal, Lawrenson, A. Kennedy, Whelan, Thompson, Dalglish, Lee, Rush, Johnston, Souness*

A convincing victory in this pulsating match added extra impetus to Liverpool's charge to the title. They continued unbeaten to the end of the season with a run of 13 wins and three draws in their final 16 matches. Ronnie Whelan opened the scoring before Graeme Sharp brought the home side level, but any hopes Everton had of earning any points were dashed in the second half with goals from Graeme Souness and Craig Johnston.

## 6ᵗʰ November 1982

First Division
**Everton 0**
**Liverpool 5**
Rush 4, Lawrenson
*Attendance: 52,741*
**Everton:** *Southall, Borrows, Bailey, Keeley, Wright, McMahon, Heath, Johnson (Richardson), Sharp, King, Sheedy*
**Liverpool:** *Grobbelaar, Neal, Kennedy, Thompson, Johnston, Hansen, Dalglish (Hodgson), Lee, Rush, Lawrenson, Souness*

An outstanding individual performance from Ian Rush gave Liverpool an emphatic win at Goodison Park and the score could easily have been double, yet the Reds went in with only a 1-0 advantage at half-time. The Welsh striker netted his first on 11 minutes and then grabbed another six minutes into the second half. Defender Mark Lawrenson got in on the action four minutes later, before Rush added two more in the final quarter of the game to complete the rout.

## 19ᵗʰ March 1983

First Division
**Liverpool 0**
**Everton 0**
*Attendance: 44,737*
**Liverpool:** *Grobbelaar, Neal, Kennedy, Lawrenson, Whelan, Hansen, Dalglish, Lee, Rush, Johnston, Souness (Hodgson)*
**Everton:** *Arnold, Stevens, Bailey, Ratcliffe, Higgins, Richardson, Irvine (Ainscow), McMahon, Sharp, Heath, Sheedy*

The 1982–83 season saw Bob Paisley announce his retirement, bringing the curtain down on a Liverpool career that had spanned six decades, before handing over the managerial reins to Joe Fagan. This goalless draw did not harm the defence of their First Division title as they had built up such a lead over their challengers that even a run of five defeats and one draw in their final six games enabled them to finish nine points ahead of second-placed Watford.

## 6ᵗʰ November 1983

First Division

**Liverpool 3**

Rush, Robinson, Nicol

**Everton 0**

*Attendance:* 40,875

**Liverpool:** *Grobbelaar, Neal, Kennedy, Lawrenson, Nicol, Hansen, Dalglish, Lee, Rush, Robinson, Souness*

**Everton:** *Southall, Harper, Bailey, Ratcliffe, Higgins, Steven, Irvine, Heath, Sharp, King, Sheedy*

Kenny Dalglish destroyed Everton at Anfield as the Merseyside derby went national via television. Everton were powerless to combat the skills of Dalglish, who was involved in all three goals that brought Liverpool victory and a place, once more, at the top of the First Division. It was hardly an exaggeration to suggest that if Everton did succeed in bringing the Brazilian Nunes to Goodison Park, they would have needed Zico and Socrates as well to counter the champions in this sort of mood. But for the vigilance of Mark Higgins, Kevin Ratcliffe and goalkeeper Neville Southall, the Anfield team might have built a score of record derby proportions. The first Liverpool goal came when Dalglish sent Nicol away on the left in the 17ᵗʰ minute and a crisply driven cross forced Southall to dive from his line to parry. Inevitably Rush was there to accept the rebound but the champions had to wait until the 60ᵗʰ minute for their second. Dalglish sent in a low cross, the ball eluded Southall and Robinson netted. Six minutes from time, Dalglish and Rush combined to allow Mark Lawrenson to drive the ball in from the right. Steve Nicol decorated a personal performance of quality with a headed goal to match.

## 3rd March 1984

First Division

**Everton 1**

Harper

**Liverpool 1**

Rush

*Attendance: 51,245*

**Everton:** *Southall, Stevens, Bailey, Ratcliffe, Mountfield, Reid, Steven (Harper), Heath, Sharp, Gray, Sheedy*

**Liverpool:** *Grobbelaar, Neal, Kennedy, Lawrenson, Whelan, Hansen, Robinson, Lee (Nicol), Rush, Johnston, Souness*

Every neutral was delighted for Everton after this match, but it was a dangerous delusion to imagine that when the two sides met again in the League Cup Final that Liverpool's long decades of arrogant win-everything one-upmanship would end. Liverpool remained essentially bigger, stronger and better and their extra class – glaringly obvious throughout the first half – created the belief that they could and should have done more than they did. They had fuel left in their tank whereas Everton sweated every liquid ounce of passionate effort in their second-half determination to emerge from the shadow of Anfield and improve a record of only one win in 25 League meetings. Everton may argue that they were robbed of the victory that would have taken them to Wembley in even greater heart by Graeme Sharp's inept penalty attempt – too soft and too straight to stand any chance of beating Bruce Grobbelaar – but it was just as debatable whether it should have been awarded in the first place. The only department in which Liverpool failed to master Everton significantly was commitment.

## 25th March 1984

League Cup Final (at Wembley)

**Everton 0**

**Liverpool 0**

*Attendance: 100,000*

**Everton:** *Southall, Stevens, Bailey, Ratcliffe, Mountfield, Reid, Irvine, Heath, Sharp, Richardson, Sheedy (Harper)*

**Liverpool:** *Grobbelaar, Neal, Kennedy, Lawrenson, Whelan, Hansen, Dalglish, Lee, Rush, Johnston (Robinson), Souness*

For all-round quality, ability, effort and incident this was one of the most stirring and memorable matches in the history of the League Cup. Even the absence of goals was compensated by many that might have been. Liverpool could claim that they still held more of the individual aces with the essentially higher class of their biggest names but for Everton the trumps were hearts . . . the hearts of players who refused to accept second place. The match itself fell neatly into compartments. Everton dominated the first half with the passion of their play but they allowed the emotion of it all to drain their energy and expose them to the constant threats of Liverpool's more coldly calculated approach. It might have cost them the trophy if, even into extra-time, they hadn't managed to continue to dredge up reserves from an inexhaustible supply to create so many marvellous memories. Liverpool would take heart from a conviction that their greatest stars would surely shine more brightly the second time around. Kenny Dalglish flitted into the game only intermittently though the occasional flashes were brilliant. Ian Rush – rightly rated the deadliest finisher in British football – was guilty of a couple of appalling lapses while Mark Lawrenson, normally so composed in defence, was on edge throughout against the darting thrusts of Adrian Heath and the muscular hustle of Graeme Sharp. The midfield men who had so often come to the rescue – Sammy Lee, Ronnie Whelan and Craig Johnston (replaced by Mike Robinson for extra-time) all took an uncomfortably long time to settle as Liverpool were never allowed to find their famous composure in the first half. Everton's claims that they should have had a seventh-minute penalty seemed amply justified when Heath beat goalkeeper Bruce Grobbelaar on the edge of his area and hooked the ball towards goal; a shot that Alan Hansen clearly handled in his race back to cover. That was just one of several frights Liverpool had to suffer under the pressure achieved by the pure persistence of the two Everton men in the centre of their midfield, the militant Peter Reid and the elegant Kevin Richardson. Liverpool – particularly Graeme Souness, who was booked just before half-time after the most blatant of spiteful tackles – needed a distinctly hairy-chested approach to survive. They were being panicked uncharacteristically into too many errors. That would have cost them a goal in the 35th minute but for Grobbelaar's sharpness in saving after Whelan had carelessly put Kevin Sheedy in for a left-foot drive. Neville Southall, the Welshman in magnificent form in Everton's goal, was far less active than Grobbelaar until the second half, but even his reflexes could not possibly have rescued him in the 64th minute. Rush was standing almost under the bar when he hooked a cross from Alan Kennedy over it. Everton came under intense pressure in the closing minutes, but the fresh legs of Robinson still couldn't carry him clear of a tackle by left-back John Bailey. Bailey was also swift enough to catch Sammy Lee just two minutes from time.

## 28th March 1984

League Cup Final replay (at Maine Road)

**Liverpool 1**

Souness

**Everton 0**

*Attendance: 52,089*

**Liverpool:** *Grobbelaar, Neal, Kennedy, Lawrenson, Whelan, Hansen, Dalglish, Lee, Rush, Johnston, Souness*

**Everton:** *Southall, Stevens, Bailey, Ratcliffe, Mountfield, Reid, Irvine (King), Heath, Sharp, Richardson, Harper*

The sustained pressure that Liverpool could apply more relentlessly than any other team in the land during the 1980s finally paid off. They made the League Cup their own as they won the competition for the fourth successive year. But at least Everton had the satisfaction of making the replay as memorable as the Wembley meeting. Until they tired, exhausted by their efforts, they had kept the match balanced on a knife-edge. No one could argue about the superb quality of the goal that broke the deadlock in the 22nd minute, nor about the enormous influence of the man who scored it – skipper Graeme Souness. He was in at the start of a move that flowed through four passes before it came back to him on the edge of the box. He turned brilliantly to leave Kevin Richardson tackling thin air and struck his shot so firmly that Neville

Southall was still preparing to dive when it was past him. Everton had had the best of the early chances when a cross from Alan Harper was turned into the path of Peter Reid for a firm drive that forced a full-length dive from Bruce Grobbelaar. Liverpool tried to cash in immediately from their goal and came close to another when Kenny Dalglish took too long to create time and room for a shot as he twisted and turned in a crowded penalty area. Once again, as at Wembley, there were frantic Everton appeals for a penalty when Adrian Heath, always their most persistent and dangerous attacker, was tackled by Phil Neal. But this time referee Robinson seemed justified in denying it. A superbly timed tackle by Lawrenson robbed Heath in the 75th minute after he had been put through. Although Everton continued to exert tremendous pressure, Liverpool looked sharper in their counter-attacks with Dalglish, Souness, Craig Johnston and Ian Rush all having chances to extend their lead.

## 18th August 1984

FA Charity Shield (at Wembley)
**Everton 1**
Grobbelaar (og)
**Liverpool 0**
*Attendance:* **100,000**
**Everton:** *Southall, Stevens, Bailey, Ratcliffe, Mountfield, Reid, Steven, Heath, Sharp, Bracewell, Richardson*
**Liverpool:** *Grobbelaar, Neal, A. Kennedy, Lawrenson, Whelan, Hansen, Dalglish, Lee (Walsh), Rush, Nicol, Wark*

When FA Cup holders Everton met First Division champions Liverpool at Wembley for the traditional season opener, few would have predicted the scorer of the game's only goal. Liverpool were playing their first competitive match following Graeme Souness' departure to Sampdoria and many felt that they were a weaker side without him as Everton's midfield duo of Peter Reid and Paul Bracewell dictated the play. The goal that decided the match, however, was scored by Bruce Grobbelaar in the 55th minute. Having saved a Graeme Sharp shot, the ball bounced off several players' legs before the Liverpool keeper's attempted clearance ended up in the back of his own net.

## 20th October 1984

First Division

**Liverpool 0**

**Everton 1**

Sharp

*Attendance: 45,545*

**Liverpool:** *Grobbelaar, Neal, Kennedy, Lawrenson, Whelan, Hansen, Dalglish, Robinson, Rush, Wark, Mølby*

**Everton:** *Southall, Stevens, Van Den Hauwe, Ratcliffe, Mountfield, Reid, Steven, Heath, Sharp, Bracewell, Harper*

Everton registered their first win at Anfield since March 1970 when Graeme Sharp produced a stunning volley three minutes into the second half to score the only goal of the game. Having not won a League match since early September and not scored a goal in their previous four matches in the same competition, Liverpool were strangely not firing on all cylinders and it was the Everton players who shone most brightly. The Goodison Park club would go on to finish the season as First Division champions, with their city neighbours 13 points behind in second place.

## 23rd May 1985

First Division

**Everton 1**

Wilkinson

**Liverpool 0**

*Attendance: 51,045*

**Everton:** *Southall, Stevens, Bailey, Ratcliffe, Van Den Hauwe, Richardson, Harper, Wilkinson, Gray, Atkins (Wakenshaw), Sheedy*

**Liverpool:** *Grobbelaar, Neal, Beglin, Mølby, Nicol, Hansen, Dalglish, Whelan, Rush, Lee, Wark*

Without the usual pressures and tensions of a Mersey derby, both sides were able to relax and produce some fine football in a game in which only local pride was at stake. Everton were short of five of their Wembley team and gave a home debut to former Grimsby striker Paul Wilkinson. Liverpool were also missing Paul Walsh and Danish international Jan

Mølby played in central defence in the absence of the injured Mark Lawrenson and Gary Gillespie. Despite the lack of tension, it was still fiercely competitive and shortly before the interval Kevin Richardson and Jim Beglin were booked for fouls in separate incidents. Liverpool's John Wark missed a chance of opening the scoring when he missed a penalty in the 55th minute. It proved a costly miss because Wilkinson pounced to score for Everton in the 68th minute. Everton had also threatened when an Andy Gray header from Kevin Sheedy's free-kick was turned against the post by Bruce Grobbelaar. Beglin completed the clearance as Alan Harper threatened.

## 21st September 1985

First Division
**Everton 2**
Sharp, Lineker
**Liverpool 3**
Dalglish, Rush, McMahon
*Attendance: 51,509*
**Everton:** *Southall, Stevens, Van Den Hauwe, Ratcliffe, Marshall (Heath), Harper, Steven, Lineker, Sharp, Bracewell, Sheedy*
**Liverpool:** *Grobbelaar, Nicol (Neal), Beglin, Lawrenson, Whelan, Hansen, Dalglish, Johnston, Rush, Mølby, McMahon*

Liverpool's enthralling victory over Everton was captured for posterity by the cameras of Thames Television but the bad news for football fans was that no one in England would ever see it. The action was filmed strictly for export only. The 51,509 fans who crammed into Goodison were the lucky ones. Liverpool – three up through Kenny Dalglish, Ian Rush and Steve McMahon – hung on for dear life as Everton surged back with goals from Graeme Sharp and Gary Lineker.

## 22nd February 1986

First Division
**Liverpool 0**
**Everton 2**
Ratcliffe, Lineker

*Attendance:* **45,445**
**Liverpool:** *Grobbelaar, Lee, Beglin, Lawrenson, Whelan, Hansen, Gillespie, Johnston, Rush, Mølby (MacDonald), McMahon*
**Everton:** *Southall, Stevens, Pointon, Ratcliffe, Van Den Hauwe, Reid, Steven, Lineker, Sharp, Bracewell (Harper), Richardson*

Bruce Grobbelaar gifted this game to Everton with the kind of horrendous error that had suddenly become all too familiar. In the previous Anfield spectacular against Manchester United, it was his slip-up that allowed Colin Gibson to score in the 1-1 draw. This time he allowed a 30-yard shot from Kevin Ratcliffe to creep under his body, through his arms and over the line. It broke the deadlock and soon afterwards Gary Lineker wrapped it up with Everton's second. Early in the first half, Grobbelaar had also been involved in a misunderstanding with Mark Lawrenson that almost cost Liverpool a goal. It was all very well to walk on his hands and perform other circus antics, but Grobbelaar was in danger of forgetting the very basics of his trade . . . safe keeping and catching. He was a magnificent athlete, agile, brave and quick as a cat. Twice he made stunning saves but they counted for nothing when he allowed the long-range shot, which neither dipped nor swerved, to go through him. There was no hiding place and the 45,000-plus crowd mocked him mercilessly. Afterwards he avoided the eyes of those who wanted a simple explanation of why he had lost a shot that a schoolboy keeper would have saved with one hand. The fury of the Liverpool fans was easy to understand. Those incredibly still trying to get into the ground 10 minutes before the final whistle who had been following the match were stunned into silence. Anfield became a celebration of blue and white.

## 10th May 1986

FA Cup Final (at Wembley)
**Everton 1**
Lineker
**Liverpool 3**
Rush 2, Johnston
*Attendance:* **98,000**

**Everton:** *Mimms, Stevens (Heath), Van Den Hauwe, Ratcliffe, Mountfield, Reid, Steven, Lineker, Sharp, Bracewell, Sheedy*
**Liverpool:** *Grobbelaar, Lawrenson, Beglin, Nicol, Whelan, Hansen, Dalglish, Johnston, Rush, Mølby, MacDonald*

Liverpool emerged triumphant from their Wembley encounter to become only the third team thus far in the 20th century to register the League and FA Cup Double (after Tottenham Hotspur in 1961 and Arsenal in 1971) but Liverpool chairman John Smith voiced his belief that this feat would never be repeated by a player-manager. Kenny Dalglish had fulfilled that role with aplomb and had by then won all the major honours in the domestic game. Everton had taken the lead when Peter Reid set up the lightning-fast Gary Lineker to open the scoring and they looked in total command at the start of the second half. Ian Rush took advantage of a dreadful mistake by Gary Stevens to equalize and Craig Johnston put Liverpool ahead. Everton were caught out hopelessly going for goal and Rush collected his second. But at the heart of all Liverpool's goals was the Great Dane, Jan Mølby, who finally wrestled midfield supremacy from Reid and Paul Bracewell. Lineker stood accused of showing his good and bad qualities at Wembley. His 40th goal of a remarkable first season with Everton illustrated his speed and sharpness, but he also failed to control the ball when presented with a second chance. Both Lineker and Rush, it was rumoured, were being tempted by moves abroad.

## 16th August 1986

FA Charity Shield (at Wembley)
**Everton 1**
Heath
**Liverpool 1**
Rush
*Attendance:* **88,231**
**Everton:** *Mimms, Harper, Power, Ratcliffe, Marshall, Langley, Steven, Heath, Sharp, Richardson, Sheedy (Adams [Wilkinson])*
**Liverpool:** *Grobbelaar (Hooper), Venison, Beglin, Lawrenson, Whelan, Hansen, McMahon, Johnston, Rush, Mølby, MacDonald (Dalglish)*

Liverpool, as First Division champions and FA Cup holders, took on runners-up Everton in the FA Charity Shield as Merseyside once again decamped to Wembley. Kenny Dalglish joked afterwards that half an hour's football was his limit, but Liverpool didn't see the funny side of what their player-manager said – until he came on as a second-half substitute they had lacked firepower. Dalglish's first touch of the game was a brilliant pass out to the wing. His use of the ball after that was in a different class; he organized the midfield and also hit the post. It was Dalglish who set up the equalizing goal for Ian Rush after Adrian Heath had put Everton ahead. Howard Kendall looked to have bought well in the close season and the kids he brought in to patch-up his injury-hit side showed once again that Everton would be Championship contenders.

## 16th September 1986

Screen Sport Super Cup Final, first leg
**Liverpool 3**
Rush 2, McMahon
**Everton 1**
Sheedy
*Attendance:* **20,660**
**Liverpool:** *Hooper, Venison, Beglin, Lawrenson, Whelan (Mølby), Gillespie, Dalglish, Nicol, Rush, MacDonald, McMahon*
**Everton:** *Mimms, Billing, Power, Ratcliffe, Marshall, Langley, Adams, Wilkinson, Sharp, Steven, Sheedy (Aspinall)*

Ian Rush produced a super show once again to torment Everton. The Juventus-bound striker scored twice and was denied a hat-trick only by a foul by Ian Marshall who was rightly booked. Marshall was lucky not to be sent off for the 78th-minute trip as Rush was homing in on goal. Kevin Sheedy equalized Rush's first goal with a 25-yard free-kick but Steve McMahon and then Rush sank Everton.

## 30th September 1986

Screen Sport Super Cup Final, second leg
**Everton 1**
Sharp (pen)

**Liverpool 4**
Rush 3, Nicol
*Attendance: 26,068*
**Everton:** *Mimms, Billing, Power, Ratcliffe, Mountfield, Steven, Adams, Heath, Sharp, Wilkinson, Sheedy (Aspinall [Pointon])*
**Liverpool:** *Grobbelaar, Gillespie, Beglin, Lawrenson, Whelan, Hansen, Wark, Nicol (Venison), Rush, Mølby, McMahon (Walsh)*

Ian Rush moved to within three goals of the derby record of the legendary Dixie Dean with a hat-trick against Everton in the second leg of the Screen Sport Super Cup Final at Goodison. The Welsh international was now within sight of Dean's tally of 19 goals in Merseyside derbies and had at least two more matches in which to crack the record before moving to Juventus. Liverpool's other goal came from Steve Nicol to give them overall victory by a 7-2 aggregate scoreline after Graeme Sharp had notched a late consolation for Everton from the penalty spot.

## 23rd November 1986

First Division
**Everton 0**
**Liverpool 0**
*Attendance: 48,247*
**Everton:** *Southall, Harper, Power, Ratcliffe, Mountfield, Langley (Wilkinson), Steven, Heath, Sharp, Adams, Sheedy*
**Liverpool:** *Grobbelaar, Gillespie, Beglin, Lawrenson, Whelan, Hansen, Walsh, Nicol, Rush, Mølby, McMahon*

Ian Rush, still looking for three goals to equal the legendary Dixie Dean's record of 19 scored in Merseyside derbies, reckoned he was robbed of one of them at Goodison. Referee George Courtney disallowed a 22nd-minute effort by Rush for a push on Everton's Derek Mountfield. Rush argued that it was a goal and that Mountfield had lost sight of the ball as the wind took it. Just two minutes later, Adrian Heath had a strong penalty appeal turned down.

## 21ˢᵗ January 1987

League Cup Quarter-final
**Everton 0**
**Liverpool 1**
Rush
*Attendance: 53,323*
**Everton:** *Southall, Stevens, Pointon (Wilkinson), Ratcliffe, Mountfield, Power (Snodin), Steven, Heath, Sharp, Harper, Sheedy*
**Liverpool:** *Grobbelaar, Gillespie, Beglin (Venison), Lawrenson, Whelan, Hansen, Walsh, Johnston, Rush, Mølby, McMahon (Irvine)*


Ian Rush struck a dramatic late winner for Liverpool to ease the pain of losing full-back Jim Beglin with a shattering injury in this League Cup clash at Goodison Park. With Beglin in hospital after breaking his leg midway through the first half, Rush popped up six minutes from time to fire Liverpool into the Semi-finals. It was his 26ᵗʰ goal of the season and a dream climax for the Liverpool faithful. Liverpool had enough problems as they tried to stem the waves of Everton attacks, despite making a promising start in which they forced a couple of early corners. Midfield man Steve McMahon also needed treatment for a groin injury as Liverpool stuck valiantly to their task. The unfortunate incident with Beglin brought the normally high temperature of a derby match to fever pitch and as Liverpool struck forward, Paul Walsh shot narrowly wide of the far post. Liverpool's cause was not helped when McMahon – who had already scored eight League Cup goals that season – failed to emerge for the second half. Recent signing Alan Irvine took his place and Liverpool were forced to reshuffle their pack yet again but they came close to snatching the lead after 57 minutes. Irvine, operating on the left side of midfield, broke down the flank and found Walsh on the edge of the Everton penalty area. Walsh neatly controlled the ball and hammered in a tremendous shot from 20 yards which beat Neville Southall, only to rebound across goal from the inside of a post. Everton's frustration was illustrated when Graeme Sharp was booked for elbowing Jan Mølby in the face and after 76 minutes Walsh was again unlucky. He had been a live wire in the Liverpool attack and Everton tried to play their new ace 13 minutes from the end when £840,000 signing Ian Snodin came on as substitute for Paul Power. But the finale belonged to Rush, who raced clear to pick up a through-ball from Walsh and hammered past the grounded Southall for a spectacular winner.

## 25th April 1987

First Division
**Liverpool 3**
McMahon, Rush 2
**Everton 1**
Sheedy
*Attendance:* **44,827**
**Liverpool:** *Hooper, Gillespie, Venison, Ablett, Whelan, Hansen, Spackman, Johnston, Rush, Mølby, McMahon*
**Everton:** *Southall, Stevens, Power, Ratcliffe, Watson, Reid, Steven, Heath, Clarke, Snodin, Sheedy*

Ian Rush equalled Dixie Dean's Mersey derby record of 19 goals then insisted that the Kop faithful should release their hold on him. Liverpool fans found it hard to agree after his two-goal strike had sunk Everton, but Rush was convinced he was not irreplaceable. Liverpool's impressive win over Everton was merely a last defiant stand in a Championship destined for Goodison. Once manager Kenny Dalglish handed over the crown to Howard Kendall he was left with the biggest headache in football – finding Ian Rush's successor. Paul Walsh, struggling to find any sort of goal form, was dropped to the bench. Dalglish didn't pick himself, perhaps finally accepting that it was time to quit as a player and concentrate on management, and his biggest signing so far – John Aldridge – had started just one game since arriving from Oxford for £750,000. Rush laid on the early strike for Steve McMahon with a superb pass across the face of the box. Kevin Sheedy curled in an unstoppable 25-yard free-kick into the top corner for the equalizer. On the stroke of half-time, Ronnie Whelan's corner was flicked on at the near post by Craig Johnston and Rush finished it off with a close-range header. The killer third goal came when Everton were pushing hard for an equalizer; Kevin Ratcliffe missed Gary Ablett's cross and Rush latched onto it. Neville Southall got a hand to the ball but couldn't stop it trickling over the line. Modestly, Rush was thinking more of Liverpool's cause than personal glory and would have settled for 2-1 as long as his club won.

## 28th October 1987

League Cup Third Round
**Liverpool 0**
**Everton 1**
Stevens
*Attendance:* **44,071**
**Liverpool:** *Grobbelaar, Lawrenson, Gillespie, Nicol, Whelan, Hansen, Beardsley, Aldridge, Johnston, Barnes, McMahon*
**Everton:** *Southall, Stevens, Van Den Hauwe, Ratcliffe, Watson, Reid, Steven, Heath, Sharp, Snodin, Wilson*

Gary Stevens drilled home a dramatic winner for Everton seven minutes from the end of this thriller. Stevens netted with a 25-yarder that appeared to take a deflection off Liverpool's Gary Gillespie on the way. Liverpool had the lurking figure of John Barnes breaking dangerously from midfield to link with front men Peter Beardsley and John Aldridge. He made his first run after 14 minutes, cutting down the left and waltzing effortlessly past two tackles before flicking the ball inside to Ronnie Whelan. But the chance was wasted when Whelan sent his shot high into the Kop. Everton should have had a gift goal right on half-time when Lawrenson miscued the ball to Graeme Sharp, but the Everton striker hit his shot straight at Bruce Grobbelaar.

## 1st November 1987

First Division
**Liverpool 2**
McMahon, Beardsley
**Everton 0**
*Attendance:* **44,760**
**Liverpool:** *Grobbelaar, Gillespie, Lawrenson, Nicol, Whelan, Hansen, Beardsley, Aldridge, Johnston, Barnes, McMahon*
**Everton:** *Southall, Stevens, Van Den Hauwe, Ratcliffe, Watson, Reid, Steven, Clarke (Mountfield), Sharp, Snodin, Wilson*

Peter Beardsley responded to taunts of "what a waste of money" with a blistering strike to destroy Everton at Anfield. Millions of TV viewers saw Liverpool's £1.9 million striker hit the knockout goal – his first in five games – that clinched this battle and sent the Reds back to the top of the First Division. With the brilliant John Barnes having a hand in both goals –Everton old boy Steve McMahon grabbed the first after 36 minutes – the watching nation were given ample evidence that Liverpool had invested wisely in the man to lead them to the title. Beardsley was the highest-priced player in British football, but Barnes had been justly hogging the headlines and the limelight since his move to Anfield. England manager Bobby Robson, overjoyed at the transformation in Barnes since his move to Merseyside, called for more goals from Beardsley to justify his ranking as one of the best forwards in Europe. Robson would certainly have relished the way Beardsley showed his quality finishing in this game. His power was awesome as he unleashed a whiplash half-volley that crashed into the roof of the net behind goalkeeper Neville Southall in the 73rd minute. It was a gem of a goal from the moment Barnes had cheekily back-heeled the ball to McMahon whose cross clipped the foot of John Aldridge and Beardsley reacted superbly. Barnes' excellent first-time through-ball enabled McMahon to open the scoring in the first half and set up a victory that wiped out the bitter memory of their League Cup defeat to Everton four days earlier. The title was the prize that manager Kenny Dalglish coveted most and this win put his team nine points ahead of defending champions and arch-rivals Everton with three games in hand. Arsenal's weekend reign as First Division leaders lasted a mere 24 hours. Not even the Gunners' remarkable record-breaking run of 11 successive wins – eight of them in the League – was enough to keep Liverpool at bay. Liverpool possessed such a wealth of talent that newcomer Ray Houghton and stalwart Jan Mølby were the substitutes . . . and not even needed! Nearly 90,000 people had crammed into Anfield in the last week for these two exciting derbies. A bumper gate of 44,760 turned out for this game even though it was live on television. Liverpool came out on top in a pinball match of raw aggression, unflinching challenges and fearless tackling. These were the hallmarks of the most competitive fixture on the English football calendar. It was hard to produce moments of inspiration with hardly an inch of space in which to manoeuvre. Somehow Barnes and Beardsley managed it though, and that is a tribute to their quality. Liverpool's margin of victory might have been more emphatic when John Aldridge finished off a flying move involving Barnes and Beardsley again only for Aldridge to be marginally offside.

## 21st February 1988

FA Cup Fifth Round
**Everton 0**
**Liverpool 1**
Houghton
*Attendance: 48,270*
**Everton:** *Southall, Stevens, Pointon, Van Den Hauwe, Watson, Reid (Harper), Steven, Heath, Sharp, Snodin, Power*
**Liverpool:** *Grobbelaar, Ablett, Venison, Nicol, Spackman, Hansen, Beardsley, Aldridge, Houghton, Barnes, McMahon*

Ray Houghton's match-winner kept Liverpool on course for the League and FA Cup Double – and inflicted revenge on the one side to blemish their incredible season. The satisfaction was deep for Kenny Dalglish's men, who had been knocked out of the League Cup by Everton way back in October – Liverpool's only defeat in 33 games that season. It was not a classic, but it had the raw commitment and excitement of a world title fight between two heavyweights, and it had the watching TV millions on a knife-edge. The difference between the Merseyside giants was that Liverpool had a knockout punch in the brilliance of Peter Beardsley and John Barnes. They were backed by the aggression and motivation of England's newest international, Steve McMahon. Beardsley and Barnes, that £2.8 million dynamic duo, carved out the winner with crisp inter-passing 15 minutes from the end. It was finished off by Ray Houghton on his Merseyside derby debut. Ian Rush, watching his beloved Liverpool march on, must have realized that the money they received for him from Juventus had been wisely invested. There was no apparent danger when Gary Ablett took a throw-in to Barnes, having a strangely quiet game sporting his new-look haircut. But a one-two shuffle between England pair Barnes and Beardsley made vital inroads along the flank. Beardsley produced the perfect pass into Barnes' stride. His accurate cross allowed Houghton to steal ahead of full-back Neil Pointon and beat Neville Southall with a downward header. Having joined from Oxford United, Houghton justified his £800,000 price tag with the fifth and most important goal of his Liverpool career so far. Everton were in their 10th major Cup tie of 1988 and their eighth that month. But after 13½ hours of toil in the FA Cup, following marathons against Sheffield Wednesday and Middlesbrough, their season now rested on Wednesday's League Cup Semi-final second leg at Arsenal.

## 20th March 1988

First Division

**Everton 1**

Clarke

**Liverpool 0**

*Attendance: 44,162*

**Everton:** *Southall, Stevens, Pointon, Van Den Hauwe, Watson, Reid, Steven, Clarke (Heath), Sharp, Harper, Sheedy (Power)*

**Liverpool:** *Grobbelaar, Gillespie, Ablett, Nicol, Spackman (Mølby), Hansen, Beardsley, Johnston, Houghton, Barnes, McMahon*

Bruce Grobbelaar let beating the 14-year-old Leeds United record slip through his fingers at Goodison Park. Grobbelaar, the Clown Prince of keepers who tended to specialize in TV clangers, dropped the ball from Trevor Steven's inswinging corner and Wayne Clarke struck to make Everton record-wreckers. Grobbelaar had been in brilliant form throughout Liverpool's phenomenal run to equal Leeds' 29-game unbeaten run from the start of a season. The Zimbabwe-born goalkeeper had been guilty of far worse mistakes and certainly could not take, single-handedly, the blame for Liverpool's failure to reach the magic 30-game figure. It was a measure of consistently outstanding performances that Clarke's winner, in the true sniffer tradition of his brother Allan, was only the third to beat Grobbelaar in the previous 17 matches. Everton would still surrender their Championship crown to their Merseyside rivals, but at least they had the enormous satisfaction of being the only team to beat Liverpool that season – and they'd done it twice! Perfectionist Grobbelaar would kick himself for letting the ball out of his grasp, even though under enormous pressure from Graeme Sharp. Dave Watson, who must have impressed the watching England manager Bobby Robson, swung at the loose ball before it fell invitingly to Clarke. Clarke's one major contribution – he was substituted later in the game – was the perfect finish. His 10th goal of the season – the 14th overall for Everton and 69th of his career – would rank as one of the most significant he was ever likely to score. It certainly provided pleasure for Allan Clarke, new manager of Barnsley, and goalscorer extraordinaire in the Leeds team under Don Revie. Clarke Senior was on duty for local radio and would have been grateful that Leeds' old record was not overtaken. But Liverpool would be bitterly disappointed at not rewriting the record books. For one of the very few times that season, they failed to score, rarely troubling goalkeeper Neville Southall. In midfield, Peter Reid gradually edged ahead of Steve McMahon in their battle royal. It was an important point for Reid to make in front of Robson, with positions in England's midfield department being hotly contested for the upcoming European Championships. When Reid hobbled from the field with a thigh injury early in the FA Cup Fifth Round tie in February, Everton's hopes went with him and Liverpool marched on towards Wembley. The effort of trying to rule the midfield left both Reid and McMahon nursing injuries that could jeopardize their places in the England squad. McMahon was deservedly shown the yellow card for a reckless late tackle on Neil Pointon that left the full-back writhing on the floor. The large crowd and the millions watching at home were privileged to witness another Merseyside encounter of breathtaking pace, commitment and skill. Liverpool could still win the Double, the first club in history to do it twice – and all inside three seasons. On balance though, this was deservedly Everton's day and no one could begrudge them that in a season otherwise dominated by their great rivals.

# 11ᵗʰ December 1988

First Division
**Liverpool 1**
Houghton
**Everton 1**
Clarke (pen)
*Attendance:* 42,372
**Liverpool:** *Hooper, Ablett, Venison, Nicol, Whelan, Burrows, Beardsley, Aldridge (Rush), Houghton, Barnes, McMahon*
**Everton:** *Southall, Snodin, Van Den Hauwe, Ratcliffe, Watson, Bracewell (Reid), Steven, McCall, Clarke, Cottee, Wilson*

Superman Neville Southall broke Liverpool's hearts in this breathless, non-stop television spectacular. After the match even Kenny Dalglish conceded that Everton had been denied what looked like a perfectly good Wayne Clarke winner by a controversial refereeing decision. The dazzling Welsh international keeper produced an astonishing one-handed save from a close-range cannonball by England man John Barnes. It was the game's crucial moment and came in the 34ᵗʰ minute with Liverpool already in the lead and threatening to run away with it. Their goal, which had been threatening for so long, came after 30 minutes. The ever-dangerous Barnes played the role of creator after robbing Stuart McCall in midfield. Barnes timed his pass perfectly through Everton's defence to beat their offside trap and put Ray Houghton clean away. Not even Southall had any chance as Houghton raced past him before guiding the ball home. Liverpool were now in rampant mood and three minutes later the second goal seemed certain. John Aldridge crossed from the right and Barnes stormed in to crack the ball powerfully. The Kop was already celebrating what they thought was a certain goal, but somehow Southall twisted in mid-air and turned the ball over the bar. It was unbelievable. He made another stunning save early in the second half with Liverpool again on the rampage. This time Aldridge was clean through, but again Southall anticipated brilliantly to dive to his right and save at point-blank range. Everton steadily fought their way back into the match. After 50 minutes they were rewarded with a vital equalizer when Trevor Steven cut into the box only to be clumsily brought down by David Burrows and up stepped the cool Clarke to crack home the penalty. Liverpool suddenly lost their poise and amazingly, five minutes after that goal, came Clarke's disallowed effort. It was relentless football, but the final drama came 15 minutes from the end and again Southall played a major part. Liverpool had brought on ace striker Ian Rush for Aldridge, and immediately the Kop were screaming for action. Skipper Ronnie Whelan put Rush through into the box, again catching Everton's defence flat-footed, and a goal seemed on. But the defiant Southall was off his line in a flash to fling himself forward just as Rush was about to shoot, and the striker's hurried shot sent the ball zooming over the crossbar. The battle was over but for the 42,000-plus fans and the millions watching on TV it was a game to savour, and those moments of Southall magic would take some forgetting. For Liverpool, inspired by a great display from Steve Nicol, there was the promise to their fans that they were still on course to keep their First Division title.

## 3rd May 1989

First Division
**Everton 0**
**Liverpool 0**
*Attendance: 45,994*
**Everton:** *Southall, McDonald, Van Den Hauwe, Ratcliffe, Watson, Bracewell, Nevin, Steven, Sharp, Cottee, Sheedy (McCall)*
**Liverpool:** *Grobbelaar, Ablett, Staunton, Nicol, Whelan, Hansen, Beardsley, Aldridge (Rush), Houghton, Barnes, McMahon*

Tony Cottee warned Arsenal boss George Graham not to rule out Liverpool after this match. The £2 million striker who turned down Graham for a move to Everton believed the First Division title race was still wide open. The draw left Liverpool five points adrift of leaders Arsenal, but the Anfield side still had five matches to play. Everton appealed for a penalty when Cottee appeared to be fouled in the second half by Gary Ablett. But Cottee sportingly insisted that the decision by referee Neil Midgeley had been the right one. Kenny Dalglish was sucking throat pastilles at the end after almost losing his voice in Liverpool's first competitive match since the tragedy of the FA

Cup Semi-final at Hillsborough. Liverpool's return to football normality, always destined to be traumatic and tearful, could have proved to have been the day that their hopes of picking up the pieces of their sorrowful season turned out to be an impossible dream. Both physically and mentally, Liverpool were shown to be fallible after so much suffering and anguish. Their phenomenal run prior to Hillsborough – 11 straight wins, nine of them in the League – was from a different team of a bygone age. The 18 days of mourning on Merseyside, counselling the bereaved, had taken its toll. It had shown that the Liverpool players were humans after all, not soccer supermen. At the end of what was always going to be an emotional resumption at Goodison, they didn't have three points, but they had their dignity – and for many that was enough. For the professionals inside Anfield, this was a day of bitter footballing disappointment. For the neutrals, and there were millions watching throughout Europe on television, this was a day when English football showed the world its compassion. English football was not all about mindless hooligans. It was about passionate football, fervent fans, high-class, top-speed soccer – and caring. The memories would linger on, and they included some of the most touching moments ever witnessed inside a soccer stadium in this country. When memories of Steve McMahon's biting tackles, the goalmouth scrambles at both ends and the arguments over a possible Everton penalty had faded, the occasion itself would live long in the minds of those who were there. Liverpool's rehabilitation as a soccer team was an anti-climax, but it was not the central event. There was no trivia, no inflatables, no celebrations from Everton fans who may have seen their side deny their rivals another Championship. There was simply a sporting handshake and polite applause from both sets of supporters. The atmosphere was set when chairmen John Smith of Liverpool and Phil Carter or Everton, followed by managers Kenny Dalglish and Colin Harvey, led out their teams to a tumultuous reception. Over the loudspeaker came the announcement that hushed the crowd: "On 15 April at Hillsborough the game of football, the City of Liverpool, and the nation witnessed a terrible tragedy. 95 [later to rise to 96] football supporters lost their lives . . . To our friends at Liverpool we say your loss is our loss." Observing a minute's silence, fans turned out not just to pay homage, but also to vote with their feet that they want the game to go on. Although this one was scoreless, goalkeepers Neville Southall and Bruce Grobbelaar had much to do with that.

## 20<sup>th</sup> May 1989

FA Cup Final (at Wembley)
**Everton 2**
McCall 2
**Liverpool 3**
Aldridge, Rush 2
*Attendance:* **82,800**
**Everton:** *Southall, McDonald, Van Den Hauwe, Ratcliffe, Watson, Bracewell (McCall), Nevin, Steven, Sharp, Cottee, Sheedy (Wilson)*
**Liverpool:** *Grobbelaar, Ablett, Staunton (Venison), Nicol, Whelan, Hansen, Beardsley, Aldridge (Rush), Houghton, Barnes, McMahon*

Kenny Dalglish, deep in the bowels of Wembley Stadium, reflected on all his marvellous former glories as a player and manager, and without hesitation confirmed this was the best one for him. Dalglish as a player won every domestic honour in both Scotland and England, and he was also a European Cup winner three times. In his first season as a manager he led Liverpool to the League and Cup Double. It had been a career full of highlights, but he spoke from the heart about the greatest moment of his sporting life – winning the 1989 Memorial Cup Final. The sheer delight and personal accomplishment at delivering the FA Cup, in the name of those who perished at Hillsborough, to the survivors and to the families of the bereaved, oozed from him. Liverpool's manager never sat down, despite the heat, during the enthralling 120 minutes. After the tragedy of Hillsborough, Dalglish and his players set out on a Cup crusade. The burden was immense, the strain incalculable. Nottingham Forest were swamped by the emotion in the Semi-final. It was a great credit to Liverpool that they didn't crack under the strain at Wembley. Dalglish genuinely felt sympathy, even felt sorry for their Merseyside rivals in defeat, but he was single-minded. That was the platform for his success. He wanted to be a winner, nothing else would do and he needed to be a winner on this occasion. He pulled off one of the most daring FA Cup Final substitutions. There would be many managers prepared to substitute a striker who had scored potentially the winning goal. Yet, equally, there wouldn't be many managers who would have a player of the quality of Ian Rush sitting on the bench. In the 73rd minute he took off John Aldridge and called up Rush, who sank Everton with two brilliant goals in extra-time. Liverpool had taken an early lead with a scintillating goal from Aldridge, making up for his penalty miss against Wimbledon the previous year, Everton eventually equalized with a last-gasp goal from substitute Stuart McCall. Rush's double, setting a new record of 21 goals in Merseyside derbies, finally won the FA Cup despite another McCall equalizer.

## 23rd September 1989

First Division
**Everton 1**
Newell
**Liverpool 3**
Barnes, Rush 2
*Attendance: 42,453*
**Everton:** *Southall, Snodin, Pointon (McDonald), Ratcliffe, Watson, Whiteside (Rehn), Nevin, McCall, Sharp, Newell, Sheedy*
**Liverpool:** *Grobbelaar, Hysén, Burrows, Nicol, Whelan, Hansen, Beardsley, Venison, Rush, Barnes, McMahon*

Liverpool's Peter Beardsley reckoned he saw it coming. He predicted in the dressing room that Ian Rush would shatter Everton in this dramatic clash and Rush the destroyer was back with a vengeance. It was Beardsley who gave him the ammunition for two goals in two minutes to silence the blue half of Merseyside. Mike Newell had given the home side the lead after 18 minutes when he kept his head and slid the ball past the advancing Bruce Grobbelaar, but their advantage lasted less than a quarter of an hour when John Barnes headed Beardsley's cross powerfully into the net.

## 3rd February 1990

First Division

**Liverpool 2**

Barnes, Beardsley (pen)

**Everton 1**

Sharp

*Attendance: 38,730*

**Liverpool:** *Grobbelaar, Hysén, Venison, Nicol, Whelan, Hansen, Beardsley, Burrows, Rush, Barnes, McMahon*

**Everton:** *Southall, Snodin, McDonald, Ratcliffe, Watson, Whiteside, Nevin (Newell), McCall, Sharp, Keown, Sheedy*

The headlines after this match were all about John Barnes' confirmation that he intended to leave Merseyside to play abroad. After scoring a fabulous goal to help Liverpool to a thrilling 2-1 win over Everton, Barnes said that his future would eventually lie with a foreign club. The England star, whose performances had made him the envy of top clubs all over Europe, talked frankly about his position at Anfield and his eventual desires for pastures new. But Liverpool knew that if they hung on to him until the end of his contract they would only receive a maximum of £800,000 whereas by selling him before they could command a fee which could have been as much as £5 million. This win put Liverpool three points clear at the top of the First Division, with the Anfield side having played two more games than second-placed Aston Villa.

# Chapter Nine

# The 1990s

The dominance that Merseyside had exerted over the rest of the country during the 1980s practically vanished as the 1990s arrived. Liverpool's record haul of 18 League titles came to an end although they remained a top-10 side, while Everton spent much of the decade in the bottom half of the table and only staved off relegation at the end of the 1997–98 season due to a better goal difference than Bolton Wanderers. The two clubs fared better in cup competitions with two FA Cup triumphs (Liverpool in 1992 and Everton in 1995) and a League Cup victory (Liverpool in 1995), but Merseyside football was in the doldrums following the recent trophy-laden decades.

## Record in the 1990s

**Everton**

| Season | League | P | W | D | L | F | A | Pts | Pos |
|--------|--------|---|---|---|---|---|---|-----|-----|
| 1990–91 | Div 1 | 38 | 13 | 12 | 13 | 50 | 46 | 51 | 9 |
| 1991–92 | Div 1 | 42 | 13 | 14 | 15 | 52 | 51 | 53 | 12 |
| 1992–93 | Prem | 42 | 15 | 8 | 19 | 53 | 55 | 53 | 13 |
| 1993–94 | Prem | 42 | 12 | 8 | 22 | 42 | 63 | 44 | 17 |
| 1994–95 | Prem | 42 | 11 | 17 | 14 | 44 | 51 | 50 | 15 |
| 1995–96 | Prem | 38 | 17 | 10 | 11 | 64 | 44 | 61 | 6 |
| 1996–97 | Prem | 38 | 10 | 12 | 16 | 44 | 57 | 42 | 15 |
| 1997–98 | Prem | 38 | 9 | 13 | 16 | 41 | 56 | 40 | 17 |
| 1998–99 | Prem | 38 | 11 | 10 | 17 | 42 | 47 | 43 | 14 |
| 1999–2000 | Prem | 38 | 12 | 14 | 12 | 59 | 49 | 50 | 14 |

**FA Cup**

| 1990–91 | 1-2 v West Ham United (Quarter-final) |
| 1991–92 | 0-1 v Chelsea (Fourth Round) |

| | |
|---|---|
| 1992–93 | 0-0, 1-2 v Wimbledon (Third Round) |
| 1993–94 | 1-1, 2-3 v Bolton Wanderers (Third Round) |
| 1994–95 | 1-0 v Manchester United (Final) |
| 1995–96 | 2-2, 1-2 v Port Vale (Fourth Round) |
| 1996–97 | 2-3 v Bradford City (Fourth Round) |
| 1997–98 | 0-1 v Newcastle United (Third Round) |
| 1998–99 | 1-4 v Newcastle United (Quarter-final) |
| 1999–2000 | 1-2 v Aston Villa (Quarter-final) |

## League Cup

| | |
|---|---|
| 1990–91 | 1-2 v Sheffield United (Third Round) |
| 1991–92 | 1-4 v Leeds United (Fourth Round) |
| 1992–93 | 2-2, 0-1 v Chelsea (Fourth Round) |
| 1993–94 | 0-1 v Manchester United (Fourth Round) |
| 1994–95 | 2-3, 1-1 v Portsmouth (Second Round) |
| 1995–96 | 0-0, 2-4 v Millwall (Second Round) |
| 1996–97 | 1-1, 2-3 v York City (Second Round) |
| 1997–98 | 1-4 v Coventry City (Third Round) |
| 1998–99 | 1-1 v Sunderland (Fourth Round) |
| 1999–2000 | 1-1, 0-1 v Oxford United (Second Round) |

## Europe

| | |
|---|---|
| 1990–91 | Did not qualify |
| 1991–92 | Did not qualify |
| 1992–93 | Did not qualify |
| 1993–94 | Did not qualify |
| 1994–95 | Did not qualify |
| 1995–96 | European Cup Winners' Cup: 0-0, 0-1 v Feyenoord (Second Round) |
| 1996–97 | Did not qualify |
| 1997–98 | Did not qualify |
| 1998–99 | Did not qualify |
| 1999–2000 | Did not qualify |

## Liverpool

| Season | League | P | W | D | L | F | A | Pts | Pos |
|--------|--------|---|---|---|---|---|---|-----|-----|
| 1990–91 | Div 1 | 38 | 23 | 7 | 8 | 77 | 40 | 76 | 2 |
| 1991–92 | Div 1 | 42 | 16 | 16 | 10 | 47 | 40 | 64 | 6 |
| 1992–93 | Prem | 42 | 16 | 11 | 15 | 62 | 55 | 59 | 6 |
| 1993–94 | Prem | 42 | 17 | 9 | 16 | 59 | 55 | 60 | 8 |
| 1994–95 | Prem | 42 | 21 | 11 | 10 | 65 | 37 | 74 | 4 |
| 1995–96 | Prem | 38 | 20 | 11 | 7 | 70 | 34 | 71 | 3 |
| 1996–97 | Prem | 38 | 19 | 11 | 8 | 62 | 37 | 68 | 4 |
| 1997–98 | Prem | 38 | 18 | 11 | 9 | 68 | 42 | 65 | 3 |
| 1998–99 | Prem | 38 | 15 | 9 | 14 | 68 | 49 | 54 | 7 |
| 1999–2000 | Prem | 38 | 19 | 10 | 9 | 51 | 30 | 67 | 4 |

## FA Cup

| | |
|--|--|
| 1990–91 | 0-0, 4-4, 0-1 v Everton (Fifth Round) |
| 1991–92 | 2-0 v Sunderland (Final) |
| 1992–93 | 2-2, 0-2 v Bolton Wanderers (Third Round) |
| 1993–94 | 1-1, 0-1 v Bristol City (Third Round) |
| 1994–95 | 1-2 v Tottenham Hotspur (Quarter-final) |
| 1995–96 | 0-1 v Manchester United (Final) |
| 1996–97 | 2-4 v Chelsea (Fourth Round) |
| 1997–98 | 1-3 v Coventry City (Third Round) |
| 1998–99 | 1-2 v Manchester United (Fourth Round) |
| 1999–2000 | 0-1 v Blackburn Rovers (Fourth Round) |

## League Cup

| | |
|--|--|
| 1990–91 | 1-3 v Manchester United (Third Round) |
| 1991–92 | 0-1 v Peterborough United (Fourth Round) |
| 1992–93 | 1-1, 1-2 v Crystal Palace (Fourth Round) |
| 1993–94 | 1-1, 2-2 (3-4 on pens) v Wimbledon (Fourth Round) |
| 1994–95 | 2-1 v Bolton Wanderers (Final) |
| 1995–96 | 0-1 v Newcastle United (Fourth Round) |
| 1996–97 | 1-2 v Middlesbrough (Quarter-final) |
| 1997–98 | 2-1, 0-2 v Middlesbrough (Semi-final) |
| 1998–99 | 1-3 v Tottenham Hotspur (Fourth Round) |
| 1999–2000 | 1-2 v Southampton (Third Round) |

### Europe

| | |
|---|---|
| 1990–91 | Liverpool banned from European competition |
| 1991–92 | UEFA Cup: 0-2, 1-2 v Genoa (Fourth Round) |
| 1992–93 | European Cup Winners' Cup: 2-4, 0-2 v Spartak Moscow (Second Round) |
| 1993–94 | Did not qualify |
| 1994–95 | Did not qualify |
| 1995–96 | UEFA Cup: 0-0, 0-1 v Brøndby (Second Round) |
| 1996–97 | European Cup Winners' Cup: 0-3, 2-0 v Paris St Germain (Semi-final) |
| 1997–98 | UEFA Cup: 0-3, 2-0 v Strasbourg (Second Round) |
| 1998–99 | UEFA Cup: 1-3, 0-1 v Celta Vigo (Third Round) |
| 1999–2000 | Did not qualify |

## The Matches

## 22nd September 1990

First Division

**Everton 2**

Hinchcliffe, Hysén (og)

**Liverpool 3**

Beardsley 2, Barnes (pen)

*Attendance:* **39,847**

**Everton:** *Southall, Atteveld, Hinchcliffe, Ratcliffe, Watson, Milligan (McDonald), Nevin, McCall, Sharp, Newell (Cottee), Ebbrell*

**Liverpool:** *Grobbelaar, Hysén, Burrows, Venison, Whelan, Gillespie, Beardsley, Houghton, Rush, Barnes, McMahon*

After this match, Kenny Dalglish's team were halfway to beating Tottenham's 11-win start to their Double-winning season of 30 years earlier. Liverpool's six wins from six games led Graeme Sharp to believe that no one could stop a rampant Liverpool adding another record to Anfield's collection. The Everton striker shrugged off his disappointment to issue a warning to the rest of the First Division. Liverpool's only defeat of the calendar year had come at Spurs the previous March and, ironically, their 11th fixture of the current season would be at White

Hart Lane. Before then, they were expected to take full points from Sunderland (away), Derby (home), Norwich (away) and Chelsea (home) – four teams in the bottom half of the table. Dalglish's men were glad to have survived Everton's late bombardment. Two more goals from Peter Beardsley and a disputed penalty from John Barnes had Liverpool coasting after 69 minutes but Andy Hinchcliffe's first goal for Everton followed by a Glenn Hysén own goal reduced them to near panic at the end. Only an 89th-minute save by Bruce Grobbelaar from Ray Atteveld's blockbuster prevented a draw.

## 9th February 1991

First Division
**Liverpool 3**
Mølby, Speedie 2
**Everton 1**
Nevin
*Attendance: 38,127*
**Liverpool:** *Grobbelaar, Hysén, Burrows, Nicol, Whelan (Carter), Ablett, Speedie (Beardsley), Staunton, Venison, Barnes, Mølby*
**Everton:** *Southall, McDonald, Ebbrell, Ratcliffe, Watson, Milligan, Nevin, McCall, Sharp, Sheedy, Beagrie (Cottee)*

Ronnie Whelan cleared Peter Beagrie of blame after suffering a fractured tibia in this Merseyside derby. The unlucky Liverpool star was ruled out for up to six weeks following a tangle with Everton winger Beagrie early in the second half and would miss two key matches – the FA Cup Fifth Round clash with Everton plus the title crunch with Arsenal on 3rd March – but he had not written off the season. Two opportunist goals by David Speedie inside three minutes swung a pulsating game for Liverpool, taking his tally to three goals in two games since his controversial £675,000 move from Coventry City. Some doubted the wisdom of Kenny Dalglish's shock swoop, but Pat Nevin – who gave Everton hope with an equalizer – had no doubts that his former Chelsea team-mate would provide value for money. Speedie guided home a Jan Mølby free-kick with a clever header and then applied a deft touch to direct David Burrows' strike past Neville Southall.

## 17ᵗʰ February 1991

FA Cup Fifth Round
**Liverpool 0**
**Everton 0**
*Attendance: 38,323*
**Liverpool:** *Grobbelaar, Hysén, Burrows, Nicol, Mølby, Ablett, Speedie (Beardsley), Staunton, Rush, Barnes, McMahon (Venison)*
**Everton:** *Southall, McDonald, Ebbrell, Ratcliffe, Watson, Keown, Atteveld, McCall, Sharp, Sheedy (Cottee), Nevin*

Jimmy Hill stated that the tackle which put Steve McMahon into hospital with a serious leg injury following this match was his own fault. The top BBC pundit issued his outspoken verdict during the televized FA Cup Merseyside derby when the England midfielder was injured in a first-half tackle with John Ebbrell in which Everton claimed they were robbed by a controversial "no penalty" decision. McMahon's 11ᵗʰ-minute collision with Ebbrell left him writhing in agony while the Everton man, who also needed treatment, shouted angrily into his ear. Salford referee Neil Midgeley awarded a free-kick to Everton but the match erupted again when Pat Nevin was denied what appeared to be a clear penalty. Midgeley ignored the posse of furious Everton players when Nevin hit the deck under a challenge from Gary Ablett, and the Scottish winger had to reject suggestions that he had become a diver. The only thing missing from this thriller was goals, and that was due to outstanding goalkeeping.

## 20ᵗʰ February 1991

FA Cup Fifth Round replay
**Everton 4**
Sharp 2, Cottee 2
**Liverpool 4**
Beardsley 2, Rush, Barnes
*Attendance: 37,766*
**Everton:** *Southall, Atteveld (McCall), Hinchcliffe, Ratcliffe, Watson, Keown, Nevin (Cottee), McDonald, Sharp, Newell, Ebbrell*
**Liverpool:** *Grobbelaar, Hysén, Burrows, Nicol, Mølby, Ablett, Beardsley, Staunton, Rush, Barnes, Venison*

Supersub Tony Cottee was Everton's saviour in a match that manager Howard Kendall described as one of the greatest FA Cup ties of all time. Striker Cottee came off the bench to score two life-savers in an amazing eight-goal thriller. Incredibly, Kenny Dalglish's team led four times – but Everton clawed their way back to force a second replay at Goodison Park. While a 37,766 crowd gave the players a standing ovation, Liverpool were left to reflect on a defensive nightmare that allowed their greatest rivals to come back so many times. It was the first time that Liverpool had conceded four goals in a game since they were hammered by Southampton in October 1989 – and it was the highest-scoring derby since Liverpool beat Everton 7-4 at Anfield during the 1932–33 season. This replay, in contrast to the previous match's goalless version, was full of raw excitement to produce the highest-scoring Cup tie between these Merseyside giants in their long history. The intensity of the tackles and the quality of the Liverpool goals was punctuated by some comic relief in the wobbly Liverpool defence. One or two goals that Liverpool conceded bordered on the farcical. Everton were allowed to strike back an incredible four times. Peter Beardsley took centre stage from the outset with a timely reminder to Dalglish and England manager Graham Taylor that his talents could no longer be kept on ice. It had been one of the big mysteries at Anfield why Dalglish had kept Beardsley out of his side, and the purchase of David Speedie seemed to push Beardsley further into the shadows. Speedie celebrated his 31st birthday by taking the seat on the bench that seemed to be permanently reserved for Beardsley, who struck after 33 minutes when Ian Rush pinched the ball from under the feet of Kevin Ratcliffe. The Welsh ace chipped the ball over Neville Southall only to be stunned as Andy Hinchcliffe cleared off the line but Beardsley was perfectly placed to unleash a first-time shot to beat Southall and ricochet in off a defender. The first of Everton's four marvellous comeback goals came after 47 minutes. Everton attacked with purpose down the right, the ball was scrambled away to Hinchcliffe lurking on the left flank, and his early cross was met with a powerful header by Graeme Sharp. Bruce Grobbelaar, in his frantic effort to push the ball out, appeared to push it onto the post and then into the net. The cracks in the Liverpool defence appeared again when Glenn Hysén and

Gary Ablett both tackled each other and crashed to the ground, leaving Pat Nevin with only Grobbelaar to beat. But Nevin tried a tricky chip and fluffed it as the ball flew well over the top. That was perhaps the only chance Everton had of actually taking the lead. Liverpool duly went back in front, even though Everton had them pinned down in their own half. With second-half substitute Stuart McCall snapping at Jan Mølby's heels in the 71st minute, the Dane cleverly kept the ball moving in a build-up that involved David Burrows and Steve Nicol. When it came to Beardsley, he rode one challenge and let fly from just outside the box past Southall into the top corner. That goal sparked three in the space of a spectacular six minutes. Everton equalized in the 73rd minute when Mike Newell's header bounced awkwardly for Nicol, and his back-pass eluded Grobbelaar and left Sharp free to run the ball into an open goal. Grobbelaar and his defenders were in a mess, and it was left to the Reds' attack to come to their rescue. Beardsley's short corner and a Mølby cross in the 77th minute found Rush, who delivered a free header into the corner. It looked Liverpool's game, but it was far from over. In the last minute of normal time, Cottee – who had come on just three minutes earlier as substitute for Nevin – scored Everton's third equalizer. It seemed harmless enough as Liverpool were in possession, but a costly ricochet left Cottee free and Ablett's desperate lunge couldn't stop him collecting his 12th goal of the season. Amazingly, the thrills intensified during extra-time. Southall produced two outstanding saves, the best from a Barry Venison header, and in the 102nd minute Liverpool were back in the lead for a fourth time. John Barnes, quiet by his own high standards for so much of the game, burst into life as he cut inside Neil McDonald. He suddenly produced a wicked curler from outside the angle of the penalty box that whipped past Southall into the top corner. Surely Everton couldn't come back again – but they did with just six minutes left. Hysén let Mølby's back-pass go through his legs to Grobbelaar and the ever-alert Cottee – for so long the nearly man of Goodison Park – hungrily latched on to the ball and grabbed his second goal of this magical night.

## 27th February 1991

FA Cup Fifth Round second replay

**Everton 1**

Watson

**Liverpool 0**

*Attendance: 40,201*

**Everton:** *Southall, McDonald, Hinchcliffe, Ratcliffe, Watson, Keown, Atteveld (Nevin), McCall, Sharp, Newell, Ebbrell*

**Liverpool:** *Grobbelaar, Hysén, Venison (Speedie), Nicol, Mølby, Ablett, Beardsley, Houghton, Rush, Barnes, Staunton*

Kenny Dalglish had been haunted by sleepless nights that drove him out of Anfield – and that nightmare now belonged to Ronnie Moran. Life after Dalglish proved a misery for caretaker boss Moran, losing the First Division leadership and being dumped out of the FA Cup by their Merseyside rivals in the space of five days. It hadn't taken Moran long to discover that life at the top with Liverpool carried with it the sort of burden that forced Dalglish to crack. It was blue murder for him as Everton marched triumphantly into an FA Cup Quarter-final at West Ham thanks to a rare goal from defender Dave Watson, who had started his career at Anfield. Dalglish walked out after Liverpool conceded four at Goodison the previous week and the shock 3-1 defeat on the plastic pitch at Luton – Moran's first game in charge – was quickly followed by the end of any dreams of Liverpool landing the Double. Everton went ahead after just 12 minutes and clung to that advantage. While Watson was the goalscoring hero, Neville Southall was the man of the match with three world-class saves, and Stuart McCall ran as far and as long as Alan Ball used to do for Everton and England. Ian Rush was left wondering how he missed Liverpool's best chance in the 65th minute, glancing a header the wrong side of the post from close range after a brilliant cross from Steve Nicol. But the credit for Everton's triumph and Liverpool's agony could only go to Southall. It had seemed improbable that he could produce a better performance than he had achieved the previous week at Goodison – but he did. Both Rush and Nicol were amazed at his skills as he conjured two saves in the space of seven minutes early in the second half. The telling goal once more emphasized Liverpool's vulnerability in the air at the back. Ray Atteveld's free-kick was flicked on by Graeme Sharp and Watson got in a header. Martin Keown was left clear at the far post but his shot was superbly saved by Grobbelaar's outstretched foot and Jan Mølby's attempts to clear failed as the ball fell to Watson. The big defender whacked the ball on the volley giving Grobbelaar no chance.

## 31st August 1991

First Division
**Liverpool 3**
Burrows, Saunders, Houghton
**Everton 1**
Newell
*Attendance: 39,072*
**Liverpool:** *Grobbelaar, Burrows, Ablett, Nicol, Whelan (Marsh), Tanner, Saunders, Houghton, McManaman, Walters (Rosenthal), McMahon*
**Everton:** *Southall, Harper, Ebbrell, McDonald, Watson, Keown (Ratcliffe), Ward, Beardsley, Newell, Cottee (Warzycha), Sheedy*

Peter Beardsley received the sympathy of the Kop as Liverpool ensured there was no happy return for Anfield's celebrated old boy. With just over an hour gone, Everton trailing 3-0 and Beardsley a largely anonymous figure, the Liverpool fans chanted "What a waste of talent!" It was meant as a tribute to a player whose skill entertained them for four seasons and secondly as a cruel indictment of Everton's inept display. Beardsley, at £1 million the most expensive player to cross Merseyside, responded to the chant by suddenly coming out of his shell to set up Mike Newell for Everton's late goal. David Burrows rifled his first ever goal for Liverpool after just 48 seconds. If that wasn't bad enough for Everton, Dean Saunders added a second 14 minutes later. Everton never looked like coming back, especially after Ray Houghton got a third.

## 28th December 1991

First Division

**Everton 1**

Johnston

**Liverpool 1**

Tanner

*Attendance:* **37,681**

**Everton:** *Southall, Jackson, Harper, Ebbrell, Watson, Keown, Warzycha (Nevin), Beardsley, Johnston, Ward, Beagrie*

**Liverpool:** *Grobbelaar, Jones, Ablett, Nicol, Wright (McManaman), Tanner, Saunders, Houghton, Marsh, Mølby, Thomas*

Liverpool came into this match having drawn five of their previous eight League games so were looking for three points to drag themselves up the table. In the end, though, they had to settle for another stalemate. Their unlikely goal hero was defender Nick Tanner who scored his only League goal for the club in the 41st minute. A Dean Saunders corner was helped on by Michael Thomas for Tanner to force the ball past Mark Ward and over the line. The Reds' lead lasted just 20 minutes, though, when Mo Johnston's shot crept inside the post to set up a thrilling finale. The last half an hour provided goalmouth action at both ends and the crowd rewarded the players with a standing ovation after 90 minutes.

## 7th December 1992

Premier League

**Everton 2**

Johnston, Beardsley

**Liverpool 1**

Wright

*Attendance:* **35,826**

**Everton:** *Southall, Horne, Ablett, Snodin (Rideout), Watson, Keown, Kenny, Beardsley, Barlow, Johnston, Unsworth (Beagrie)*

**Liverpool:** *Hooper, Marsh, Wright, Nicol, Piechnik, Hutchison (Stewart), McManaman, Redknapp, Rosenthal (Walters), Barnes, Jones*

Former Kop stars Peter Beardsley and Gary Ablett combined to leave Graeme Souness with a red face – and Everton in blue heaven. Souness controversially sold both players to Liverpool's greatest rivals in his turbulent first season as Anfield chief and it was almost inevitable they would come back to haunt him with a vengeance. Beardsley scored a sensational late winner from Ablett's pass to leave Souness squirming and Goodison boss Howard Kendall breathing a huge sigh of relief. The win, only Everton's second in 10 matches, eased some of the pressure building on Kendall in a season that started so promisingly but had soured badly. Now Kendall hoped this first League derby win since March 1988 could provide the springboard for a rapid climb away from the relegation zone. But Liverpool were left wondering just how they let this game slip away after being almost totally in command for the first hour. Mark Wright set a low-key derby clash alight in the 62$^{nd}$ minute, squeezing in front of Martin Keown to score with a towering header from Mike Marsh's corner. It was a sweet moment for the England defender in his first start for a month after falling out of favour with Souness. But Wright's joy at the fourth goal of his topsy-turvy season lasted only two minutes as Everton finally came to life as an attacking force. It was Mo Johnston, who had had such a nightmare time since his £1.5 million move from Rangers 11 months earlier, who was the surprise scorer. There looked no danger when Johnston, with his back to goal on the edge of the area, received Ian Snodin's pass. But he neatly slipped Torben Piechnik before curling a low shot past the outstretched hands of Mike Hooper and into the net via the inside of the far post. Liverpool recovered well from Johnston's equalizer and were desperately unlucky not to regain the lead. Barnes hit the post with a volley after a clever one-two with Steve McManaman and seconds later forced Neville Southall into a flying save. The goals had brought the game vibrantly to life and then it was Everton's turn to go close, with first the rejuvenated Johnston and then the ever-dangerous Beardsley sending diving headers inches off-target. At this point Everton, with the worst home record in the Premier League, would surely have been grateful for a draw but six minutes from time they grabbed their shock winner. Beagrie held off a Rob Jones challenge to feed Ablett and his astute pass picked out Beardsley lurking on the edge of the area. The little Geordie, whom many considered to be a giveaway at £1 million, checked to his right to make space before hammering the sweet shot past Hooper.

## 20th March 1993

Premier League

**Liverpool 1**

Rosenthal

**Everton 0**

*Attendance:* **44,619**

**Liverpool:** *James, Burrows, Harkness, Nicol, Wright (Mølby), Whelan, McManaman (Rosenthal), Hutchison, Rush, Barnes, Walters*

**Everton:** *Southall, Jackson, Hinchcliffe, Snodin, Watson, Ablett, Ward (Radosavijevic), Beardsley, Cottee, Kenny (Barlow), Ebbrell*

One of the most notable absentees for this match was Bruce Grobbelaar, the Liverpool goalkeeper having joined Stoke City on loan with his guaranteed starting position in the side slowly being undermined by David James. It was not quite a relegation crunch but both teams were in the bottom half of the table and desperate for the three points. With Mark Wright limping off after 10 minutes, Jan Mølby took centre stage and showed his range of passing talents but was forced to play for the final quarter of the game with a torn hamstring. Hobbling by the end, the Great Dane collected the ball in midfield before setting John Barnes loose down the left wing. The England winger fed Ian Rush who managed to find Ronnie Rosenthal and the Israeli scored the only goal of the game 40 seconds into injury time.

## 18th September 1993

Premier League

**Everton 2**

Ward, Cottee

**Liverpool 0**

*Attendance:* **38,157**

**Everton:** *Southall, Holmes, Hinchcliffe, Ebbrell, Jackson, Ablett, Ward, Horne, Cottee, Rideout, Beagrie (Radosavijevic)*

**Liverpool:** *Grobbelaar, Nicol, Dicks, Whelan, Wright, Ruddock, Clough, Redknapp, Rush, Walters (Rosenthal), McManaman (Stewart)*

Extraordinary scenes followed Mark Ward's opening goal for Everton shortly before the half-hour mark when Bruce Grobbelaar chasing after, and squared up to, Liverpool team-mate Steve McManaman to berate him for the lacklustre clearance to the edge of the penalty area that gave Ward the opportunity to shoot for goal. The visitors had given a debut to former West Ham defender Julian Dicks but were missing the craft of Jan Mølby and failed to create many clear-cut chances. Liverpool had Grobbelaar to thank for keeping them in the match for so long with the veteran keeper saving from Matt Jackson, John Ebbrell, Mark Ward and Tony Cottee, but even his superhuman efforts could not prevent defeat. With Dicks failing to clear the danger, the ball fell to Cottee and the Everton striker made no mistake to double the home side's advantage with just five minutes to go.

## 13th March 1994

Premier League

**Liverpool 2**

Rush, Fowler

**Everton 1**

Watson

*Attendance:* **44,281**

**Liverpool:** *James, Jones, Dicks, Redknapp, Wright, Ruddock, McManaman, Whelan, Rush, Barnes (Thomas), Fowler*

**Everton:** *Southall, Jackson, Hinchcliffe, Ebbrell, Watson, Snodin, Radosavijevic (Horne), Stuart, Cottee, Angell (Rideout), Beagrie*

Robbie Fowler, the kid who grew up an Everton fan, was the toast of the Kop after this match. The Toxteth teenager celebrated his return from a broken leg by scoring a sensational winner for Liverpool and it ensured Fowler, only 18, a place in the record books as the last player to score a derby goal in front of the famous Kop terrace, which was due to be pulled down in the summer and replaced by an all-seater stand. During his two-month lay-off, Fowler had vowed to be back in time to make his derby debut and boss Roy Evans took a gamble by playing him with just 19 minutes of reserve football under his belt. Evans needn't have worried because one of the most natural finishers in the English game simply picked up where he left off with his 16th goal in just 24 senior games and it was a goal to savour as Merseyside celebrated 100 years of English football's most historic local war. There were just two minutes left of the first half when Brett Angell lost possession to John Barnes on the half-way line. Fowler, who learned his craft from Ian Rush, timed his run perfectly onto Barnes' through-pass to beat the offside trap. He was coolness personified as he looked up, waited for Neville Southall to move to cover his near post and then promptly dispatched a perfect shot just inside the far post. Fowler's return gave Liverpool the attacking impetus they had lacked since Evans had taken over six games earlier. But it was a goal from the kid's mentor, Rush, that brought Liverpool back into a frantic game after Everton, looking for their first double over their rivals for nearly 10 years, had taken a shock lead. It came from skipper Dave Watson, who went up with a posse of players to get his head to a superbly flighted 20th-minute free-kick from Serbian import Radosavijevic. But straight from the kick-off Rush stunned Everton with an equalizer. The ball was swept back to Julian Dicks and his long through-pass caught Everton's back four still celebrating. While they hesitated, Rush was onto it with all his typical predatory instincts and, as the ball bounced up, he volleyed past Southall from 15 yards. Everton's lead had lasted precisely 30 seconds and it was Rush's 25th goal in 32 derby appearances. Remarkably, despite that impressive record, it was the Welshman's first in an Anfield derby for seven years. The King of the Kop had vowed to score in front of the famous terrace – and did it with style. The goals lit up an even but scrappy first half which lacked nothing in commitment and passion but was too frantic for real quality. Liverpool certainly had their chances to run up a far more convincing scoreline following their shambolic 2-0 defeat at Goodison earlier in the season.

## 21ˢᵗ November 1994

Premier League

**Everton 2**

Ferguson, Rideout

**Liverpool 0**

*Attendance: 39,866*

**Everton:** *Southall, Jackson (Rideout), Ablett, Ebbrell, Watson, Unsworth, Horne, Parkinson, Amokachi (Limpar), Ferguson, Hinchcliffe*

**Liverpool:** *James, Jones, Bjørnebye (Redknapp), Scales, Babb, Ruddock, McManaman, Mølby, Rush, Barnes, Fowler*

Bad boy Duncan Ferguson had shrugged off the latest problem in his turbulent career to become the toast of Everton. The Rangers loan star had been arrested for an alleged drink-driving offence but put the skids under high-riding Liverpool with his first goal in seven games since starting his temporary move south of the border. With substitute Paul Rideout latching onto a David James blunder before sliding in the second in the last minute, new boss Joe Royle made a dream start to his Goodison reign. Everton's second win of a traumatic season lifted them over Leicester and Ipswich and off the bottom of the Premiership for the first time since 10ᵗʰ September and Royle would have been hoping this well-deserved victory would prove the impetus for a rapid climb away from the danger zone. Liverpool, themselves hoping for a win that would have closed the gap on leaders Manchester United to two points, ended the game well beaten. Liverpool had strong appeals for a second-half penalty waved away by referee Dermot Gallagher when Rideout appeared to handle an Ian Rush effort while both Rob Jones and Steve McManaman flashed shots just wide.

## 24ᵗʰ January 1995

Premier League

**Liverpool 0**

**Everton 0**

*Attendance: 39,505*

**Liverpool:** *James, Jones, Bjørnebye, Scales, Babb, Ruddock, McManaman, Redknapp, Rush, Barnes, Fowler*

**Everton:** *Southall, Jackson, Burrows, Ebbrell, Watson, Unsworth, Horne, Parkinson, Ferguson, Rideout, Hinchcliffe*

Joe Royle's dogs of war sunk their teeth into Liverpool at Anfield – and tore a point out of a rugged Mersey derby battle. Everton snapped and snarled their way through a brutal clash and Liverpool didn't like it one little bit. But this sometimes gory and ultimately goalless draw would do far more for Everton's survival hopes than it would for the title prospects of their rivals. It left Roy Evans' side nine points behind Blackburn, who had a game in hand, and looking to the two Cup competitions for any realistic hope of landing silverware at the end of the season. In the end, though, it lifted resurgent Everton another two places up the table. While they missed out on their first derby double for a decade, they could still draw consolation from the fact that this was the first time since 1985–86 they had taken four points in a season from Liverpool. Royle had sacrificed the flair of Anders Limpar, Vinny Samways, Graham Stuart and Daniel Amokachi for the players he called his dogs of war. Men like Barry Horne, John Ebbrell and Joe Parkinson could run and battle all day – and they were winning bravery medals by the bucketload.

## 18ᵗʰ November 1995

Premier League
**Liverpool 1**
Fowler
**Everton 2**
Kanchelskis 2
*Attendance:* **40,818**
**Liverpool:** *James, Wright, Scales, Babb (Thomas), Jones, McAteer, Barnes, Harkness (Ruddock), McManaman, Fowler, Rush*
**Everton:** *Southall, Jackson, Watson, Short, Ablett (Unsworth), Kanchelskis, Ebbrell, Parkinson, Limpar, Stuart, Rideout*

Ian Rush urged Liverpool to consider a radical tactical rethink after this match to keep their fading title hopes alive. The Anfield skipper believed his team had become too predictable and should mix the long-ball approach with their renowned passing game. Derby game specialist Andrei Kanchelskis kick-started Everton's season with a smash-and-grab double that plunged Roy Evans' team into a bout of serious self-analysis. The first came when Kanchelskis' pace allowed him to reach an Anders Limpar pass to power the ball home, while his second came courtesy of a right-foot rocket. Robbie Fowler grabbed his 13th goal of the season a minute from time but Liverpool's third successive defeat followed an all-too-familiar pattern – bags of possession, but precious little penetration.

## 16th April 1996

Premier League
**Everton 1**
Kanchelskis
**Liverpool 1**
*Fowler Attendance: 40,120*
**Everton:** *Southall, Hottiger, Hinchcliffe, Ebbrell, Watson, Unsworth, Kanchelskis, Horne, Ferguson, Amokachi (Stuart), Grant*
**Liverpool:** *James, McAteer, Jones, Scales, Wright, Ruddock (Thomas), McManaman, Redknapp (Rush), Collymore, Barnes, Fowler*

Goal thief Robbie Fowler salvaged Liverpool's Merseyside derby pride at rain-lashed Goodison Park when he popped up three minutes from the end of a mistake-ridden match to grab a dramatic equalizer and deny Everton their first double over their bitter rivals for 11 years. A draw may have been a fair result – but that result did neither team any good. It finally killed off Liverpool's lingering title hopes and left Everton struggling to make fifth spot and qualify for the next season's UEFA Cup. Derby specialist Andrei Kanchelskis' first-half goal looked set to give Joe Royle his third win in four derbies since taking over as Goodison boss, but with the seconds ticking away Stan Collymore's superb cross provided Fowler with the chance to stab in his 36th goal of the season. It had been fitting that Collymore should have been the provider: he was Liverpool's best player. Collymore had been denied a goal himself by the crossbar and two outstanding Neville Southall saves – but he would have been satisfied with his outstanding contribution. Everton bossed the first half when Liverpool looked totally ill-at-ease on a waterlogged pitch that severely hampered their fluent style, but they bounced back superbly after a half-time roasting from Roy Evans and Fowler's equalizer gave them a deserved point. It had been no surprise when Kanchelskis put Everton ahead after 18 minutes. Neville Southall's huge clearance bounced over Mark Wright and David James lost out to John Ebbrell as the ball skidded towards the byline. Ebbrell somehow managed to screw his shot from an almost impossible angle against the crossbar. As the ball dropped, Kanchelskis bundled aside Rob Jones to chest down and ram his shot home from six yards. The Ukrainian raider had carried his love of derby games from Manchester to Merseyside. The previous season he scored four for United in their two games against City and he opened his Everton account with two at Anfield in a 2-1 win. This strike was his sixth in six games, giving him 13 for the season and underlined Royle's belief that he spent £5 million on a goalscoring front man rather than an old-fashioned winger. Collymore and David Unsworth squared up to each other after just two minutes to set the tone for a passionate but untidy game. Neil Ruddock, returning from this third suspension of the season, was cautioned after only six minutes for a late challenge on Tony Grant. Liverpool had David James to thank for keeping the score down in the first half. The giant keeper made outstanding stops from Duncan Ferguson and Daniel Amokachi, but Liverpool were a different side after the break. Collymore always looked the likeliest man to break Everton hearts. He rattled the bar with a 30-yard blockbuster then saw Southall acrobatically save two other long-range efforts. Liverpool were running out of time when Evans decided to throw on Ian Rush and Michael Thomas for Ruddock and Jamie Redknapp. Collymore's swinging cross eluded the Everton defence and Fowler latched onto it like a shot at the far post.

## 20th November 1996

Premier League
**Liverpool 1**
Fowler
**Everton 1**
Speed
*Attendance:* 40,751

**Liverpool:** *James, Bjørnebye, Wright, Ruddock, Matteo, McAteer, Redknapp, McManaman (Collymore), Barnes, Thomas, Fowler*
**Everton:** *Southall, Barrett, Hinchcliffe, Unsworth, Watson, Parkinson, Kanchelskis (Ferguson), Stuart, Barmby, Grant, Speed*

Liverpool's hopes of returning to the top of the Premiership were hit by their Royle curse at Anfield. Roy Evans' team had forgotten what it was like to savour the sweet taste of a derby victory since Joe Royle had taken command of Everton. It was two years ago that Royle launched his reign at Goodison with a shock 2-0 victory over their rivals – and since then he'd continued an unbeaten sequence of a win and three draws. Liverpool were just eight minutes away from the win that would have leapfrogged them a point clear of Newcastle at the top after Robbie Fowler headed in his ninth goal of an eight-game purple patch, but Royle had put the pride and resilience back into Everton. It was no real surprise when Gary Speed glanced home an equalizer that stretched their unbeaten run to seven games. The Welsh ace had sparked Everton to their biggest League win for 25 years the previous Saturday with a hat-trick in the 7-1 humiliation of Southampton and that night he was the toast of the blue half of Merseyside thanks to his seventh goal of the season. The point was no more than Everton deserved after they had bossed long spells of a pulsating clash. The Reds weren't helped by a worrying hamstring injury to their key man, Steve McManaman. He pulled up after just eight minutes, came back on after treatment but was clearly not happy and was replaced by Stan Collymore. Evans' decision to send on his £9.5 million buy instead of Patrik Berger stunned many – but Stan the Man, out of favour this season, helped to turn the game Liverpool's way. He forced Liverpool's corner after 25 minutes and from Stig Inge Bjørnebye's kick Mark Wright saw a towering header cleared off the line by Speed. Everton's relief was short-lived because Liverpool took the lead from a 30th-minute corner. Dave Watson headed Bjørnebye's kick back to the Norwegian who quickly fed Jamie Redknapp and his cross found Fowler unmarked. The equalizer came in the 82nd minute. Dominic Matteo, like Nicky Barmby, an impressive derby debutant, fouled Graham Stuart just outside the box. Set-piece specialist Andy Hinchcliffe swung over his cross and Speed rose to plant a superb header just inside the far post. Everton had two chances to snatch a dramatic winner with Bjørnebye hacking the ball off the line after a scramble following David Unsworth's challenge on James. Then, in injury time, substitute Duncan Ferguson – on at half-time for Andrei Kanchelskis – shot too close to James.

## 16<sup>th</sup> April 1997

Premier League
**Everton 1**
Ferguson
**Liverpool 1**
Redknapp
*Attendance:* **40,177**
**Everton:** *Southall, Barrett, Unsworth, Short (Ball), Watson, Dunne, Stuart, Branch, Ferguson, Thomsen (Barmby), Speed*
**Liverpool:** *James, Kvarme, Bjørnebye, Wright, Harkness, Jones (McAteer), Redknapp, McManaman, Barnes, Thomas, Fowler*

The race for the Premier League Championship erupted into all-out war with Robbie Fowler seeing red as Liverpool hit the self-destruct button yet again. Fowler, the Premiership's leading scorer, was sent off in shame along with Everton defender David Unsworth for fighting as a high-octane clash of the Mersey clans caught light seven minutes from the end. The brawling pair had to be pulled apart by team-mates . . . and even then it wasn't over. After referee Stephen Lodge dismissed them both, Fowler went back for more by foolishly flicking his hand into Unsworth's face. Liverpool physio Mark Leather and assistant boss Doug Livermore raced onto the pitch to pull him away and escort him down the tunnel. Unsworth was held back by police and stewards to prevent any further clashes on the way to the dressing rooms. The trouble had been brewing for a while, with Unsworth and Fowler niggling away at each other. Their simmering feud finally erupted when the burly Unsworth sent Fowler crashing to the floor with a crude challenge. Fowler simply flipped and went straight for his opponent as the game went on. Finally, Barnsley official Lodge caught sight of the punch-up and took the only action that was open to him. It was a dramatic end to a night that could well have signalled the end of Liverpool's title dream. This frustrating draw left them two points adrift of Manchester United, having played a game more. Scottish braveheart Duncan Ferguson was the man who plunged the dagger into Liverpool's hearts with a stunning 66th-minute equalizer. There looked little danger when Steve Harkness headed away a Graham Stuart cross but Ferguson, with his back to goal 20 yards out, turned superbly and buried a fierce shot past David James and into the bottom corner of the net. It cancelled out Jamie Redknapp's first ever derby goal in the 26th minute. Immediately after Ferguson's strike, Neville Southall marked his 40th Mersey derby appearance with a brilliant save from Redknapp. Southall then stood and watched in utter relief as first Fowler's header cannoned off the bar and then saw his shot strike the outside of a post. Maybe it was the frustration of those near-misses that led to Fowler's moment of madness later in the game. No one had worked harder than the little Scouser to bring about the victory Liverpool so badly needed. He had supplied a pass to send Steve McManaman away for the cross from which Redknapp slid in to score. The lead was no more than Liverpool deserved at that stage. Everton had suffered a worrying blow after only 17 minutes when Craig Short tumbled over Fowler and injured his neck. Everton took a while to reorganize but could have been level at the break but for two outstanding saves by James – first from Ferguson's towering header and then from Claus Thomsen's close-range volley. Liverpool, in control for most of the first half, had to spend much of the second period on the back foot as Everton bombarded their penalty area with crosses. It was ironic, then, that their equalizer should come from an outstanding piece of skill by Ferguson on the deck. Liverpool simply couldn't seem to break their Mersey jinx. They hadn't beaten their bitter rivals in the last six encounters but the latest result in the depressing sequence was likely to prove the most costly.

## 18th October 1997

Premier League
**Everton 2**
Ruddock (og), Cadamarteri
**Liverpool 0**

*Attendance:* 40,112

**Everton:** *Southall, Barrett, Hinchcliffe, Williamson, Watson, Short, Stuart, Cadamarteri (Ball), Ferguson, Oster (McCann), Speed*

**Liverpool:** *James, Bjørnebye, Kvarme, Ruddock, McManaman, Thomas, McAteer, Ince, Berger (Leonhardsen), Riedle (Owen), Fowler*

Roy Evans took his Liverpool side to Strasbourg following this derby defeat. Much of the talk after the game was about whether Karl-Heinz Riedle and Patrik Berger would be fit for the UEFA Cup clash. Both had limped out of the 2-0 humiliation at Everton, Riedle with a groin strain and Berger with an Achilles injury. Evans, though, dismissed the European clash as a reason for such a dismal Goodison display that saw Liverpool fail to break their sequence of not having won a Mersey derby match in seven attempts. The home side took the lead just before the interval when Gary Speed flicked on Andy Hinchcliffe's corner and the unfortunate Neil Ruddock turned the ball into his own net. Their second was much more dramatic and came courtesy of 18-year-old Danny Cadamarteri. The youngster dispossessed Bjørn Tore Kvarme on the left before cutting inside Ruddock and unleashing a low shot that beat David James.

## 23rd February 1998

Premier League
### Liverpool 1
Ince
### Everton 1
Ferguson
*Attendance:* 44,501

**Liverpool:** *James, Harkness, Jones, Kvarme, Leonhardsen, Ince, Redknapp, Carragher, McManaman, Fowler (Murphy), Owen*

**Everton:** *Myhre, Ward, Ball, Tiler, Watson, Bilić, Farrelly, Thomsen, Ferguson, Cadamarteri (Oster), Madar (McCann)*

Duncan Ferguson signed off for a spell in soccer's sinbin by virtually killing off Liverpool's title hopes. Big bad Fergie went some way to making amends for the red card that would remove him from Everton's relegation battle for the next three games. Certainly Everton fans were prepared to forgive him anything after he struck a superb goal that extended his remarkable unbeaten sequence against their Merseyside foes to eight games. Paul Ince scrambled an equalizer which may have salvaged some local pride for Liverpool but did little for their hopes of catching Manchester United. Roy Evans' team remained nine points adrift of the leaders with 11 games to go and second place now looked the best they could expect – and even then they faced a tough battle to shake off the attentions of Arsenal, Chelsea and Blackburn Rovers. It could have been worse for Liverpool as Mickaël Madar had missed a sitter – after a David James blunder – which would have made it 2-0 and the Frenchman's embarrassment at missing an open goal deepened moments later when Ince notched the equalizer after Slaven Bilić's clearance had bounced off Claus Thomsen to leave the Liverpool skipper with a chance he converted with assurance. Everton, though, finished the game much the happier team and Ferguson showed what it meant to him by spurning handshakes to give a fist-clenching salute to the blue section of a capacity crowd – Anfield's biggest since the Kop was made all-seater four years earlier. Ferguson, who had never been on the losing side in a Mersey battle, would have licked his lips in anticipation when he saw Liverpool's makeshift defence. Evans was without six defenders and while his team was never going to compete with the giant Scot in the air, they worked hard to deprive him of decent service. They coped pretty well, despite their lack of height, but just one lapse proved so costly. It came in the 58th minute when they were caught flat-footed from Michael Ball's long throw. Madar nodded the ball down and Ferguson's right boot did the rest as he swivelled to bury his ninth goal of the season – and his third in Mersey derbies. It came against the run of play, but Everton should have wrapped it up when Madar shot wide with the goal at his mercy after James had collided with Rob Jones and Ferguson had headed the ball into the Frenchman's path. Ince, Liverpool's own Captain Marvel, sparked a frantic late onslaught with his desperately needed equalizer after 68 minutes but Liverpool finished a frustrated team. It was now four years since they had tasted a derby win and it might have been different had Michael Owen twice not squandered the sort of chance he'd been scoring in his sleep during a remarkable debut season. Twice Steve McManaman put him clear, but on the first occasion the youngster dragged his shot wide and with the second he drove his shot straight at Thomas Myhre. Norwegian Myhre also frustrated Øyvind Leonhardsen and Jamie Redknapp in an impressive derby debut. He had a daunting task taking over from Neville Southall but the veteran Welshman would have been the first to applaud Myhre's display. It contrasted sharply with another jittery show from James. Everton produced the sort of commitment and work-rate which had typified their recent derby performances. Liverpool matched them in that department and bossed most of the game without enjoying a lot of luck. Every time a glimmer of a chance opened up for them, an Everton body seemed to get in the way and when the defensive fortress was breached there was always Myhre to come to the rescue.

## 17ᵗʰ October 1998

Premier League
**Everton 0**
**Liverpool 0**
*Attendance: 40,185*
**Everton:** *Myhre, Cleland, Ball, Short, Watson, Unsworth, Collins, Grant (Cadamarteri), Ferguson, Bakayoko (Ward), Hutchison*
**Liverpool:** *James, Bjørnebye, Carragher (Kvarme), Staunton, Heggem, Redknapp (McAteer), Berger (Riedle), McManaman, Ince, Owen, Fowler*

This match went down in the history books as one of the most uninspiring Merseyside derbies ever. True, there was passion and commitment – seven bookings are testimony to that – but there was little in the way of creativity or flair. Everton fans were left still waiting at the end of the match to witness their first goal that season at Goodison Park, although new signing Ibrahima Bakayoko glanced a Michael Ball header just wide in the first minute. Michael Owen could have wrapped it up in the closing stages but was shut out by man of the match Dave Watson.

## 3rd April 1999

Premier League

**Liverpool 3**

Fowler 2 (1 pen), Berger

**Everton 2**

Dacourt, Jeffers

*Attendance: 44,852*

**Liverpool:** *James, Heggem (Gerrard), Matteo, Staunton, Song, Redknapp, McManaman, Ince, Berger, Fowler (Riedle), Owen Everton: Myhre, Short, Ball, Unsworth, Watson, Materazzi (Weir), Gemmill, Barmby (Jeffers), Campbell, Dacourt, Branch (Cadamarteri)*

After the painful bore draw at Goodison Park earlier in the season, this match was anything but dull with Olivier Dacourt opening the scoring after just 41 seconds. The Frenchman – one of several derby debutants who included Kevin Campbell and Scott Gemmill – latched onto Steve Staunton's defensive header to unleash a 30-yard rocket past David James. Robbie Fowler equalized from the penalty spot 15 minutes later but his goal celebrations proved controversial when he dropped to his knees and pretended to snort the goal-line. The striker claimed his second just six minutes later when he headed home a Patrik Berger corner while the Czech got on the scoresheet himself when he volleyed the ball into the net with eight minutes remaining. Francis Jeffers reduced the deficit two minutes later and Danny Cadamarteri was denied a dramatic late equalizer when Steven Gerrard cleared off the line with James stranded.

## 27th September 1999

Premier League

**Liverpool 0**

**Everton 1**

Campbell

*Attendance: 44,802*

**Liverpool:** *Westerveld, Hyypiä, Carragher, Staunton, Heggem, Berger, Hamann (Meijer), Redknapp, Šmicer (Camara), Owen, Fowler (Gerrard)*

**Everton:** *Gerrard, Weir, Ball, Xavier, Dunne, Gough, Collins, Barmby, Campbell, Hutchison, Jeffers*

No one was prepared for the frenzied scenes of bare-knuckle fighting that ignited this Merseyside derby. In what was almost a surreal incident, Everton flyweight Francis Jeffers gave about six stone to Sander Westerveld as he traded punches with the Liverpool keeper in the penalty area 15 minutes from time. The little Everton striker got nothing more than a red card, along with Westerveld, for his efforts. Liverpool – who had used all their substitutes – were forced to put full-back Steve Staunton in goal and he went on to produce the save of the match. This match underlined the commitment and passion of both teams as the game boiled over in the dying seconds in a flurry of red cards. Liverpool substitute Steven Gerrard was also dismissed, on the stroke of full-time, for an appalling waist-high challenge on Kevin Campbell that caught the Everton forward in a place that cranked his voice up a couple of octaves. It could have been worse – referee Mike Riley was guilty of a dereliction of duty when he chose the soft option in failing to dismiss Michael Owen in the first half. Owen produced an awful challenge when he miscontrolled a through-ball and lunged into a horrendous assault on David Weir. It was frustration at losing a run on goal, rather than any great malice, that caused him to perpetrate the ugly deed. Even so, it was a two-footed horror show that deserved a red card but Riley clearly lacked the authority to control such a passionate, high-tempo match as he displayed a series of mistakes, which also saw him miss another brutal challenge from Everton's Don Hutchison. In the frenzy of all this action, it was easy to overlook the merits of a wonderful display by Everton, who turned in a gritty, accomplished performance to completely outplay their local rivals. A solitary and well-crafted goal by Campbell hardly did justice to a dominant display from Walter Smith's side, who created virtually all the chances and could have won more easily. Quite simply, Liverpool lost because they never matched Everton's desire or ability to move the ball with pace and precision. Too many players were clearly not match-fit and, as manager Gérard Houllier conceded, they were never at the races. It took just four minutes for Liverpool to fall behind. Nick Barmby started the move on the left, but Jeffers contributed a superb turn and an even better pass to put Campbell in behind the back line. The Everton striker took one touch and slammed the ball goalwards. Even though Westerveld got a hand to it, he could not deflect it from its course into the corner of the net.

## 21st April 2000

Premier League
**Everton 0**
**Liverpool 0**
*Attendance: 40,052*
**Everton:** *Gerrard, Dunne, Pembridge (Ball), Unsworth, Weir, Xavier, Collins, Barmby (Ward), M. Hughes (Jeffers), Hutchison, S. Hughes*
**Liverpool:** *Westerveld, Carragher, Matteo, Hamann, Henchoz, Hyypiä, Gerrard, Thompson (Heggem), Heskey (Fowler), Owen, Berger*

That this game finished goalless was beyond comprehension for most of the spectators. Michael Owen had three opportunities to put Liverpool in front but was thwarted each time by Paul Gerrard, while Mark Hughes unbelievably shot wide when clear through in the second half. But the biggest controversy was the manner in which referee Graham Poll ended the match. In the final minute, Sander Westerveld took a free-kick that bounced off the back of Don Hutchison. The Everton player had not retreated the 10 yards required by law yet when the ball careered into the Liverpool net and the Blues began to celebrate. Poll, however, had other ideas and claimed he had blown for full-time as the ball was kicked and before it had crossed the line so declared the game a draw.

# Chapter Ten

# The 21st Century

While Everton's League record improved so they were more consistently a top-10 team, neither Merseyside club could top the Premier League in its first 20 years. Liverpool did, however, come close with second-place finishes behind Arsenal in 2001–02 and Manchester United in 2008–09. Numerous managers came and went on Merseyside with Everton's David Moyes staying the longest and Cup competitions became more important in the absence of League success. Liverpool added two FA Cups, three League Cups, a UEFA Cup and a Champions League to their trophy cabinet while Everton's best showing was a 2009 FA Cup Final defeat at the hands of Chelsea.

## Record in the 21st Century

**Everton**

| Season | League | P | W | D | L | F | A | Pts | Pos |
|--------|--------|-----|-----|-----|-----|-----|-----|-----|-----|
| 2000–01 | Prem | 38 | 11 | 9 | 18 | 45 | 59 | 42 | 16 |
| 2001–02 | Prem | 38 | 11 | 10 | 17 | 45 | 57 | 43 | 15 |
| 2002–03 | Prem | 38 | 17 | 8 | 13 | 48 | 49 | 59 | 7 |
| 2003–04 | Prem | 38 | 9 | 12 | 17 | 45 | 57 | 39 | 17 |
| 2004–05 | Prem | 38 | 18 | 7 | 13 | 45 | 46 | 61 | 4 |
| 2005–06 | Prem | 38 | 14 | 8 | 16 | 34 | 49 | 50 | 11 |
| 2006–07 | Prem | 38 | 15 | 13 | 10 | 52 | 36 | 58 | 6 |
| 2007–08 | Prem | 38 | 19 | 8 | 11 | 55 | 33 | 65 | 5 |
| 2008–09 | Prem | 38 | 17 | 12 | 9 | 55 | 37 | 63 | 5 |
| 2009–10 | Prem | 38 | 16 | 13 | 9 | 60 | 49 | 61 | 8 |
| 2010–11 | Prem | 38 | 13 | 15 | 10 | 51 | 45 | 54 | 7 |
| 2011–12 | Prem | 38 | 15 | 11 | 12 | 50 | 40 | 56 | 7 |
| 2012–13 | Prem | 38 | 16 | 15 | 7 | 55 | 40 | 63 | 6 |

## FA Cup

| | |
|---|---|
| 2000–01 | 0-3 v Tranmere Rovers (Fourth Round) |
| 2001–02 | 0-3 v Middlesbrough (Quarter-final) |
| 2002–03 | 1-2 v Shrewsbury Town (Third Round) |
| 2003–04 | 1-1, 1-2 v Fulham (Fourth Round) |
| 2004–05 | 0-2 v Manchester United (Fifth Round) |
| 2005–06 | 1-1, 1-4 v Chelsea (Fourth Round) |
| 2006–07 | 1-4 v Blackburn Rovers (Third Round) |
| 2007–08 | 0-1 v Oldham Athletic (Third Round) |
| 2008–09 | 1-2 v Chelsea (Final) |
| 2009–10 | 1-2 v Birmingham City (Fourth Round) |
| 2010–11 | 0-1 v Reading (Fifth Round) |
| 2011–12 | 1-2 v Liverpool (Semi-final) |
| 2012–13 | 0-3 v Wigan Athletic (Quarter-final) |

## League Cup

| | |
|---|---|
| 2000–01 | 1-1, 1-1 (2-4 on pens) v Bristol Rovers (Second Round) |
| 2001–02 | 1-1 (4-5 on pens) v Crystal Palace (Second Round) |
| 2002–03 | 1-4 v Chelsea (Fourth Round) |
| 2003–04 | 0-0 (4-5 on pens) v Middlesbrough (Fourth Round) |
| 2004–05 | 1-3 v Arsenal (Fourth Round) |
| 2005–06 | 0-1 v Middlesbrough (Third Round) |
| 2006–07 | 0-1 v Arsenal (Fourth Round) |
| 2007–08 | 1-2, 0-1 v Chelsea (Semi-final) |
| 2008–09 | 0-1 v Blackburn Rovers (Third Round) |
| 2009–10 | 0-2 v Tottenham Hotspur (Fourth Round) |
| 2010–11 | 1-1 (3-4 on pens) v Brentford (Third Round) |
| 2011–12 | 1-2 v Chelsea (Fourth Round) |
| 2012–13 | 1-2 v Leeds United (Third Round) |

## Europe

| | |
|---|---|
| 2000–01 | Did not qualify |
| 2001–02 | Did not qualify |
| 2002–03 | Did not qualify |
| 2003–04 | Did not qualify |
| 2004–05 | Did not qualify |

| | |
|---|---|
| 2005–06 | Champions League: 1-2, 1-2 v Villarreal (Third Qualifying Round) |
| 2006–07 | Did not qualify |
| 2007–08 | UEFA Cup: 0-2, 2-0 (2-4 on pens) v Fiorentina (Round of 16) |
| 2008–09 | UEFA Cup: 2-2, 1-2 v Standard Liège (First Round) |
| 2009–10 | Europa League: 2-1, 0-3 v Sporting CP (Round of 32) |
| 2010–11 | Did not qualify |
| 2011–12 | Did not qualify |
| 2012–13 | Did not qualify |

## Liverpool

| Season | League | P | W | D | L | F | A | Pts | Pos |
|---|---|---|---|---|---|---|---|---|---|
| 2000–01 | Prem | 38 | 20 | 9 | 9 | 71 | 39 | 69 | 3 |
| 2001–02 | Prem | 38 | 24 | 8 | 6 | 67 | 30 | 80 | 2 |
| 2002–03 | Prem | 38 | 18 | 10 | 10 | 61 | 41 | 64 | 5 |
| 2003–04 | Prem | 38 | 16 | 12 | 10 | 55 | 37 | 60 | 4 |
| 2004–05 | Prem | 38 | 17 | 7 | 14 | 52 | 41 | 58 | 5 |
| 2005–06 | Prem | 38 | 25 | 7 | 6 | 57 | 25 | 82 | 3 |
| 2006–07 | Prem | 38 | 20 | 8 | 10 | 57 | 27 | 68 | 3 |
| 2007–08 | Prem | 38 | 21 | 13 | 4 | 67 | 28 | 76 | 4 |
| 2008–09 | Prem | 38 | 25 | 11 | 2 | 77 | 27 | 86 | 2 |
| 2009–10 | Prem | 38 | 18 | 9 | 11 | 61 | 35 | 63 | 7 |
| 2010–11 | Prem | 38 | 17 | 7 | 14 | 59 | 44 | 58 | 6 |
| 2011–12 | Prem | 38 | 14 | 10 | 14 | 47 | 40 | 52 | 8 |
| 2012–13 | Prem | 38 | 16 | 13 | 9 | 71 | 43 | 61 | 7 |

## FA Cup

| | |
|---|---|
| 2000–01 | 2-1 v Arsenal (Final) |
| 2001–02 | 0-1 v Arsenal (Fourth Round) |
| 2002–03 | 0-0, 0-2 v Crystal Palace (Fourth Round) |
| 2003–04 | 1-1, 0-1 v Portsmouth (Fifth Round) |
| 2004–05 | 0-1 v Burnley (Third Round) |
| 2005–06 | 3-3 (3-1 on pens) v West Ham United (Final) |
| 2006–07 | 1-3 v Arsenal (Third Round) |
| 2007–08 | 1-2 v Barnsley (Fifth Round) |

| 2008–09 | 1-1, 0-1 v Everton (Fourth Round) |
| 2009–10 | 1-1, 1-2 v Reading (Third Round) |
| 2010–11 | 0-1 v Manchester United (Third Round) |
| 2011–12 | 1-2 v Chelsea (Final) |
| 2012–13 | 2-3 v Oldham Athletic (Fourth Round) |

### League Cup

| 2000–01 | 1-1 (5-4 on pens) v Birmingham City (Final) |
| 2001–02 | 1-2 v Grimsby Town (Third Round) |
| 2002–03 | 2-0 v Manchester United (Final) |
| 2003–04 | 2-3 v Bolton Wanderers (Fourth Round) |
| 2004–05 | 2-3 v Chelsea (Final) |
| 2005–06 | 1-3 v Crystal Palace (Third Round) |
| 2006–07 | 3-6 v Arsenal (Quarter-final) |
| 2007–08 | 0-2 v Chelsea (Quarter-final) |
| 2008–09 | 2-4 v Tottenham Hotspur (Fourth Round) |
| 2009–10 | 1-2 v Arsenal (Fourth Round) |
| 2010–11 | 2-2 (2-4 on pens) v Northampton Town (Third Round) |
| 2011–12 | 2-2 (3-2 on pens) v Cardiff City (Final) |
| 2012–13 | 1-3 v Swansea City (Fourth Round) |

### Europe

| 2000–01 | UEFA Cup: 5-4 v Alavés (Final) |
| 2001–02 | Champions League: 1-0, 2-4 v Bayer Leverkusen (Quarter-final) |
| 2002–03 | Champions League: first group stage; UEFA Cup: 1-1, 0-2 v Celtic (Quarter-final) |
| 2003–04 | UEFA Cup: 1-1, 1-2 v Marseille (Fourth Round) |
| 2004–05 | Champions League: 3-3 (3-2 on pens) v AC Milan (Final) |
| 2005–06 | Champions League : 0-1, 0-2 v Benfica (First Knockout Round) |
| 2006–07 | Champions League: 1-2 v AC Milan (Final) |
| 2007–08 | Champions League: 1-1, 2-3 v Chelsea (Semi-final) |
| 2008–09 | Champions League: 1-3, 4-4 v Chelsea (Quarter-final) |
| 2009–10 | Champions League: first group stage; Europa League 0-1, 2-1 (away goals) v Atlético Madrid (Semi-final) |
| 2010–11 | Europa League: 0-1, 0-0 v SC Braga (Round of 16) |
| 2011–12 | Did not qualify |

2012–13    Europa League: 0-2, 3-1 (away goals) v Zenit St Petersburg
           (Round of 32)

# The Matches

## 29th October 2000

Premier League
**Liverpool 3**
Barmby, Heskey, Berger (pen)
**Everton 1**
Campbell
*Attendance: 44,718*
**Liverpool:** *Westerveld, Ziege, Babbel, Hyypiä, Berger, Hamann, Gerrard (Carragher), Barmby, McAllister, Heskey, Fowler (Šmicer)*
**Everton:** *Gerrard, Watson, Ball (Naysmith), Xavier, Weir, Gravesen, Nyarko, Gascoigne, Campbell, Pembridge, Tal (Moore)*

Gérard Houllier's side secured an ultimately comfortable victory over old enemies Everton but not before displaying a character swing that would alarm Dr Jekyll. It was a performance that summed up perfectly their schizophrenic season, lurching from the sublime to the ridiculous in two hugely contrasting halves. The win took Liverpool to third in the table and, perhaps more importantly, gave them only their second victory in 13 derby matches. Given Everton's stirring contribution, it was a display – in the second half at least – that warranted praise, particularly towards Emile Heskey. It was his stunning goal that turned the game in Liverpool's favour and one that summed up his attributes perfectly . . . pace, power and an instinctive finish that possessed deadly venom. After an almost spookily predictable opening goal from Nick Barmby, Liverpool had lost control and belief to such an extent that Everton were level and threatening to run away with the match. Cue Heskey. A nagging, muscular presence all afternoon, his goal was as delicious as it was timely. On 55 minutes, with the game in the balance, he powered onto a weak defensive header from Everton sub Gary Naysmith and unleashed a shot that skidded across the turf like a Barnes Wallis special. It was enough to burst through Everton keeper

Paul Gerrard's dam, and throw the floodgates open for the home side. One moment of lapsed concentration on 76 minutes meant there was no way back for Everton, and again it was the unfortunate Naysmith who was the culprit. The young Scotland defender failed to control a Sander Westerveld clearance as the ball bounced in front of him and allowed Vladimír Šmicer to sprint towards the penalty area. When Thomas Gravesen lunged desperately in an attempt to stop him, referee Paul Durkin had little option but to point to the spot. Given the conditions, he was perhaps harsh to dismiss Gravesen – who had looked Everton's best performer alongside Paul Gascoigne – and when he trudged off he took Everton's last hopes with him. Patrik Berger lashed home the penalty and victory was sealed. The remaining minutes proved something of an anti-climax, though such serenity was in complete contrast to a mad opening as Barmby's goal ignited already combustible passions. It was his first League goal for Liverpool, and a belter too – even if you had very little chance of finding an Evertonian in agreement. When Christian Ziege's shot was deflected by Abel Xavier, Barmby was the first to react to send a tracer of a header into the top of the net. There was more than a hint of a foul from Fowler on Michael Ball but, if any justice was required, Everton applied it six minutes later. From an Idan Tal corner, David Weir rose above the exposed Barmby at the far post to head back for Kevin Campbell to steer his header into the net with Reds keeper Westerveld AWOL.

## 16th April 2001

Premier League
**Everton 2**
Ferguson, Unsworth (pen)
**Liverpool 3**
Heskey, Babbel, McAllister
*Attendance:* **40,260**
**Everton:** *Gerrard, Watson (Pistone), Unsworth, Gough (Alexandersson), Weir, Ball, Nyarko, Gemmill, Campbell, Ferguson, Xavier*
**Liverpool:** *Westerveld, Henchoz, Babbel, Hyypiä, Carragher, Šmicer, Hamann, McAllister, Bišćan, Heskey, Fowler (Vignal)*

## EVERTON vs LIVERPOOL

Even by derby standards, this one scaled new heights in sheer nail-biting tension and unbelievable storyline. It had it all, and then more: 11 yellow cards and one red; two penalties that should not have been given and were – one of them missed; and two that should have been given that were not. All in all, a far from vintage display of refereeing by Jeff Winter. There were two incredible comebacks, four incredible goals and, finally, a winner with the last kick of the game from 44 yards from a man who should not even still have been on the pitch. There was also a bust-up at the end where the Liverpool assistant boss was involved in an ugly exchange with an Everton player that has no place in football. Yet, Gary McAllister's astonishing free-kick breathed new life into Liverpool's Champions League hopes. It was a fairytale end to a fantasy football match, giving Liverpool their first win at Goodison Park for over 11 years and, more importantly, three points that allowed them to narrow the gap on Ipswich to six points with two games in hand. Nothing though could possibly be as drama-laden as McAllister's winner, not least because Everton would argue that he should have been dismissed for a second bookable offence just seconds before his jaw-dropping goal. The veteran Scot appeared to handle a pass from David Unsworth and that – allied to his earlier booking for dissent – should have required him to make the long walk that Igor Biščan endured earlier for his own two bookings. Referee Winter though – as he had done all evening – simply missed the crucial offence and waved play on before blowing for a Liverpool free-kick moments later, a decision not without controversy as well because Niclas Alexandersson appeared to win the ball cleanly. With the game in the third minute of injury time, McAllister picked up the ball and miraculously spotted Paul Gerrard dashing too far across his goal-line. With incredible accuracy and even more incredible audacity, he fired the ball into the far corner of the net. It was cruel on Everton but probably no more than Liverpool deserved because, even when they had Biščan dismissed on 77 minutes, they kept battling to the end, despite a missed penalty from Robbie Fowler. Both were slightly unlucky because Biščan's second offence was hardly serious, although his earlier elbow on Michael Ball probably was. Fowler, for his part, stroked a penalty on the hour that was almost perfect, apart from the fact that he hit the inside of the post and not the back of the net. Everton would claim that the referee was wrong again because Fowler won the penalty in dubious circumstances when he theatrically tumbled over Richard Gough. It was a miss that appeared costly, because it would have given Liverpool a 3-1 lead and put the game beyond Everton, but instead inspired them to what appeared to be a remarkable comeback. They had trailed early and with a goal of certain irony given that Everton had clearly entered the game with the sole intention of launching the ball forward high and early, aiming at their twin towers of Duncan Ferguson and Kevin Campbell. Before the bombing operation could even get properly under way, though, Liverpool had travelled down Route One themselves. Everton, predictably, had sent in a high and hopeful ball towards Ferguson that looked like it had been handled by Jamie Carragher. Whatever the legality of the challenge, Liverpool were away and running when Dietmar Hamann smashed the loose ball towards Emile Heskey. The big striker still seemed to have plenty to do but the Everton defence parted and Heskey was left with the simple task of charging unattended close enough to goal to unleash an unstoppable right-foot shot. The response came on the stroke of half-time when a long ball from defence saw Ferguson get above an uncomfortable-looking Sami Hyypiä. Even though Carragher did well with a lunging tackle to stop Campbell in his tracks, the ball broke invitingly for Ferguson to smash home. Liverpool's second came just after the interval when Hamann picked up a defensive header from Dave Watson's free-kick into the Liverpool box. The German marched forward and delivered a superb pass to Fowler, who provided an equally skillful cross from the left which Ball could only deflect into the path of Markus Babbel. The unlikely marauder gleefully stabbed home a right-foot shot from 12 yards. Both sides had decent penalty claims turned down – a trip on Vladimír Šmicer and a blatant Hamann hand ball – before yet another controversial decision seemed to give Everton an amazing point. Winter decided that Hyypiä had held down Ferguson and Unsworth remained calm to convert the penalty seven minutes from time.

# 15th September 2001

Premier League

**Everton 1**

Campbell

**Liverpool 3**

Gerrard, Owen (pen), Riise

*Attendance: 39,554*

**Everton:** *Gerrard, Watson, Naysmith, Stubbs, Weir, Unsworth (Gascoigne), Alexandersson (Hibbert), Gravesen, Campbell, Ferguson, Xavier (Radzinski)*

**Liverpool:** *Dudek, Henchoz, Hyypiä, Riise, Carragher, Vignal, Murphy (McAllister), Hamann, Gerrard (Šmicer), Heskey, Owen*

Everton drew first blood in this early-season encounter when Kevin Campbell collected a flick-on from Duncan Ferguson, turned Sami Hyypiä and thundered the ball past Jerzy Dudek to open the scoring for the home side within five minutes. It wasn't long, though, before Liverpool's talisman Steven Gerrard levelled the match after a poor defensive header failed to clear the danger in the Everton penalty area. The midfielder left Gary Naysmith in his wake and drove the ball past Paul Gerrard into the far corner of the net. The Everton keeper prevented his near namesake doubling his tally with a right-handed save but was unable to do anything about Michael Owen's penalty after David Unsworth had fouled Emile Heskey. Didi Hamann wasted a glorious opportunity to extend Liverpool's lead shortly before the interval but, early in the second half, John Arne Riise netted the Reds' third. Latching onto a pass from Danny Murphy, the Norwegian managed to turn Steve Watson before steering the ball past the helpless Gerrard. Although the home side created several chances as Liverpool took their foot off the pedal, it was the red half of Merseyside which was celebrating at the final whistle.

# 23rd February 2002

Premier League

**Liverpool 1**

Anelka

**Everton 1**

Radzinski

*Attendance: 44,371*
**Liverpool:** *Kirkland, Henchoz, Xavier, Hyypiä, Riise, Wright (Heskey), Murphy, Hamann, McAllister (Šmicer), Anelka, Owen*
**Everton:** *Simonsen, Clarke, Pistone, Stubbs, Weir, Carsley, Linderoth (Gravesen), Gemmill, Campbell, Ginola (Radzinski), Naysmith*

Both sides were desperate for the three points – with Everton facing the growing threat of relegation and Liverpool trying to keep in touch with Premiership leaders Manchester United – so this draw was not of particular use to either club. As often happens in derby matches, the game was played at a frantic pace and quality was at a premium with tackles frequently punctuating the run of play, but it was Liverpool who created the majority of the early chances. Steve Simonsen saved from John Arne Riise and Nicolas Anelka and it was surprising that the first booking was only served shortly before the interval. The second half saw Tomasz Radzinski and Thomas Gravesen replacing David Ginola and Tobias Linderoth and the changes paid dividends just seven minutes later. Alessandro Pistone and Gary Naysmith exchanged passes to allow the Italian defender to cross from the left into the path of Radzinski. His mis-hit shot took Chris Kirkland by surprise and the ball bobbled in off the post to give the visitors the lead. Emile Heskey was brought on to give added impetus to the Liverpool attack and Michael Owen wasted two opportunities to level the match before Anelka scored his first Premiership goal since his arrival from Paris St Germain on loan two months earlier. Both sides had chances to score before the final whistle, with a Danny Murphy header being tipped over the bar by Simonsen and Kirkland saving from Radzinski.

## 22nd December 2002

Premier League
**Liverpool 0**
**Everton 0**
*Attendance: 44,025*
**Liverpool:** *Kirkland, Henchoz, Hyypiä, Riise, Carragher, Traore (Heskey), Murphy, Gerrard, Diao (Šmicer), Baroš, Owen*
**Everton:** *Wright, Hibbert (Watson), Pistone, Stubbs, Weir, Pembridge, Carsley, Gravesen, Campbell, Radzinski (Rooney), Naysmith*

In other circumstances, battling away against a fired-up Everton for a goalless draw might have been seen as a reasonable return, but Liverpool were supposed to be streets ahead of their neighbours, not a point behind – the first time they had trailed their fiercest rivals at Christmas in 18 years. The boos from the Kop that greeted the final whistle were proof of a slump that had, whether Gérard Houllier liked it or not, turned into a full-blown crisis. Liverpool's lack of width had been aggravated by a failure to get their full-backs forward and emphasized the poor quality of their play. For all the lung-busting effort and commitment – despite Steven Gerrard's horror tackle on Gary Naysmith – Liverpool never looked like breaking down Everton. Richard Wright made two diving stops to foil John Arne Riise, the first after a well-worked corner then a run from half-way just before the break but – apart from gathering a shot from substitute Vladimír Šmicer and watching a close-range header from fellow replacement Emile Heskey go wide – the Everton keeper was not tested. Everton's method, with two hard-working lines of four – with Alessandro Pistone outstanding on the left – leaving Tomasz Radzinski and Kevin Campbell to forage alone – was extremely simplistic. Yet it was more than enough to snuff out what little threat Liverpool offered as they resorted to far too many optimistic long balls in the vague direction of Michael Owen and Milan Baroš. Title pretenders must have more than that and while Everton offered little innovation of their own, they always looked to exploit the deficiencies of Djimi Traore down the left. Radzinski should have done better on the turn when David Weir flicked on Thomas Gravesen's throw, and then the Canadian's ball defeated Traore's lunge to free Lee Carsley, whose far-post chip was clawed behind by Chris Kirkland. The arrival of wonderkid Wayne Rooney added to Everton's self-belief. Kirkland, who had clattered into the substitute as they chased down a loose ball, was lucky when Heskey's baulk on Campbell went undetected after he had dropped the ball. Heskey miscontrolled after Gerrard's quick free-kick sent him in on goal but Everton, who did not shirk a single tackle, were beginning to sense glory. It nearly came in the shape of Rooney 17 minutes from time. The prodigy managed to spin away from Sami Hyypiä to hammer the ball towards goal, with a deflection off Stéphane Henchoz diverting the ball past Kirkland but off the bar. Owen might have stolen a victory as tempers boiled over late on.

## 19th April 2003

Premier League

**Everton 1**

Unsworth (pen)

**Liverpool 2**

Owen, Murphy

*Attendance: 40,162*

**Everton:** *Wright, Yobo, Unsworth, Stubbs, Weir, Carsley, Watson (Ferguson), Gravesen (Gemmill), Campbell, Rooney, Naysmith*

**Liverpool:** *Dudek, Riise, Carragher, Traore, Murphy, Hamann, Gerrard, Bišćan (Diao), Baroš (Diouf), Heskey, Owen*

Both sides were riding high in the Premier League and pushing for Champions League qualification as the 2002–03 campaign began to reach its climax, but it was Liverpool who were the happiest following another victory at Goodison Park. Michael Owen opened the scoring after 31 minutes with his first goal from open play in 10 Merseyside derbies. The diminutive striker worked his way infield from the left-half touchline, past Steve Watson and Joseph Yobo, before unleashing an unstoppable shot that flew inside Richard Wright's near post. Everton equalized shortly before the hour mark when David Unsworth converted from the spot after Jamie Carragher had been judged to have needlessly and wildly fouled Gary Naysmith. The parity only lasted seven minutes, however, as Danny Murphy curled in a long-range effort from 30 yards to secure the points for Liverpool. Everton finished the match with nine men after both David Weir and Naysmith received second yellow cards in the final nine minutes.

## 30th August 2003

Premier League

**Everton 0**

**Liverpool 3**

Owen 2, Kewell

*Attendance: 40,200*

**Everton:** *Simonsen, Pistone, Unsworth (Gravesen), Stubbs, Yobo, Pembridge, Watson, Rooney, Radzinski, Linderoth (Ferguson), Naysmith*

**Liverpool:** *Dudek, Finnan, Hyypiä, Carragher, Bišćan, Kewell, Šmicer (Murphy), Gerrard, Baroš (Heskey), Diouf (Riise), Owen*

Liverpool continued their impressive recent run at Goodison Park with an emphatic victory over their neighbours that gave them their first win of the new season. All eyes were on the two star strikers – Michael Owen and Wayne Rooney – and it was the Liverpool forward who came out on top. Owen was clinical in his finishing whereas his Everton counterpart had a number of chances but could not capitalize on any of them. The first half was drawing to a close when Harry Kewell found Owen who slotted the ball past Steve Simonsen and in off the post to give the visitors the lead. Seven minutes after the restart and Owen had doubled his tally once Milan Baroš had outwitted Joseph Yobo. Rooney's frustration culminated in a booking – one of three yellow cards handed out to each team – while Owen's final contribution to the scoreline was to outmanoeuvre Simonsen and cross the ball for Kewell to shoot past the desperately lunging Gary Naysmith.

## 31st January 2004

Premier League
**Liverpool 0**
**Everton 0**
*Attendance: 44,056*
**Liverpool:** *Dudek, Henchoz, Finnan, Hyypiä, Carragher, Kewell, Hamann, Gerrard, Le Tallec, Cheyrou, Owen*
**Everton:** *Martyn, Hibbert, Naysmith, Stubbs, Pistone, Gravesen, Rooney (Watson), Ferguson (Carsley), Radzinski (Jeffers), Nyarko, Kilbane*

In sharp contrast to many a Merseyside derby, this clash produced only one yellow card – Thomas Gravesen after 37 minutes – and no goals, which was surprising because the scoreline could quite easily read 5-5 at the full-time whistle. Everton had Nigel Martyn to thank for their clean sheet as the former England goalkeeper thwarted efforts from Steven Gerrard, Dietmar Hamann and Harry Kewell. The one time he was beaten, however, Tony Hibbert was there to clear Anthony Le Tallec's header off the line. Martyn's counterpart, Jerzy Dudek, was just as busy preventing Wayne Rooney, Duncan Ferguson and Alan Stubbs from finding the back of the net. The visiting fans were incensed though that referee Steve Bennett failed to award a penalty following a Jamie Carragher hand ball and that Tomasz Radzinski was denied a free-kick on the edge of the box after being fouled by Sami Hyypiä.

## 11th December 2004
Premier League
**Everton 1**
Carsley
**Liverpool 0**
*Attendance: 40,552*
**Everton:** *Martyn, Hibbert, Pistone, Stubbs, Weir, Carsley, Osman (Watson), Gravesen (Yobo), Bent (Ferguson), Cahill, Kilbane*
**Liverpool:** *Kirkland, Hyypiä, Riise, Josemi, Carragher, Kewell, Gerrard, Diao (Alonso), Hamann (Núñez), Sinama-Pongolle (Traore), Mellor*

Everton recorded their first win over Liverpool since September 1999 (and their first at Goodison since October 1997) with a single Lee Carsley goal in the 68th minute proving to be the difference. The three valuable points pushed Everton up to second in the Premiership table. Receiving the ball from Leon Osman just outside the 18-yard box, Carsley curled the ball around two Liverpool players and past the unsighted Chris Kirkland. The first half had been peppered with intense tackles but few scoring chances; of the few to arise, Tim Cahill caused consternation among the Blues supporters with an unbelievable headed miss while Neil Mellor could only direct his header into the waiting hands of Nigel Martyn. After the interval, Salif Diao volleyed over from 18 yards out before Steven Gerrard came closest to scoring an equalizer when Martyn tipped his shot over the bar.

## 20th March 2005
Premier League
**Liverpool 2**
Gerrard, García
**Everton 1**
Cahill

*Attendance: 44,224*
**Liverpool:** *Dudek, Finnan, Riise, Pellegrino, Carragher, Warnock (Núñez), Gerrard, García, Hamann (Bišćan), Baroš, Morientes (Šmicer)*
**Everton:** *Martyn, Hibbert, Pistone (Watson), Stubbs, Weir, Carsley, Osman, Yobo (Beattie), Bent (Ferguson), Cahill, Kilbane*

If ever Liverpool's season could be encapsulated in one match, then it was in this quite insane Merseyside derby. Even in pulsating, dramatic, stirring victory, even as they secured what could be an absolutely vital three points, they still managed somehow to contrive to make life harder for themselves. While the whole Liverpool team celebrated on the pitch at the end of the match as if they had just lifted the Premiership, the reality was that with four serious injuries and one ridiculous dismissal, the task of overhauling Everton in the table remained as difficult as ever, even if the gap was narrowed to four points. Goals from skipper Steven Gerrard and Luis García were just enough to repel a comeback from their neighbours which saw Tim Cahill set up a passionate finale after Milan Baroš saw red. The Anfield team deserved their win, especially for a commanding first-half display inspired by Gerrard and Jamie Carragher, but with injuries to Fernando Morientes, Stephen Warnock, Didi Hamann and Luis García – and a three-match ban for Baroš – they paid a heavy price. For all Liverpool's dominance, Everton could feel aggrieved. For instance, they could point to the fact that the free-kick from which Gerrard scored the opening goal should not have been awarded. The referee saw a foul on García on the edge of the box when it was clear he had already lost control and was looking for the award when Tony Hibbert took both ball and man with his tackle. Even so, the visiting side only had themselves to blame for the shambles of a wall that allowed Gerrard to pick his spot on 27 minutes and fire in a side-foot shot into the unprotected far corner of the net. If that was bad, the killer second goal five minutes later was worse. Again, there was a suspicion of the referee ruling against the visitors when he ignored a blatant high challenge from Hamann on Leon Osman, but the danger should still have been extinguished. As the free ball fell to Morientes, his shot from 30 yards was at best hopeful and Everton keeper Nigel Martyn should have dealt comfortably with the swirling effort. Instead, he timidly pushed it onto the crossbar, fell backwards into the net, and was an embarrassed observer as García nodded home the rebound. But Martyn at least made a quite outstanding save from the hapless Baroš when, on 69 minutes, the Czech raced through, dummied the keeper and shot towards the empty net only to see Martyn stick out a foot for a miraculous stop. In Baroš, they had a striker who too often displayed a lack of intelligence with his lack of an instinctive finish. His dismissal on 76 minutes was brainless, and not just because he left Liverpool with 10 men for a hairy final 15 minutes in a match his side dared not lose. Morientes limped from the game with a thigh injury that would sideline him for three weeks and García limped throughout the second half. Many felt that Rafa Benítez would not tolerate Baroš for much longer, because that sort of behaviour – a horrible, ludicrous challenge on Alan Stubbs – undermined his side so badly. Worse was the host of chances that Baroš missed. He was sent through on at least three occasions and never looked like finding the net. Cahill scored a fine goal with a right-foot shot almost immediately after Baroš trudged off to set up a stirring finale in which the visitors only just came up short.

## 28th December 2005

Premier League
**Everton 1**
Beattie
**Liverpool 3**
Crouch, Gerrard, Cissé
*Attendance: 40,158*
**Everton:** *Martyn, Hibbert, Valente, Yobo, Weir, Davies (McFadden), Arteta, Cahill, Beattie, Neville, Kilbane*
**Liverpool:** *Reina, Finnan, Hyypiä, Carragher, Warnock, Kewell (Riise), Gerrard (García), Alonso, Sissoko, Cissé, Crouch (Morientes)*

After emulating Bob Paisley and Joe Fagan by lifting the European Cup, Rafa Benítez was rekindling the glory days of Kenny Dalglish. Not since 1989, when King Kenny reigned at Anfield, had Liverpool won nine straight League games and not even Dalglish's magnificent side of 1987–88 – which had Alan Hansen, Barry Venison, Gary Gillespie and

Steve Nicol at the back – could match the current generation's record of 762 minutes without conceding a goal. Peter Crouch continued his hot scoring streak for Liverpool, while Phil Neville and Mikel Arteta were sent off late on to compound Everton's misery. Liverpool quickly settled into their passing game and they carved out the first chance when Djibril Cissé volleyed wide from Steven Gerrard's free-kick. It came as little surprise when Liverpool took the lead in the 11th minute when the rejuvenated Crouch bagged his sixth goal in seven games. Everton failed to clear their lines properly and Momo Sissoko headed the ball forward for Cissé to lay it off for Gerrard. He nodded it through to set up Crouch and he rounded Nigel Martyn to score. The odds on an Everton recovery lengthened considerably when Gerrard doubled Liverpool's advantage six minutes later with his 14th goal of an already prolific campaign. This time Everton twice passed up opportunities to clear their lines and when the ball fell to Gerrard he cut inside before hitting a 25-yard shot past the unsighted Martyn. It very nearly got worse for Everton and Cahill was fortunate to escape with just a booking when he scythed down Xabi Alonso. The Blues were in disarray and Cissé wasted a great chance to make it 3-0 when he blazed over from six yards out on the right. Everton regrouped and twice threatened Pepe Reina's goal in the space of a minute. First Kevin Kilbane's header from Arteta's cross came off Steve Finnan and bounced just wide and from the resultant corner Joseph Yobo headed over. James Beattie did manage to put the ball in the Liverpool net but the assistant referee was already flagging because the ball had crossed the line before Cahill put in his cross. Beattie was not to be denied though, and three minutes before the interval he got his head to Simon Davies' overhead kick from Kilbane's knock-down to pull a goal back with his fifth strike of the season. It ended Liverpool's club record run without conceding a goal although any thoughts of an Everton comeback were dampened just 74 seconds into the second half when Cissé scored a fine solo goal to restore Liverpool's two-goal cushion. Harry Kewell sent the French striker scampering down the left wing and he skinned David Weir before planting the ball perfectly beyond Martyn and into the far corner. The goal knocked the stuffing out of Everton and, with Liverpool back in full control, Gerrard went close to his second with a dipping free-kick.

Gerrard was determined to get a second goal and he rifled another drive just inches wide of Martyn's left-hand post. Everton's misery was compounded on 68 minutes when Neville was sent off for a second bookable offence after chopping down Sissoko and, deep into injury time, Arteta followed him off after picking up a second yellow card.

## 25th March 2006

Premier League

**Liverpool 3**

Neville (og), García, Kewell

**Everton 1**

Cahill

*Attendance: 44,923*

**Liverpool:** *Reina, Finnan, Hyypiä, Riise, Carragher, Kewell (Warnock), Gerrard, García, Alonso, Sissoko, Crouch (Morientes)*

**Everton:** *Wright, Hibbert, Naysmith, Stubbs, Weir, Neville, Kilbane (van der Meyde), Cahill, Beattie, Osman, McFadden (Ferguson)*

Even the dismissal of Steven Gerrard for two bookable offences within two minutes before the game was even 20 minutes old could not give Everton the impetus needed to overcome the Reds. Liverpool's tactic of leaving Peter Crouch up front as a lone target man was proving troublesome for the Everton defenders and it wasn't a surprise when the home side scored just before the break. The goal, however, came about from Phil Neville heading a Xabi Alonso corner into his own net. Shortly after the interval, Crouch flicked on for Luis García to lift his shot over Richard Wright and double Liverpool's lead. A triple substitution was being lined up by Everton manager David Moyes when his side won a corner from which Tim Cahill reduced the deficit, but any hopes of netting an equalizer were dashed when substitute Andy van der Meyde was dismissed for an arm in the face of Xabi Alonso just five minutes after entering the fray. With 10 minutes to go, Harry Kewell put the tie beyond doubt when he gratefully accepted the ball from Steve Finnan and slotted it past the despairing Everton keeper.

## 9th September 2006

Premier League

**Everton 3**

Cahill, Johnson 2

**Liverpool 0**

*Attendance:* **40,004**

**Everton:** *Howard, Hibbert, Naysmith, Lescott, Yobo, Carsley, Arteta (Valente), Neville, Johnson, Cahill, Osman (Beattie)*

**Liverpool:** *Reina, Finnan, Hyypiä, Aurelio, Carragher, Gerrard, García, Alonso, Sissoko (Pennant), Fowler (Riise), Crouch (Kuyt)*

Everton continued their unbeaten start to the new campaign with a decisive victory over neighbours Liverpool that gave them their biggest Merseyside derby win since 1964. Man of the match was undoubtedly Andy Johnson, the Everton striker who was well on his way to justifying his club record £8.6 million price tag, but it was Tim Cahill who opened the scoring when he pounced on a loose ball to nutmeg keeper Pepe Reina after 24 minutes. Johnson grabbed his first shortly after the half-hour mark when he latched onto a Lee Carsley pass, skinned Jamie Carragher and slid the ball into the back of the net. The two combined again in the final minute to put the icing on the cake as far as Evertonians were concerned – following up a Carsley volley, Johnson delighted in nodding in the ball after Reina's fumble. Liverpool, in truth, failed to gel and rarely troubled the Everton goal despite the introduction of new arrivals Dirk Kuyt and Jermaine Pennant as second-half substitutes.

## 3rd February 2007

Premier League

**Liverpool 0**

**Everton 0**

*Attendance:* **44,234**

**Liverpool:** *Reina, Finnan, Agger, Riise, Carragher, Gerrard, Alonso, Pennant, Crouch, Bellamy (Fowler), Kuyt*

**Everton:** *Howard, Hibbert, Lescott, Stubbs, Yobo, Carsley, Arteta, Neville, Johnson (Anichebe), Cahill, Osman*

Rafa Benítez angered Evertonians with his pre-match comments about the Blues being a small club, but honours ended even in this 205th competitive meeting between the two sides. The visitors ensured that their defence was watertight and Liverpool were forced to resort to pumping long balls up to Peter Crouch in the hope that the ungainly England international could produce an individual piece of magic. Alan Stubbs and Joseph Yobo easily dealt with any threat presented by the home side and Joleon Lescott – drafted in to play at left-back instead of centre-back – contained the darting runs of Jermaine Pennant. The closest the home side came to scoring was when Stubbs intercepted to deny Dirk Kuyt with 13 minutes remaining, while Everton's best chance fell to Andy Johnson but Jamie Carragher and Pepe Reina combined to deny the Blues striker.

## 20th October 2007

Premier League
**Everton 1**
Hyypiä (og)
**Liverpool 2**
Kuyt 2 (2 pens)
*Attendance:* 40,049
**Everton:** *Howard, Hibbert, Lescott, Stubbs, Yobo, Jagielka, Arteta, Neville, Yakubu (McFadden), Anichebe (Baines), Osman*
**Liverpool:** *Reina, Finnan, Hyypiä, Riise, Carragher, Gerrard (Lucas), Benayoun (Babel), Mascherano, Sissoko (Pennant), Voronin, Kuyt*

This match was full of controversy with red cards, penalties and an own goal thrown in. Without a doubt, Liverpool were lucky to come away from Goodison with all three points despite giving Everton a head start after 38 minutes when Sami Hyypiä turned an Alan Stubbs cross into his own net off the post. Pushing for a second goal after half-time, Everton were caught on the break and paid the price when Tony Hibbert was dismissed for a foul on Steven Gerrard after 54 minutes. Dirk Kuyt took responsibility for the spot-kick and made no mistake from 12 yards to level the score. The Dutchman was the perpetrator of a dangerous two-footed tackle on Phil Neville 10 minutes later that referee Mark Clattenburg should have punished with a red card rather than a lenient yellow. Andriy Voronin, Momo Sissoko and John Arne Riise all had chances as Liverpool failed to take advantage of their extra man, but the winning goal did eventually come. Derby debutant and second-half substitute Lucas' shot was handled on the line by Neville in stoppage time and the referee had no alternative other than to award another penalty and flash the red card again. Kuyt netted his second successful spot-kick of the game but Liverpool were fortunate not to concede a penalty of their own in the dying seconds when Jamie Carragher wrestled Joleon Lescott to the ground but play was waved on much to Everton's disgust.

## 30th March 2008

Premier League
**Liverpool 1**
Torres
**Everton 0**
*Attendance: 44,295*
**Liverpool:** *Reina, Hyypiä, Riise, Carragher, Skrtel, Gerrard (Crouch), Alonso, Babel (Benayoun), Lucas, Torres (Pennant), Kuyt*
**Everton:** *Howard, Hibbert, Lescott, Jagielka, Yobo, Carsley, Arteta, Neville (Baines), Yakubu, Osman, Pienaar (Fernandes)*

They were the Kings of Merseyside for another season but this derby victory over a lacklustre Everton summed up an Anfield season in one frustrating 90 minutes. Rafa Benítez's side started with menacing intent and a real sense of purpose, but after taking the lead they lost their way and were clinging on until a late Steven Gerrard-inspired rally. Caution was intrinsic in Benítez's tactical approach and it was clear that – after creating at least five golden opportunities in the first period – they decided to ensure they hung on to what they had, a precious lead courtesy of Fernando Torres. Torres tired after the break and without him Liverpool lacked a cutting edge. When that finally dawned on Everton, they started believing they could get something from the game. They didn't because they lacked energy with their tiny squad finally reaching breaking point. The Reds' skipper took control of the game with his intelligent, powerful running and crisp, clever passing. Torres opened the scoring on seven minutes. Yakubu dallied on the edge of the box when Gerrard's corner was cleared and Xabi Alonso and Dirk Kuyt worked the ball to the striker who wasn't going to miss from 10 yards out. From there, it could have been an avalanche. Torres saw one shot blocked and another saved. Kuyt then missed a free header from four yards and Babel performed a similar feat from John Arne Riise's cross. Lucas also missed a golden chance from close range and Gerrard smashed a dipping 25-yard volley against the upright with Tim Howard beaten. It should have been game over but after the interval Liverpool shut up shop far too early and almost paid the price. The closest Everton came to a goal was when Leon Osman headed wide from Mikel Arteta's cross and then Tony Hibbert saw a good chance blocked after a mistake from Liverpool keeper Pepe Reina.

## 27ᵗʰ September 2008

Premier League

**Everton 0**

**Liverpool 2**

Torres 2

*Attendance:* 39,574

**Everton:** *Howard, Hibbert (Saha), Lescott, Jagielka, Yobo, Neville, Fellaini, Cahill, Yakubu, Arteta, Osman*

**Liverpool:** *Reina, Dossena, Arbeloa, Carragher, Skrtel, Gerrard, Riera (Aurelio), Alonso (Lucas), Keane (Pennant), Torres, Kuyt*

David Moyes would have been thankful for Everton's away form from the start of the 2008–09 season (two wins and a draw from three games) because Liverpool condemned his side to their third consecutive home defeat with a double from Fernando Torres leaving the Toffees still looking for their first point at Goodison Park. The Anfield club, on the other hand, had only dropped two points from their first six League games and sat proudly in second place in the Premiership, with the same number of points as leaders Chelsea. While Liverpool dominated in terms of possession, the best chances of the first half fell to Everton and the crowd had to wait until the hour for a goal. Then two came along within the space of three minutes. Robbie Keane's cross from the left was accurately dispatched by Torres and the Spaniard claimed his double when he thundered a loose ball into the roof of the net from 12 yards out. Two more Liverpool goals were disallowed (Dirk Kuyt and Torres) before Tim Cahill earned himself a straight red on 80 minutes for a rash challenge on Xabi Alonso.

## 19th January 2009

Premier League
**Liverpool 1**
Gerrard
**Everton 1**
Cahill
*Attendance: 44,382*
**Liverpool:** *Reina, Hyypiä, Aurelio, Carragher, Skrtel, Gerrard, Riera (Babel), Alonso, Keane (Benayoun), Torres (Lucas), Kuyt*
**Everton:** *Howard, Hibbert, Baines, Jagielka, Lescott, Neville, Osman, Anichebe, Cahill, Arteta, Pienaar*

Handed the advantage by a typical piece of brilliance by Steven Gerrard – the perfect response to the baying predictions of the gloating Everton fans who taunted him throughout – Liverpool should have finished the job. Their failure to do so illuminated the flaw at the heart of their title challenge, a flakiness that originated with manager Rafa Benítez. If anything summed up that lack of killer instinct, it was the moment Tim Cahill struck with the bite of a viper to end Liverpool's victory chants and leave Manchester United on top of the table. Title-winning sides knew that championships are gained with steel and grit, by digging in under pressure and winning games you didn't really deserve to. For Liverpool, this should have been one of those; a major milestone on the hunt for the Holy Grail. Only the most staunch of Liverpool supporters would have claimed that this was a vintage Liverpool performance and the stand-out player on the pitch was Phil Jagielka. But, 30 seconds after Victor Anichebe was left appealing in vain for a spot-kick at the other end, Gerrard demonstrated his unerring instincts for the grand occasion. The Reds skipper received Albert Riera's square ball and from

30 yards drilled the ball past Tim Howard and into the bottom corner at the Kop end. All Liverpool had to do was see it out, hold firm and maybe even nick a killer second but having already sacrificed Robbie Keane – whose contribution was negligible – Benítez then hauled off Fernando Torres, the most likely source of that decisive strike, and paid the price. Instead, three minutes from time, the red shirts stood and watched as Mikel Arteta's free-kick fizzed into the six-yard box where Cahill's touch flashed the ball past a helpless Pepe Reina. It was a devastating moment, bringing anguish and despair to Anfield. Not that it was unfair; even Torres would have left the stadium wondering how he failed to take the sort of chance he would expect to convert in his sleep. That miss came after 28 minutes in which Reina had been far the busier of the two goalkeepers. Reina, who had saved from Anichebe inside 35 seconds of the start, had just plunged to his right to deny Cahill's header when Sami Hyypiä launched the ball 60 yards upfield. It was one instant when Torres escaped the close attentions of Jagielka and Joleon Lescott, ghosting between the pair and bearing down on goal. The Spaniard steadied himself, committed Howard, picked his spot . . . and held his head as the shot flicked the outside of the post on its way behind.

## 25th January 2009

FA Cup Fourth Round
**Liverpool 1**
Gerrard
**Everton 1**
Lescott
*Attendance: 43,524*
**Liverpool:** *Reina, Dossena, Arbeloa, Carragher, Skrtel, Gerrard, Alonso, Babel (Riera), Mascherano, Torres, Kuyt*
**Everton:** *Howard, Hibbert, Baines, Jagielka, Lescott, Neville, Osman, Castillo (Rodwell), Cahill, Anichebe (Gosling), Pienaar*

Liverpool had the sublime skill of Fernando Torres to thank for their continued presence in the FA Cup. The Spanish striker displayed sheer genius to produce one of the most exquisite moments the competition had ever seen to create the Steven Gerrard equalizer that denied Everton an historic Cup triumph. Rafa Benítez fielded more or less his strongest side in search of victory – with the notable exception of Robbie Keane – and was clearly devastated his plan backfired. It did so because of Everton's resilience, embodied by Phil Jagielka. He was magnificent, his commitment jaw-droppingly total and he was supported by an all-English defence that performed equally admirably. It took incredible skill from Torres to breach them. His assist on 53 minutes went down as another of those impossible, immortal moments that defined the FA Cup. Somehow, in one movement, he took the ball out of the air and mystified two defenders before flicking it towards Gerrard with an action that defied physics. The Liverpool skipper seized on the chance and slammed the ball past Tim Howard at the near post. The Everton keeper could have come in for criticism for being beaten from such a narrow angle on his near side, but the shot came in awkwardly close to his feet. It was a wonder goal that Liverpool certainly needed as up until that point they had been second-best to Everton who took the lead after 27 minutes by again exposing the home side's weakness at set pieces. They had enough of a warning of Tim Cahill's danger in the air when he equalized in the League game earlier that week, but they left him unmarked again from a Steven Pienaar corner. Incredibly, Liverpool chose to mark Everton's best header of the ball with Xabi Alonso – a cruel mismatch. Cahill rose unchallenged, headed goalwards and Joleon Lescott diverted the ball into the net from close range unhindered. Everton dominated the first half and could have had a penalty when Pienaar was caught in the box by Álvaro Arbeloa. They were allowed to because Liverpool lacked the passion required in a Merseyside derby. At least they discovered it after the break. Howard redeemed himself with a fine save from Gerrard just after the equalizer, then saved well when Dirk Kuyt got clear, though the striker should have done better. Everton escaped again late on when Jagielka blocked superbly from almost on the line after Gerrard had crossed for Torres. The truth was that the visitors deserved their replay, even if Liverpool begrudged it.

## 4th February 2009

FA Cup Fourth Round replay

**Everton 1**

Gosling

**Liverpool 0**

*Attendance: 37,918*

**Everton:** *Howard, Hibbert, Baines, Jagielka, Lescott, Neville (van der Meyde), Osman, Fellaini (Gosling), Cahill, Arteta, Pienaar (Rodwell)*

**Liverpool:** *Reina, Dossena, Arbeloa, Carragher, Skrtel, Gerrard (Benayoun), Riera (Mascherano), Alonso, Lucas, Torres (Babel), Kuyt*

An incredible, unbelievable winner from teenager Dan Gosling less than two minutes from the end of extra-time – after a supremely tense contest that bordered on the hysterical – gave Everton a victory that would go down in the annals of history. The nation may have missed it when ITV amazingly went to a commercial break by mistake . . . but the Goodison fans relished every second of the cool strike that completed a miserable night for Rafa Benítez. The 19-year-old Gosling showed ice-cool calm after getting on the end of forgotten man Andy van der Meyde's cross, bamboozling the visiting defence before somehow curling a shot into the far corner via two deflections to inspire incredible scenes of jubilation. Gosling was plucked from the obscurity of Plymouth Argyle after playing just 24 games for them and he rewarded the vision of his manager David Moyes with a goal that could well prove the greatest of his career, even at such a tender age. Everton thoroughly deserved the victory and probably should have put Liverpool out of their misery much earlier. The visitors knew that the architect of their downfall was their own midfielder Lucas, who needlessly got himself sent off on 75 minutes for two naive fouls. While Gosling's finish was undoubtedly a fairytale, Liverpool's experience was the stuff of nightmares. Not only did they slump to the most sickening of defeats, but Steven Gerrard limped off barely minutes into the tie and striker Fernando Torres seemed to be struggling as he was replaced in extra-time. Without Gerrard, Liverpool looked decidedly vulnerable and Everton quickly sensed it. There was an extra spring in their step and their passing finally found its range as Mikel Arteta and Leon Osman produced some pleasant exchanges around the penalty area. From the 17th minute, it was just a question of whether they could break down the admirable visiting rearguard so brilliantly led by Jamie Carragher. When Lucas was dismissed, it was more a matter of when. Osman could have done it before the end of normal time when Arteta and Tim Cahill brilliantly combined to set him up in front of goal, but his shot crashed back off an upright with 20 minutes left. Everton came so close when Pepe Reina saved from Osman in extra-time and then sprang to his feet to produce a stunning stop from the ebullient substitute Gosling. Cahill headed just wide from a corner and it seemed like penalties were the next logical step but that was forgetting the drama and sheer romance of the FA Cup. Who better to produce a winner if one had to come than a teenager who has played just five games for his club? It was a fairytale, even if the story was spoiled by the scenes at the end when Reina and van der Meyde produced an unsightly free for all.

## 29th November 2009

Premier League
**Everton 0**
**Liverpool 2**
Yobo (og), Kuyt
*Attendance: 39,652*
**Everton:** *Howard, Heitinga, Baines, Distin, Yobo (Neill), Hibbert, Cahill (Yakubu), Bilyaletdinov, Fellaini, Pienaar, Jo (Saha)*
**Liverpool:** *Reina, Johnson, Agger, Aurélio (Riera), Insúa, Carragher, Gerrard, Mascherano, Lucas, Kuyt, N'Gog (Benayoun)*

The weather matched the mood on the blue half of Merseyside: the grey skies and rain summed up perfectly how the Evertonians felt as they trudged home disconsolately from Goodison Park. The Blues had slipped to 16th – just three points above the drop zone – and a season that had promised so much was turning into the grim relegation struggle; David Moyes predicted that there would be a silver lining to this dark cloud. Everton were the better team and had the best outfield player on the park in Steven Pienaar. Pepe Reina's outstanding save from Tim Cahill was, for Liverpool, one of those defining moments – not just of this match but perhaps the whole season. Without it Everton would have been level and, given that Liverpool had shown a tendency to collapse once conceding, there was every chance the home side would have gone on to win the game. Liverpool were pinned back and even outplayed for significant sections of the game. Liverpool's opening goal was fortunate in the extreme, as Javier Mascherano advanced in the 12th minute after almost constant Everton pressure, he was faced with precisely no options. His response was a speculative shot so bad that it may have even gone out for a throw-in. Instead it hit Joseph Yobo and ballooned into the air and beyond the despairing grasp of Tim Howard in the Everton goal. For the rest of the half, David Moyes' side advanced at will and created enough chances to have controlled the game comfortably but spurned every one. The worst was a miss at the far post by Diniyar Bilyaletdinov as he contrived to spoon wide of an open goal. Jo did find the net but had wandered offside, then Bilyaletdinov just failed to reach a fine flick from Cahill. But when Cahill got a flick onto Johnny Heitinga's free-kick it seemed Everton would get their reward. Somehow, though, Reina got down to stop it and then got up to block the rebound from Marouane Fellaini. Inevitably, Everton paid the price for such profligacy when Yobo made a horrible mistake to gift the ball to the otherwise subdued Steven Gerrard, who set up sub Albert Riera for a shot that Howard could only parry to the waiting Dirk Kuyt to convert. At the end of an absorbing, though low-quality contest, Jamie Carragher offered the best snapshot of what had happened. He took a match ball to kick to the celebrating Liverpool fans but succeeded only in slicing it horribly into the Park End, 50 metres wide of the target.

## 6th February 2010

Premier League

**Liverpool 1**

Kuyt

**Everton 0**

*Attendance:* 44,316

**Liverpool:** *Reina, Agger, Kyrgiakos, Insúa, Carragher, Gerrard, Rodríguez (Aurélio), Mascherano, Lucas, Kuyt (Skrtel), N'Gog (Babel)*

**Everton:** *Howard, Baines, Heitinga, Distin, Neville, Pienaar, Cahill, Osman (Yakubu), Donovan, Fellaini (Arteta), Saha (Anichebe)*

The talking points after this match centred largely on the thunderous tackles and the referee's performance. A two-footed lunge from Sotirios Kyrgiakos left Martin Atkinson with no choice but to show a red card to the Liverpool defender after 34 minutes, although television replays showed he did play the ball. Marouane Fellaini, however, was lucky to remain on the pitch after stamping on Kyrgiakos during that tackle while Steve Pienaar was dismissed late on after picking up his second yellow. Fellaini was unable to carry on and was replaced by Mikel Arteta, still short of match fitness. Despite being a man down for the majority of the game, Liverpool took the lead when Dirk Kuyt managed to squeeze a header past Tim Howard and Phil Neville from a corner in the 55th minute.

## 17th October 2010

Premier League
**Everton 2**
Cahill, Arteta
**Liverpool 0**
*Attendance: 39,673*
**Everton:** *Howard, Heitinga (Hibbert), Coleman, Baines, Distin, Jagielka, Neville, Cahill, Osman (Bilyaletdinov), Arteta (Beckford), Yakubu*
**Liverpool:** *Reina, Konchesky, Kyrgiakos, Carragher, Skrtel, Meireles, Gerrard, Cole (Babel), Rodríguez (Jovanović), Lucas (N'Gog), Torres*

It wasn't the chant of "Going down!" from the Gwladys Street crowd that hurt Liverpool fans the most or even the "You're getting sacked in the morning!" directed at Roy Hodgson. The most devastating arrow to their hearts was the triumphant chorus of "Easy, easy" that rang around Goodison Park at the end of this typically intense derby match. It was so viciously cutting because it was true. Everton confirmed their obvious superiority in one of the more comfortable victories they had enjoyed in recent derby history. From the start, Everton were a yard quicker to the ball and a yard ahead in terms of the wit required to gain any edge in what were always frenetic exchanges. The bare statistics suggested that Liverpool enjoyed a 67 per cent to 33 per cent advantage in possession but – until the final few minutes when Fernando Torres, David N'Gog and Raul Meireles all had good opportunities – they created little. The home side, conversely, dominated the opening half-hour, grabbed a crucial goal soon after and then defended with the swagger of a team who knew they had the winning lead. Liverpool lacked confidence, not just in front of goal in the woefully forlorn shape of Torres but behind him in the nervous passing of Joe Cole, while Maxi Rodríguez and Lucas seemed determined to pass on responsibility. Only Steven Gerrard and Jamie Carragher showed the commitment required for one of these games. Contrast that with Everton who had heroes throughout their line-up. Phil Jagielka and Mikel Arteta performed magnificently, despite both carrying hamstring injuries. What Everton had in addition was the leadership shown by Phil Neville. He provided a calming voice of authority for his side which was conspicuously absent in the opposition. Gerrard, as always, tried but his frustration with his under-performing team-mates was always bubbling near the surface and likewise Carragher, who launched into a savage attack on Torres and his unwillingness to run. For Everton, everyone was ready to work and that was never more evident than when Séamus Coleman burst down the right to deliver a cross that found Tim Cahill with the help of a deflection off Paul Konchesky. The Aussie, with some venom, converted brilliantly on the half-volley at the near post. Liverpool did start the second half brightly, but their confidence vanished visibly as the home side added another goal within five frantic minutes as Arteta slammed home a brilliant 20-yard shot after finding himself unmarked when Sotirios Kyrgiakos' headed clearance landed at his feet. From there, Everton were happy to concede possession such was their comfort in repelling what little the visitors had to offer. Their victory showed they had the desire and courage to escape the bottom three while Liverpool lay one place off the foot of the Premiership, level on points with Wolves and West Ham. Their first eight games of the season had brought just one win and three draws.

# 16th January 2011

Premier League

**Liverpool 2**

Meireles, Kuyt (pen)

**Everton 2**

Distin, Beckford

*Attendance:* 44,795

**Liverpool:** *Reina, Johnson, Agger (Kyrgiakos), Kelly, Skrtel, Meireles (Shelvey), Rodríguez, Lucas, Spearing, Torres, Kuyt*

**Everton:** *Howard, Coleman, Baines, Distin, Heitinga, Neville, Osman (Rodwell), Arteta, Fellaini, Anichebe (Bilyaletdinov), Beckford (Vaughan)*

Breathless, nerve-shredding, heart-pumping – Kenny Dalglish must have felt that nothing had changed in his 20-year absence from the Merseyside derby. But the Liverpool manager had to reflect on one crucial difference from the pulsating 4-4 draw against Everton that proved to be the last game of his first spell as Anfield manager – quality – or the lack of it. This was an exciting, open, entertaining contest that defied the usual caution of these encounters and provided as much tension as ever. Yet it was clearly a game between two teams nervously aware of their positions close to the relegation zone. Quite how the Reds managed to throw away their dominant half-time position, when they led through Raul Meireles' first goal for the club, was an enigma. Everton, to be brutal, were woeful in the first half as they wasted the possession their opponents timidly presented and then defended poorly to allow the Anfield side the chances from which Meireles eventually established a lead. They weren't helped by the form of Tim Howard in the visiting goal. He saved brilliantly from Fernando Torres on three separate occasions but Dirk Kuyt, Maxi Rodríguez and Meireles should all have done better before Liverpool opened the scoring on 29 minutes. Even then, Howard made two outstanding saves from Kuyt before Meireles, the Portugal international midfielder, seized on the loose ball as the Everton defence day-dreamed, and smashed it into the roof of the net. With the King Kenny factor inspiring an emotional homecoming for the Anfield legend, it was expected that his side would have gone on from that commanding position to take the victory they so desperately needed, especially against opponents who looked overawed by the occasion. Yet they were behind within seven minutes of the restart. The Blues were a completely different side and Liverpool couldn't cope with the physical approach they brought to the second half. Martin Skrtel had looked suspect in his positioning on set pieces all afternoon and he made one mistake too many from Mikel Arteta's corner just 40 seconds after the restart. He allowed Sylvain Distin a free header from which he made no mistake. The home side then showed their vulnerability when the impressively physical Victor Anichebe got above Martin Kelly. Leon Osman seized on the knock-down and, with Liverpool this time snoozing, his pass found Jermaine Beckford and the Blues striker made no mistake from close range. The equalizer came from a mistake by Howard who, until that point, had been the game's outstanding performer. Skrtel was left unmarked from a Meireles free-kick but slipped. Howard dived to claim the loose ball but Maxi Rodríguez got in front of the keeper to force a rash penalty. Dirk Kuyt showed confidence with the conversion to set up a big finale, but this time there was to be no late drama.

## 1st October 2011

Premier League

**Everton 0**

**Liverpool 2**

Carroll, Suárez

*Attendance:* **39,510**

**Everton:** *Howard, Coleman (Drenthe), Baines, Distin, Jagielka, Hibbert (Vellios), Cahill, Osman (Neville), Rodwell, Fellaini, Saha*

**Liverpool:** *Reina, Enrique, Carragher, Kelly, Skrtel, Downing (Bellamy), Lucas (Henderson), Adam (Gerrard), Suárez, Carroll, Kuyt*

Referee Martin Atkinson – who spotted a phantom offence unseen by anyone else – destroyed this match in terms of entertainment when he made the wrong decision despite being just three yards away from the action. Everton suffered when Jack Rodwell was sent off in the 23rd minute and while his red card was subsequently rescinded, it didn't change the outcome. The row over the sending off overshadowed the continuing emergence of Andy Carroll. The Liverpool striker had endured criticism, but his goal – which effectively settled this non-contest because 10 men were never coming back in the heat – was heralded as a landmark moment in his Anfield career. José Enrique escaped down the left and Dirk Kuyt allowed the ball to travel to Carroll who smashed it home in the 71st minute. Suárez scored the visitors' second eight minutes from time when he capitalized on a mix-up between Sylvain Distin and Leighton Baines, giving the scoreline an unbalanced look. Everton had played well enough before the Rodwell injustice to have provided a real contest.

## 13th March 2012

Premier League
**Liverpool 3**
Gerrard 3
**Everton 0**
*Attendance: 44,921*
**Liverpool:** *Reina, Enrique, Carragher, Kelly, Skrtel, Gerrard, Henderson (Kuyt), Downing, Spearing, Suárez, Carroll*
**Everton:** *Howard, Coleman (Drenthe), Baines, Distin, Jagielka, Hibbert, Pienaar, Fellaini, Rodwell, Anichebe (Jelavić), Stracqualursi (Osman)*

Steven Gerrard was the difference between the two sides – Liverpool had flailed desperately without his goals and drive in the middle yet, when he was fit, Gerrard was capable not only of winning games on his own, he could also change the entire mood around the club. His first goal beat down typical Everton verve and resistance in the first half and, six minutes after the break, before the visitors could even start their search for some sort of result that would mark David Moyes' 10th anniversary in charge, he ended the game with a single blow. It was a fine finish after good work from Luis Suárez on the right, where he exposed Sylvain Distin before slipping the ball to allow his skipper to smash gleefully into the roof of the net. He even seemed to do it on one leg at times, as he limped around the place even before the interval. Gerrard completed his hat-trick in the last minute, receiving a return pass from Suárez then dispatching a strike into the roof of the net. The game had begun at a breathless pace and rarely relented, with Liverpool impressive in their desire to get forward. With skipper Gerrard displaying the sort of drive and enthusiasm in the heart of midfield that made him one of England's few world-class assets, the home side surged at the Everton defence repeatedly. It took the formidable barrier of Tim Howard to deny them, as Gerrard burst onto a ball from Suárez and into a dangerous shooting position. Even after that fine save, Jordan Henderson seemed certain to convert the rebound, but a tremendous block by Jack Rodwell denied the winger. Soon after, Howard was in action again with an even better save from Suárez after the South American ran onto a flick by the aerially dominant Andy Carroll. Not that Liverpool had it all their own way, with Everton showing intent going forward when they could get hold of the ball. Steven Pienaar should have done much better with a fine shooting chance after brilliant work down the left from Leighton Baines, but he blasted over. Marouane Fellaini found time to steal forward at a Pienaar corner and was inches away from scoring as Pepe Reina flapped in the Liverpool goal. As so often seemed to be the case, it was when the pace dipped for a few moments that the opening goal came. Suárez chipped the ball forward in the 34th minute and it deflected off Gerrard into the path of full-back Martin Kelly – a constant attacking source for the Reds – whose shot was again saved by Howard. But as Distin turned on the loose ball, he sliced lazily and sent it spinning to Gerrard who calmly lobbed it into the roof of the net.

## 14th April 2012

FA Cup Semi-final (at Wembley)
**Everton 1**
Jelavić
**Liverpool 2**
Suárez, Carroll
*Attendance:* **87,231**
**Everton:** *Howard, Baines (Anichebe), Distin, Heitinga, Neville, Cahill, Fellaini, Gibson, Osman, Jelavić, Gueye (Coleman)*
**Liverpool:** *Jones, Johnson, Agger, Carragher, Skrtel, Gerrard, Henderson (Rodríguez), Downing (Bellamy), Spearing, Suárez, Carroll*

For 87 minutes, Kenny Dalglish must have yearned for the days when Ian Rush wore Liverpool's number 9 shirt. One Andy Carroll miss, early in the second half as Everton defended the lead plundered by Nikica Jelavić, would have embarrassed the striker. Then, with extra-time approaching, came the moment that could well provide salvation for both Carroll and Dalglish. The striker wasn't even looking towards goal when Craig Bellamy floated a free-kick into the heart of Everton's box from wide on the left but he used the back of his head to guide the ball beyond Tim Howard. After Jay Spearing and Martin Skrtel had wasted early chances for the Reds, it was the Blues who were ahead in the 24th minute. Dalglish's decision to use Daniel Agger as a left-back so he could call on Jamie Carragher backfired when both players hesitated to make a routine clearance. When Carragher swiped at the ball, it bounced off Tim Cahill into the path of Jelavić and the Croatian gave stand-in keeper Brad Jones no hope with a clinical finish. It didn't look like being Liverpool's day when Carroll missed a glorious chance two minutes after half-time. There seemed to be no way that he could miss when Stewart Downing floated in a delicious far-post cross. Carroll didn't even have to break his stride but his downward header flashed a yard wide. When Sylvain Distin's woefully underhit back-pass allowed Luis Suárez to look into the whites of Howard's eyes, there was no mercy as the Uruguayan used the outside of his right boot to guide his shot into the bottom corner. Initially, it didn't get any better for Carroll, who sent a flashing left-foot strike just wide before missing his kick from six yards with the goal gaping, but Carroll's moment came after Everton sub Séamus Coleman was lured into a needless lunge at Steven Gerrard.

## 28th October 2012

Premier League

**Everton 2**

Osman, Naismith

**Liverpool 2**

Baines (og), Suárez

*Attendance:* 39,613

**Everton:** *Howard, Coleman, Jagielka, Distin, Baines, Naismith (Oviedo), Osman, Neville, Mirallas (Gueye), Fellaini, Jelavić*

**Liverpool:** *Jones, Enrique, Agger, Skrtel, Wisdom (Henderson), Şahin (Coates), Gerrard, Allen, Sterling, Suárez, Suso (Shelvey)*

Luis Suárez displayed an almost religious zeal in this fabulous contest and it wasn't difficult to work out why. David Moyes' comments about diving provoked an inspired display that deserved to culminate in the spectacular finale only a linesman's crass error denied. At least Moyes had the good grace to admit as much afterwards, even if he rather pointedly suggested that the Liverpool striker shouldn't have been on the pitch in the final minute after a bad – although arguably accidental – challenge on Sylvain Distin. Liverpool were on the ropes and facing a knockout blow by the interval after the home side had staged a passionate fightback from the Reds' early blitz of their own, but they regrouped to dominate the last quarter of the game. It was certainly one of those games, though, high on drama and adrenaline, as Suárez showed with a furious opening that delivered two stunning Liverpool goals in the first 20 minutes. The first came when his vicious shot from the right cannoned in off the unfortunate Leighton Baines. Barely five minutes later and Liverpool were two up, this time when the Reds striker delicately clipped a header into the far corner from Gerrard's cross. Everton were helped by some shocking Liverpool defending, first when Brad Jones misplaced a punch from a corner and Leon Osman turned the gift into the net. Then both Martin Skrtel and Luis Enrique allowed Marouane Fellaini's cross to reach Steve Naismith in front of the open goal. Jones denied the outstanding Kevin Mirallas to allow Liverpool the sanctuary of the break and an astute Brendan Rodgers' half-time reshuffle gave them the second-half edge that Suárez's brilliance should have confirmed. From a Steven Gerrard free-kick, sub Sebastián Coates rose above everyone to nod down and Suárez swept the half-volley into the roof of the net. But he was pulled up halfway through his victory parade around Goodison by a shockingly late, and shockingly inaccurate, offside flag.

# 5th May 2013

Premier League

**Liverpool 0**

**Everton 0**

*Attendance: 44,991*

**Liverpool:** *Reina, Johnson, Enrique, Agger, Carragher, Gerrard, Coutinho, Henderson (Borini), Downing (Skrtel), Lucas, Sturridge*

**Everton:** *Howard, Coleman, Jagielka, Distin, Baines, Mirallas (Jelavić), Osman, Gibson, Pienaar, Fellaini, Anichebe*

It would have been an injustice in the extreme if Everton had walked away with all three points in the 220th Merseyside derby, because Liverpool dominated when it came to chances even if they were second-best when it came to dictating the tempo of the game. Gerrard was behind everything good his side did, in the first half connecting sweetly with a clever knock-down from the quietly effective Jordan Henderson for what seemed like a certain goal until Phil Jagielka's block. After the break, he raced magnificently onto a ball from Daniel Sturridge to round Tim Howard, only to see his shot cleared from the line by Sylvain Distin. There were more chances for Liverpool, thanks largely to the brilliance of Philippe Coutinho. One ball for Sturridge was sublime, but the centre-forward seemed to think he had all the time in the world, when the opposite was true even in a derby as lacklustre as this one. Sturridge showboated with his finish and was denied by the excellence of Howard, and the Liverpool striker was guilty of taking too much time earlier when he should have finished after another great ball from Henderson. Coutinho still got on the end of that one but was denied by another fine block by Distin. Everton had their moments too and succeeded in finding the back of the Liverpool net on 56 minutes. Distin scrambled above Jamie Carragher to head a corner into the net but, as the visiting fans celebrated wildly, referee Michael Oliver had his arm raised for a free-kick for a foul by Victor Anichebe on Pepe Reina. Marouane Fellaini got behind Carragher to steer a shot just wide of the post from Leighton Baines' free-kick and a deflected Anichebe effort was turned onto the bar by Reina.